Statistics 1

Steve Dobbs and Jane Miller

Series editor Hugh Neill

CAMBRIDGE UNIVERSITY PRESS
Cambridge, New York, Melbourne, Madrid, Cape Town, Singapore,
São Paulo, Delhi, Dubai, Tokyo, Mexico City

Cambridge University Press
The Edinburgh Building, Cambridge CB2 8RU, UK

www.cambridge.org
Information on this title: www.cambridge.org/9780521548939

First published 2000
Second edition 2004
7th printing 2010

Printed in the United Kingdom at the University Press, Cambridge

A catalogue record for this publication is available from the British Library

ISBN 978-0-521-54893-9 Paperback

Contents

Introduction   *page* iv

1   Representation of data   1
2   Measures of location   27
3   Measures of spread   44
4   Probability   66
5   Permutations and combinations   86
6   Probability distributions   103
7   The binomial and geometric distributions   113
8   Expectation and variance of a random variable   133
9   Correlation   148
10 Regression   175

Revision exercise   197
Practice examination papers   201
Cumulative binomial probabilities   208

Answers   214
Index   227

Introduction

Cambridge Advanced Mathematics has been written especially for the OCR modular examination. It consists of one book or half-book corresponding to each module. This book is the first Statistics module, S1.

The books are divided into chapters roughly corresponding to syllabus headings. Occasionally a section includes an important result that is difficult to prove or is outside the syllabus. These sections are marked with an asterisk (*) in the section heading, and there is usually a sentence early on explaining precisely what it is that the student needs to know.

Occasionally within the text paragraphs appear in a grey box. These paragraphs are usually outside the main stream of the mathematical argument, but may help to give insight, or suggest extra work or different approaches.

The authors have assumed that the students have access to calculators with built-in statistical functions.

Numerical work is presented in a form intended to discourage premature approximation. In ongoing calculations inexact numbers appear in decimal form like $3.456\ldots$, signifying that the number is held in a calculator to more places than are given. Numbers are not rounded at this stage; the full display could be either $3.456\,123$ or $3.456\,789$. Final answers are then stated with some indication that they are approximate, for example '1.23 correct to 3 significant figures'.

Most chapters contain practical activities. These can be used either as an introduction to a topic, or, later on, to reinforce the theory. There are plenty of exercises, and each chapter contains a miscellaneous exercise which includes some questions of examination standard. Questions which go beyond examination requirements are marked by an asterisk. At the end of the book there is a revision exercise and two practice examination papers. The authors thank Norman Morris and Owen Toller, the OCR examiners who contributed to these exercises, and also Peter Thomas and William Germain, who read the books very carefully and made many extremely useful comments.

The authors thank OCR and Cambridge University Press for their help in producing this book. However, the responsibility for the text, and for any errors, remains with the authors.

1 Representation of data

This chapter looks at ways of displaying numerical data using diagrams. When you have completed it you should

- know the difference between quantitative and qualitative data
- be able to make comparisons between sets of data by using diagrams
- be able to construct a stem-and-leaf diagram from raw data
- be able to draw a histogram from a grouped frequency table, and know that the area of each block is proportional to the frequency in that class
- be able to draw a frequency polygon from a grouped frequency table
- be able to construct a cumulative frequency diagram from a frequency distribution table.

You should be familiar with pie charts and bar charts.

1.1 Introduction

The collection, organisation and analysis of numerical information are all part of the subject called **statistics**. Pieces of numerical and other information are called **data**. A more helpful definition of 'data' is 'a series of facts from which conclusions may be drawn'.

In order to collect data you need to observe or to measure some property. This property is called a **variable**. The data which follow were taken from the internet, which has many sites containing data sources. In this example a variety of measurements was taken on packets of breakfast cereal for sale in a supermarket in the USA. Each column represents a variable. So, for example, 'mfr', 'sodium' and 'shelf' are all variables.

Datafile Name   Cereals

Description   Data which refer to various brands of breakfast cereal in a particular store. A value of −1 for nutrients indicates a missing observation.

Number of cases   77

Variable Names

1 name: name of cereal

2 mfr: manufacturer of cereal, where A = American Home Food Products; G = General Mills; K = Kellogg's; N = Nabisco; P = Post; Q = Quaker Oats; R = Ralston Purina

3 type: cold (C) or hot (H)

4 cals: calories per serving

5 fat: grams of fat

6 sodium: milligrams of sodium

7 carbo: grams of complex carbohydrates

8 shelf: display shelf (1, 2 or 3, counting from the floor)

9 mass: mass in ounces of one serving (1 ounce = 28 grams)

10 rating: a measure of the nutritional value of the cereal

name	mfr	type	cals	fat	sodium	carbo	shelf	mass	rating
100%_Bran	N	C	70	1	130	5	3	1	68
100%_Natural_Bran	Q	C	120	5	15	8	3	1	34
All-Bran	K	C	70	1	260	7	3	1	59
All-Bran_with_Extra_Fiber	K	C	50	0	140	8	3	1	94
Almond_Delight	R	C	110	2	200	14	3	1	34
Apple_Cinnamon_Cheerios	G	C	110	2	180	10.5	1	1	30
Apple_Jacks	K	C	110	0	125	11	2	1	33
Basic_4	G	C	130	2	210	18	3	1.3	37
Bran_Chex	R	C	90	1	200	15	1	1	49
Bran_Flakes	P	C	90	0	210	13	3	1	53
Cap'n'Crunch	Q	C	120	2	220	12	2	1	18
Cheerios	G	C	110	2	290	17	1	1	51
Cinnamon_Toast_Crunch	G	C	120	3	210	13	2	1	20
Clusters	G	C	110	2	140	13	3	1	40
Cocoa_Puffs	G	C	110	1	180	12	2	1	23
Corn_Chex	R	C	110	0	280	22	1	1	41
Corn_Flakes	K	C	100	0	290	21	1	1	46
Corn_Pops	K	C	110	0	90	13	2	1	36
Count_Chocula	G	C	110	1	180	12	2	1	22
Cracklin'_Oat_Bran	K	C	110	3	140	10	3	1	40
Cream_of_Wheat_(Quick)	N	H	100	0	80	21	2	1	65
Crispix	K	C	110	0	220	21	3	1	47
Crispy_Wheat_&_Raisins	G	C	100	1	140	11	3	1	36
Double_Chex	R	C	100	0	190	18	3	1	44
Froot_Loops	K	C	110	1	125	11	2	1	32
Frosted_Flakes	K	C	110	0	200	14	1	1	31
Frosted_Mini-Wheats	K	C	100	0	0	14	2	1	58
Fruit_&_Fibre_Dates,_Walnuts, _and_Oats	P	C	120	2	160	12	3	1.3	41
Fruitful_Bran	K	C	120	0	240	14	3	1.3	41
Fruity_Pebbles	P	C	110	1	135	13	2	1	28
Golden_Crisp	P	C	100	0	45	11	1	1	35
Golden_Grahams	G	C	110	1	280	15	2	1	24
Grape_Nuts_Flakes	P	C	100	1	140	15	3	1	52
Grape-Nuts	P	C	110	0	170	17	3	1	53
Great_Grains_Pecan	P	C	120	3	75	13	3	1	46
Honey_Graham_Ohs	Q	C	120	2	220	12	2	1	22

(*cont.*)

(*cont.*)

name	mfr	type	cals	fat	sodium	carbo	shelf	mass	rating
Honey_Nut_Cheerios	G	C	110	1	250	11.5	1	1	31
Honey-comb	P	C	110	0	180	14	1	1	29
Just_Right_Crunchy__Nuggets	K	C	110	1	170	17	3	1	37
Just_Right_Fruit_&_Nut	K	C	140	1	170	20	3	1.3	36
Kix	G	C	110	1	260	21	2	1	39
Life	Q	C	100	2	150	12	2	1	45
Lucky_Charms	G	C	110	1	180	12	2	1	27
Maypo	A	H	100	1	0	16	2	1	55
Muesli_Raisins,_Dates,_&_Almonds	R	C	150	3	95	16	3	1	37
Muesli_Raisins,_Peaches,_&_Pecans	R	C	150	3	150	16	3	1	34
Mueslix_Crispy_Blend	K	C	160	2	150	17	3	1.5	30
Multi-Grain_Cheerios	G	C	100	1	220	15	1	1	40
Nut_&_Honey_Crunch	K	C	120	1	190	15	2	1	30
Nutri-Grain_Almond-Raisin	K	C	140	2	220	21	3	1.3	41
Nutri-grain_Wheat	K	C	90	0	170	18	3	1	60
Oatmeal_Raisin_Crisp	G	C	130	2	170	13.5	3	1.3	30
Post_Nat._Raisin_Bran	P	C	120	1	200	11	3	1.3	38
Product_19	K	C	100	0	320	20	3	1	42
Puffed_Rice	Q	C	50	0	0	13	3	0.5	61
Puffed_Wheat	Q	C	50	0	0	10	3	0.5	63
Quaker_Oat_Squares	Q	C	100	1	135	14	3	1	50
Quaker_Oatmeal	Q	H	100	2	0	−1	1	1	51
Raisin_Bran	K	C	120	1	210	14	2	1.3	39
Raisin_Nut_Bran	G	C	100	2	140	10.5	3	1	40
Raisin_Squares	K	C	90	0	0	15	3	1	55
Rice_Chex	R	C	110	0	240	23	1	1	42
Rice_Krispies	K	C	110	0	290	22	1	1	41
Shredded_Wheat	N	C	80	0	0	16	1	0.8	68
Shredded_Wheat'n'Bran	N	C	90	0	0	19	1	1	74
Shredded_Wheat_spoon_size	N	C	90	0	0	20	1	1	73
Smacks	K	C	110	1	70	9	2	1	31
Special_K	K	C	110	0	230	16	1	1	53
Strawberry_Fruit_Wheats	N	C	90	0	15	15	2	1	59
Total_Corn_Flakes	G	C	110	1	200	21	3	1	39
Total_Raisin_Bran	G	C	140	1	190	15	3	1.5	29
Total_Whole_Grain	G	C	100	1	200	16	3	1	47
Triples	G	C	110	1	250	21	3	1	39
Trix	G	C	110	1	140	13	2	1	28
Wheat_Chex	R	C	100	1	230	17	1	1	50
Wheaties	G	C	100	1	200	17	1	1	52
Wheaties_Honey_Gold	G	C	110	1	200	16	1	1	36

Table 1.1. Datafile 'Cereals'.

The variable 'mfr' (manufacturer) has several different letter codes, for example N, G, K, Q and P.

The variable 'sodium' takes values such as 130, 15, 260 and 140.

The variable 'shelf' takes values 1, 2 or 3.

You can see that there are different types of variable. The variable 'mfr' is non-numerical: such variables are usually called **qualitative**. The other two variables are called **quantitative**, because the values they take are numerical.

Example 1.1.1
Which of the variables   (a) 'type',   (b) 'carbo',   (c) 'mass',   are quantitative and which are qualitative?

(a) 'type' is a qualitative variable, since the two different types of breakfast cereal, cold and hot, are recorded as words (letters) rather than as numbers.

(b) 'carbo' is the number of grams of complex carbohydrates. This is quantitative, since the possible values are numerical.

(c) 'mass' stands for mass in ounces. This is also quantitative, since the different possible masses per serving would be given in the form of numbers.

Quantitative numerical data can be subdivided into two categories. For example, 'sodium', the mass of sodium in grams, which can take any value in a particular range, is called a **continuous** variable. 'Display shelf', on the other hand, is a **discrete** variable: it can only take the integer values 1, 2 or 3, and there is a clear step between each possible value. It would not be sensible, for example, to refer to display shelf number 2.43.

In summary:

> A variable is **qualitative** if it is not possible for it to take a numerical value.
>
> A variable is **quantitative** if it can take a numerical value.
>
> A quantitative variable which can take any value in a given range is **continuous**.
>
> A quantitative variable which has clear steps between its possible values is **discrete**.

1.2 Stem-and-leaf diagrams

The datafile on cereals has one column which gives a rating of the cereals on a scale of 0–100. The ratings are given below.

68	34	59	94	34	30	33	37	49	53
18	51	20	40	23	41	46	36	22	40
65	47	36	44	32	31	58	41	41	28
35	24	52	53	46	22	31	29	37	36
39	45	27	55	37	34	30	40	30	41
60	30	38	42	61	63	50	51	39	40
55	42	41	68	74	73	31	53	59	39
29	47	39	28	50	52	36			

These values are what statisticians call **raw data**. Raw data are the values collected in a survey or experiment before they are categorised or arranged in any way. Usually raw data appear in the form of a list. It is very difficult to draw any conclusions from these raw data just by looking at the numbers. One way of arranging the values that gives some information about the patterns within the data is a **stem-and-leaf diagram**.

In this case the stems are the tens digits and the leaves are the units digits. You write the stems to the left of a vertical line and the leaves to the right of the line. So, for example, you would write the first value, 68, as 6|8.

The leaves belonging to one stem are then written in the same row. The stem-and-leaf diagram for these data is shown in Fig. 1.2. The **key** shows what the stems and leaves mean.

```
0 |                                                        (0)
1 | 8                                                      (1)
2 | 0 3 2 8 4 2 9 7 9 8                                   (10)
3 | 4 4 0 3 7 6 6 2 1 5 1 7 6 9 7 4 0 0 0 8 9 1 9 9 6    (25)
4 | 9 0 1 6 0 7 4 1 1 6 5 0 1 2 0 2 1 7                  (18)
5 | 9 3 1 8 2 3 5 0 1 5 3 9 0 2                          (14)
6 | 8 5 0 1 3 8                                           (6)
7 | 4 3                                                   (2)
8 |                                                        (0)
9 | 4                                                      (1)
```
Key: 6|8 means 68

Fig. 1.2. Stem-and-leaf diagram of cereal ratings.

The numbers in the brackets tell you how many leaves belong to each stem (and may be omitted). The digits in each stem form a horizontal 'block', similar to a bar on a bar chart, which gives a visual impression of the distribution. In fact, if you rotate a stem-and-leaf diagram anticlockwise through 90° it looks like a bar chart. It is also common to rewrite the leaves in numerical order; the stem-and-leaf diagram formed in this way is called an **ordered stem-and-leaf diagram**. The ordered stem-and-leaf diagram for the cereal ratings is shown in Fig. 1.3.

```
0 |                                                    (0)
1 | 8                                                  (1)
2 | 0 2 2 3 4 7 8 8 9 9                                (10)
3 | 0 0 0 0 1 1 1 2 3 4 4 4 5 6 6 6 6 7 7 7 8 9 9 9 9  (25)
4 | 0 0 0 0 1 1 1 1 1 2 2 4 5 6 6 7 7 9                (18)
5 | 0 0 1 1 2 2 3 3 3 5 5 8 9 9                        (14)
6 | 0 1 3 5 8 8                                        (6)
7 | 3 4                                                (2)
8 |                                                    (0)
9 | 4                                                  (1)
```
Key: 6|8 means 68

Fig. 1.3. Ordered stem-and-leaf diagram of cereal ratings.

When you are asked to draw a stem-and-leaf diagram you should assume that an *ordered* stem-and-leaf diagram is required.

So far the stem-and-leaf diagrams discussed have consisted of data values which are integers between 0 and 100. With suitable adjustments, you can use stem-and-leaf diagrams for other data values.

For example, the data 6.2, 3.1, 4.8, 9.1, 8.3, 6.2, 1.4, 9.6, 0.3, 0.3, 8.4, 6.1, 8.2, 4.3 could be illustrated in the stem-and-leaf diagram in Fig. 1.4.

Table 1.5 is a datafile about brain sizes which will be used in several examples.

```
0 | 3 3        (2)
1 | 4          (1)
2 |            (0)
3 | 1          (1)
4 | 3 8        (2)
5 |            (0)
6 | 1 2 2      (3)
7 |            (0)
8 | 2 3 4      (3)
9 | 1 6        (2)
```
Key: 0|3 means 0.3

Fig. 1.4. A stem-and-leaf diagram.

Datafile Name   Brain size (Data reprinted from *Intelligence*, Vol. 15, Willerman et al, 'In vivo brain size . . .', 1991, with permission from Elsevier Science)

Description   A team of researchers used a sample of 40 students at a university. The subjects took four subtests from the 'Wechsler (1981) Adult Intelligence Scale – Revised' test. Magnetic Resonance Imaging (MRI) was then used to measure the brain sizes of the subjects. The subjects' genders, heights and body masses are also included. The researchers withheld the masses of two subjects and the height of one subject for reasons of confidentiality.

Number of cases   40

Variable Names

1 gender: male or female

2 FSIQ: full scale IQ scores based on the four Wechsler (1981) subtests

3 VIQ: verbal IQ scores based on the four Wechsler (1981) subtests

4 PIQ: performance IQ scores based on the four Wechsler (1981) subtests

5 mass: body mass in pounds (1 pound = 0.45 kg)

gender	FSIQ	VIQ	PIQ	mass	height	MRI_Count
Female	133	132	124	118	64.5	816 932
Male	140	150	124	–	72.5	1 001 121
Male	139	123	150	143	73.3	1 038 437
Male	133	129	128	172	68.8	965 353
Female	137	132	134	147	65.0	951 545
Female	99	90	110	146	69.0	928 799
Female	138	136	131	138	64.5	991 305
Female	92	90	98	175	66.0	854 258
Male	89	93	84	134	66.3	904 858
Male	133	114	147	172	68.8	955 466
Female	132	129	124	118	64.5	833 868
Male	141	150	128	151	70.0	1 079 549
Male	135	129	124	155	69.0	924 059
Female	140	120	147	155	70.5	856 472
Female	96	100	90	146	66.0	878 897
Female	83	71	96	135	68.0	865 363
Female	132	132	120	127	68.5	952 244
Male	100	96	102	178	73.5	945 088
Female	101	112	84	136	66.3	808 020
Male	80	77	86	180	70.0	889 083
Male	83	83	86	–	–	892 420
Male	97	107	84	186	76.5	905 940
Female	135	129	134	122	62.0	790 619
Male	139	145	128	132	68.0	955 003
Female	91	86	102	114	63.0	831 772
Male	141	145	131	171	72.0	935 494
Female	85	90	84	140	68.0	798 612
Male	103	96	110	187	77.0	1 062 462
Female	77	83	72	106	63.0	793 549
Female	130	126	124	159	66.5	866 662
Female	133	126	132	127	62.5	857 782
Male	144	145	137	191	67.0	949 589
Male	103	96	110	192	75.5	997 925
Male	90	96	86	181	69.0	879 987
Female	83	90	81	143	66.5	834 344
Female	133	129	128	153	66.5	948 066
Male	140	150	124	144	70.5	949 395
Female	88	86	94	139	64.5	893 983
Male	81	90	74	148	74.0	930 016
Male	89	91	89	179	75.5	935 863

Table 1.5. Datafile 'Brain size'.

6 height: height in inches (1 inch = 2.54 cm)

7 MRI_Count: total pixel count from the 18 MRI scans

The stems of a stem-and-leaf diagram may consist of more than one digit. So, for example, consider the following data, which are the masses of 20 women in pounds (correct to the nearest pound), taken from the datafile 'Brain size'.

| 118 | 147 | 146 | 138 | 175 | 118 | 155 | 146 | 135 | 127 |
| 136 | 122 | 114 | 140 | 106 | 159 | 127 | 143 | 153 | 139 |

You can represent these data with the stem-and-leaf diagram shown in Fig. 1.6, which uses stems from 10 to 17.

```
10 | 6                (1)
11 | 4 8 8            (3)
12 | 2 7 7            (3)
13 | 5 6 8 9          (4)
14 | 0 3 6 6 7        (5)
15 | 3 5 9            (3)
16 |                  (0)
17 | 5                (1)
```
Key: 10|6 means 106 pounds

Fig. 1.6. Stem-and-leaf diagram of the masses of a sample of 20 women.

Two sets of data can be compared in a **back-to-back stem-and-leaf diagram**. Consider the following data, which are the masses of 18 males in pounds (correct to the nearest pound), taken from the datafile 'Brain size'.

| 143 | 172 | 134 | 172 | 151 | 155 | 178 | 180 | 186 |
| 132 | 171 | 187 | 191 | 192 | 181 | 144 | 148 | 179 |

Fig. 1.7 shows these data added to Fig. 1.6 as 'leaves' to the left of the stem. Note that the stem has been extended to 19 to accommodate the highest male mass of 192 pounds.

```
       males                         females
(0)                      10 | 6                (1)
(0)                      11 | 4 8 8            (3)
(0)                      12 | 2 7 7            (3)
(2)              4 2     13 | 5 6 8 9          (4)
(3)            8 4 3     14 | 0 3 6 6 7        (5)
(2)              5 1     15 | 3 5 9            (3)
(0)                      16 |                  (0)
(5)        9 8 2 2 1     17 | 5                (1)
(4)          7 6 1 0     18 |                  (0)
(2)              2 1     19 |                  (0)
```
Key: 10|6 means 106 pounds

Fig. 1.7. Back-to-back stem-and-leaf diagram of the masses of a sample of 20 women and 18 men.

Exercise 1A

1 The following stem-and-leaf diagram illustrates the lengths, in cm, of a sample of 15 leaves fallen from a tree. The values are given correct to 1 decimal place.

```
4 | 3                  (1)
5 | 4  0  7  3  9       (5)
6 | 3  1  2  4          (4)
7 | 6  1  6             (3)
8 |                     (0)
9 | 3  2                (2)
```
Key: 7|6 means 7.6 cm

(a) Write the data in full, and in increasing order of size.

(b) State whether the variable is (i) qualitative or quantitative, (ii) discrete or continuous.

2 Construct ordered stem-and-leaf diagrams for the following data sets.

(a) The speeds, in miles per hour, of 20 cars, measured on a city street.

41 15 4 27 21 32 43 37 18 25 29 34 28 30 25 52 12 36 6 25

(b) The times taken, in hours (to the nearest tenth), to carry out repairs to 17 pieces of machinery.

0.9 1.0 2.1 4.2 0.7 1.1 0.9 1.8 0.9 1.2 2.3 1.6 2.1 0.3 0.8 2.7 0.4

3 Construct a stem-and-leaf diagram for the following ages (in completed years) of famous people with birthdays on June 14 and June 15, as reported in a national newspaper.

75 48 63 79 57 74 50 34 62 67 60 58 30 81 51 58 91 71 67 56 74
50 99 36 54 59 54 69 68 74 93 86 77 70 52 64 48 53 68 76 75 56

4 The tensile strength of 60 samples of rubber was measured and the results, in suitable units, were as follows.

174 160 141 153 161 159 163 186 179 167 154 145 156 159 171
156 142 169 160 171 188 151 162 164 172 181 152 178 151 177
180 186 168 169 171 168 157 166 181 171 183 176 155 161 182
160 182 173 189 181 175 165 177 184 161 170 167 180 137 143

Construct a stem-and-leaf diagram using two rows for each stem so that, for example, with a stem of 15 the first leaf may have digits 0 to 4 and the second leaf may have digits 5 to 9.

5 A selection of 25 of A. A. Michelson's measurements of the speed of light, carried out in 1882, is given below. The figures are in thousands of kilometres per second and are given correct to 5 significant figures.

299.84	299.96	299.87	300.00	299.93	299.65	299.88	299.98	299.74
299.94	299.81	299.76	300.07	299.79	299.93	299.80	299.75	299.91
299.72	299.90	299.83	299.62	299.88	299.97	299.85		

Construct a suitable stem-and-leaf diagram for the data.

6 The contents of 30 medium-size packets of soap powder were weighed and the results, in kilograms correct to 4 significant figures, were as follows.

1.347	1.351	1.344	1.362	1.338	1.341	1.342	1.356	1.339	1.351
1.354	1.336	1.345	1.350	1.353	1.347	1.342	1.353	1.329	1.346
1.332	1.348	1.342	1.353	1.341	1.322	1.354	1.347	1.349	1.370

(a) Construct a stem-and-leaf diagram for the data.

(b) Why would there be no point in drawing a stem-and-leaf diagram for the data rounded to 3 significant figures?

7 Construct a back-to-back stem-and-leaf diagram to illustrate the heights of males and females in the datafile 'Brain size'.

1.3   Histograms and frequency polygons

Stem-and-leaf diagrams are quick and easy to construct for small data sets, particularly if there is an obvious choice for the values on the stem. Also, a back-to-back diagram gives a good way to compare two sets of data. For large data sets, however, it becomes tedious to construct a stem-and-leaf diagram and the resulting diagram may look messy. Different methods are usually used to display large data sets.

For large sets of data you may wish to divide the data into groups, called **classes**.

In the cereals data, the amounts of sodium may be grouped into classes as in Table 1.8.

Amount of sodium (mg)	Tally	Frequency
0–49	ⵏ ⵏ ‖	12
50–99	ⵏ	5
100–149	ⵏ ⵏ ‖	12
150–199	ⵏ ⵏ ⵏ ‖	17
200–249	ⵏ ⵏ ⵏ ⵏ ∣	21
250–299	ⵏ ‖‖	9
300–349	∣	1

Table 1.8. Data on cereals grouped into classes.

Table 1.8 is called a **grouped frequency distribution**. This table shows how many values of the variable lie in each class. The pattern of a grouped frequency distribution is decided to some extent by the choice of classes. There would have been a different appearance to the distribution if the classes 0–99, 100–199, 200–299 and 300–399 had been chosen. There is no clear rule about how many classes should be chosen or what size they should be, but it is usual to have from 5 to 10 classes.

Grouping the data into classes inevitably means losing some information. Someone looking at the table would not know the exact values of the observations in the 0–49 category. All he or she would know for certain is that there were 12 such observations.

Consider the class 50–99. This refers to cereal packets which contained from 50 to 99 mg of sodium. The amount of sodium is a continuous variable and the amounts appear to have been rounded to the nearest mg. If this is true then the class labelled as 50–99 would actually contain values from 49.5 up to (but not including) 99.5. These real endpoints, 49.5 and 99.5, are referred to as the **class boundaries**. The class boundaries are generally used in most numerical and graphical summaries of data. In this example you were not actually told that the data were recorded to the nearest mg: you merely assumed that this was the case. In most examples you will know how the data were recorded.

Example 1.3.1
For each case below give the class boundaries of the first class.

(a) The heights of 100 students were recorded to the nearest centimetre.

Height, h (cm)	160–164	165–169	170–174	. . .
Frequency	7	9	13	. . .

Table 1.9. Heights of 100 students.

(b) The masses in kilograms of 40 patients entering a doctor's surgery on one day were recorded to the nearest kilogram.

Mass, m (kg)	55–	60–	65–	. . .
Frequency	9	15	12	. . .

Table 1.10. Masses of 40 patients.

(c) A group of 40 motorists was asked to state the ages at which they passed their driving tests.

Age, a (years)	17–	20–	23–	. . .
Frequency	6	11	7	. . .

Table 1.11. Ages at which 40 motorists passed their driving tests.

(a) The minimum and maximum heights for someone in the first class are 159.5 cm and 164.5 cm. The class boundaries are given by $159.5 \leq h < 164.5$.

(b) The first class appears to go from 55 kg up to but not including 60 kg, but as the measurement has been made to the nearest kg the lower and upper class boundaries are 54.5 kg and 59.5 kg. The class boundaries are given by $54.5 \leq m < 59.5$.

(c) Age is recorded to the number of completed years, so 17– contains those who passed their tests from the day of their 17th birthday up to, but not including, the day of their 20th birthday. The class boundaries are given by $17 \leq a < 20$.

Sometimes discrete data are grouped into classes. For example, the test scores of 40 students might appear as in Table 1.12.

Score	0–9	10–19	20–29	30–39	40–59
Frequency	14	9	9	3	5

Table 1.12. Test scores of 40 students.

What are the class boundaries? There is no universally accepted answer, but a common convention is to use 9.5 and 19.5 as the class boundaries. Although it may appear strange, the class boundaries for the first class would be –0.5 and 9.5.

When a grouped frequency distribution contains continuous data, one of the most common forms of graphical display is the **histogram**. A histogram looks similar to a bar chart, but there are two important differences.

> A bar chart which represents continuous data is a histogram if
>
> - the bars have no spaces between them (though there may be bars of height zero, which look like spaces), and
> - the *area* of each bar is proportional to the frequency.

If all the bars of a histogram have the same width, the height is proportional to the frequency.

Consider Table 1.13, which gives the heights in centimetres of 30 plants.

Height, h (cm)	Frequency
$0 \leq h < 5$	3
$5 \leq h < 10$	5
$10 \leq h < 15$	11
$15 \leq h < 20$	6
$20 \leq h < 25$	3
$25 \leq h < 30$	2

Table 1.13. Heights of 30 plants.

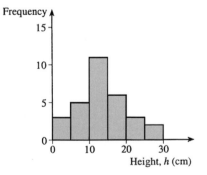

Fig. 1.14. Histogram for the data in Table 1.13.

The histogram to represent the set of data in Table 1.13 is shown in Fig. 1.14.

Another person recorded the same results by combining the last two rows as in Table 1.15, and then drew the diagram shown in Fig. 1.16.

Height, h (cm)	Frequency
$0 \le h < 5$	3
$5 \le h < 10$	5
$10 \le h < 15$	11
$15 \le h < 20$	6
$20 \le h < 30$	5

Table 1.15. Heights of 30 plants.

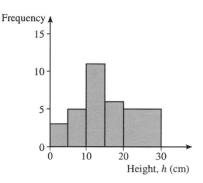

Fig. 1.16. Incorrect diagram for the data in Table 1.15.

Can you see why Fig. 1.16 is misleading?

The diagram makes it appear, incorrectly, that there are more plants whose heights are in the interval $20 \le h < 30$ than in the interval $5 \le h < 10$. It would be a more accurate representation if the bar for the class $20 \le h < 30$ had a height of 2.5, as in Fig. 1.17.

For the histogram in Fig 1.17 the areas of the five blocks are 15, 25, 55, 30 and 25. These are in the same ratio as the frequencies, which are 3, 5, 11, 6 and 5 respectively. This example demonstrates that when a grouped frequency distribution has unequal class widths, it is the area of the block in a histogram, and not its height, which should be proportional to the frequency in the corresponding interval.

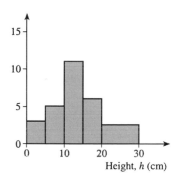

Fig. 1.17. Histogram for the data in Table 1.15.

The simplest way of making the area of a block proportional to the frequency is to make the area equal to the frequency. This means that

$$\text{width of class} \times \text{height} = \text{frequency}.$$

This is the same as

$$\text{height} = \frac{\text{frequency}}{\text{width of class}}.$$

These heights are then known as **frequency densities**.

Example 1.3.2
The grouped frequency distribution in Table 1.18 represents the heights in inches of a sample of 39 of the people from the datafile 'Brain size' (see the previous section). Represent these data in a histogram.

Height (inches)	Frequency
62–63	4
64–65	5
66–67	8
68–71	13
72–75	5
76–79	4

Table 1.18. Heights of people from the datafile 'Brain size'.

Find the frequency densities by dividing the frequency of each class by the width of the class, as shown in Table 1.19.

Height, h (inches)	Class boundaries	Class width	Frequency	Frequency density
62–63	$61.5 \le h < 63.5$	2	4	2
64–65	$63.5 \le h < 65.5$	2	5	2.5
66–67	$65.5 \le h < 67.5$	2	8	4
68–71	$67.5 \le h < 71.5$	4	13	3.25
72–75	$71.5 \le h < 75.5$	4	5	1.25
76–79	$75.5 \le h < 79.5$	4	4	1

Table 1.19. Calculation of frequency density for the data in Table 1.18.

The histogram is shown in Fig. 1.20.

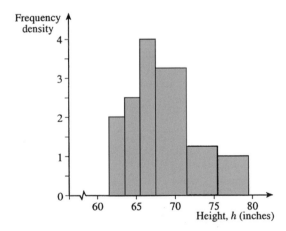

Fig. 1.20. Histogram for the data in Table 1.19.

When illustrating a frequency table with unequal class widths using a histogram, plot frequency *density* against the variable, where

$$\text{frequency density of a class} = \frac{\text{frequency of the class}}{\text{class width}}.$$

Example 1.3.3

The grouped frequency distribution in Table 1.21 summarises the masses in grams (g), measured to the nearest gram, of a sample of 20 pebbles. Represent the data in a histogram.

The problem with this frequency distribution is that the last class is open-ended, so you cannot deduce the correct class boundaries unless you know the individual data values. In this case the individual values are not given. A reasonable procedure for this type of situation is to take the width of the last interval to be twice that of the previous one. Table 1.22 and the histogram in Fig. 1.23 are constructed using this assumption.

Mass (g)	Frequency
101–110	1
111–120	4
121–130	2
131–140	7
141–150	2
over 150	4

Table 1.21. Masses of a sample of 20 pebbles.

Mass, m (g)	Class boundaries	Class width	Frequency	Frequency density
101–110	$100.5 \le m < 110.5$	10	1	0.1
111–120	$110.5 \le m < 120.5$	10	4	0.4
121–130	$120.5 \le m < 130.5$	10	2	0.2
131–140	$130.5 \le m < 140.5$	10	7	0.7
141–150	$140.5 \le m < 150.5$	10	2	0.2
over 150	$150.5 \le m < 170.5$	20	4	0.2

Table 1.22. Calculation of frequency density for the data in Table 1.21.

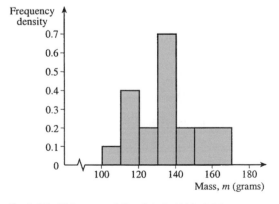

Fig. 1.23. Histogram of the data in Table 1.21.

All the previous examples of histograms have involved continuous data. You can also represent grouped discrete data in a histogram. Table 1.24 gives the class boundaries for the data in Table 1.12, which were the test scores of 40 students. Recall that the convention used is to take the class with limits 10 and 19 as having class boundaries 9.5 and 19.5. Using this convention you can find the frequency densities.

Score	Class boundaries	Class width	Frequency	Frequency density
0–9	−0.5–9.5	10	14	1.4
10–19	9.5–19.5	10	9	0.9
20–29	19.5–29.5	10	9	0.9
30–39	29.5–39.5	10	3	0.3
40–59	39.5–59.5	20	5	0.25

Table 1.24. Class boundaries for the data in Table 1.12.

Fig. 1.25 shows the histogram for the data. Notice that the left bar extends slightly to the left of the vertical axis, to the point –0.5. This accounts for the apparent thickness of the vertical axis.

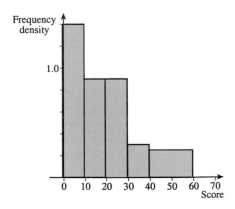

Fig. 1.25. Histogram of the data in Table 1.24.

A **frequency polygon** can be constructed by joining the midpoints of the tops of the bars in a histogram. Fig. 1.26 shows the histogram in Fig. 1.17 with a frequency polygon superimposed.

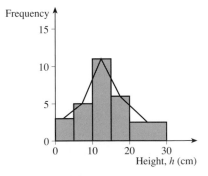

Fig. 1.26. The histogram in Fig. 1.17 with a frequency polygon superimposed.

Usually you would not display both the histogram and the frequency polygon on the same diagram. A frequency polygon can be drawn, without drawing the histogram first, by plotting the frequency density for each class at the mid-point of that class.

Example 1.3.4
Plot a frequency polygon for the data in Table 1.18.

The table below reproduces Table 1.19 with an extra column added.

Height, h (inches)	Class boundaries	Class width	Frequency	Frequency density	Mid-point
62–63	$61.5 \leq h < 63.5$	2	4	2	62.5
64–65	$63.5 \leq h < 65.5$	2	5	2.5	64.5
66–67	$65.5 \leq h < 67.5$	2	8	4	66.5
68–71	$67.5 \leq h < 71.5$	4	13	3.25	69.5
72–75	$71.5 \leq h < 75.5$	4	5	1.25	73.5
76–79	$75.5 \leq h < 79.5$	4	4	1	77.5

Table 1.27. Calculation of frequency density for the data in Table 1.18.

The frequency polygon is shown in Fig. 1.28.

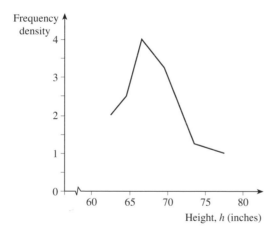

Fig. 1.28. Frequency polygon for the data in Table 1.27.

Frequency polygons are useful when comparing two or more data sets because they can be superimposed in the same diagram.

Exercise 1B

In Question 1 on the next page, the upper class boundary of one class is identical to the lower class boundary of the next class. If you were measuring speeds to the nearest m.p.h., then you might record a result of 40 m.p.h., and you would not know which class to put it in. This is not a problem in Question 1. You may come across data like these in examination questions, but it will be made clear what to do with them.

1 The speeds, in miles per hour, of 200 vehicles travelling on a motorway were measured by a radar device. The results are summarised in the following table.

Speed	30–40	40–50	50–60	60–70	70–80	over 80
Frequency	12	32	56	72	20	8

Draw a histogram to illustrate the data.

2 The mass of each of 60 pebbles collected from a beach was measured. The results, correct to the nearest gram, are summarised in the following table.

Mass	5–9	10–14	15–19	20–24	25–29	30–34	35–44
Frequency	2	5	8	14	17	11	3

Draw a histogram of the data.

3 For the data in Question 4 of Exercise 1A, form a grouped frequency table using six equal classes, starting 130–139. Assume that the data values are correct to the nearest integer.

Draw a frequency polygon of the data.

4 Thirty calls made by a telephone saleswoman were monitored. The lengths in minutes, to the nearest minute, are summarised in the following table.

Length of call	0–2	3–5	6–8	9–11	12–15
Number of calls	17	6	4	2	1

(a) State the boundaries of the first two classes.

(b) Illustrate the data with a histogram.

5 The following grouped frequency table shows the score received by 275 students who sat a statistics examination.

Score	0–9	10–19	20–29	30–34	35–39	40–49	50–59
Frequency	6	21	51	36	48	82	31

Taking the class boundaries for 0–9 as –0.5 and 9.5, represent the data in a histogram.

6 The haemoglobin levels in the blood of 45 hospital patients were measured. The results, correct to 1 decimal place, and ordered for convenience, are as follows.

    9.1 10.1 10.7 10.7 10.9 11.3 11.3 11 4 11.4 11.4 11.6 11.8 12.0 12.1 12.3
    12.4 12.7 12.9 13.1 13.2 13.4 13.5 13.5 13.6 13.7 13.8 13.8 14.0 14.2 14.2
    14.2 14.6 14.6 14.8 14.8 15.0 15.0 15.0 15.1 15.4 15.6 15.7 16.2 16.3 16.9

(a) Form a grouped frequency table with 8 classes.

(b) Draw a frequency polygon of the data.

7 Each of the 34 children in a Year 3 class was given a task to perform. The times taken in minutes, correct to the nearest quarter of a minute, were as follows.

$$4 \quad 3\tfrac{3}{4} \quad 5 \quad 6\tfrac{1}{4} \quad 7 \quad 3 \quad 7 \quad 5\tfrac{1}{4} \quad 7\tfrac{1}{2} \quad 8\tfrac{3}{4} \quad 9\tfrac{1}{2} \quad 4\tfrac{1}{2}$$

$$6\tfrac{1}{2} \quad 4\tfrac{1}{4} \quad 8 \quad 7\tfrac{1}{4} \quad 6\tfrac{3}{4} \quad 5\tfrac{3}{4} \quad 4\tfrac{3}{4} \quad 8\tfrac{1}{4} \quad 7 \quad 3\tfrac{1}{2} \quad 5\tfrac{1}{2} \quad 7\tfrac{3}{4}$$

$$8\tfrac{1}{2} \quad 6\tfrac{1}{2} \quad 5 \quad 7\tfrac{1}{4} \quad 6\tfrac{3}{4} \quad 7\tfrac{3}{4} \quad 5\tfrac{3}{4} \quad 6 \quad 7\tfrac{3}{4} \quad 6\tfrac{1}{2}$$

(a) Form a grouped frequency table with 6 equal classes beginning with $3 - 3\tfrac{3}{4}$.

(b) What are the boundaries of the first class?

(c) Draw a frequency polygon for the data.

8 The table shows the age distribution of the 200 members of a golf club.

Age	16–19	20–29	30–39	40–49	50–59	over 59
Number of members	12	40	44	47	32	25

(a) Form a table showing the class boundaries and frequency densities.

(b) Draw a histogram of the data.

9* A histogram is drawn to represent a set of data.

(a) The first two classes have boundaries 2.0 and 2.2, and 2.2 and 2.5, with frequencies 5 and 12. The height of the first bar drawn is 2.5 cm. What is the height of the second bar?

(b) The class boundaries of the third bar are 2.5 and 2.7. What is the corresponding frequency if the bar drawn has height 3.5 cm?

(c) The fourth bar has a height of 3 cm and the corresponding frequency is 9. The lower class boundary for this bar is 2.7 cm. Find the upper class boundary.

1.4 Cumulative frequency graphs

An alternative method of representing continuous data is a **cumulative frequency graph**. (Cumulative frequency graphs can also be drawn for discrete data.) The cumulative frequencies are plotted against the upper class boundaries of the corresponding class. Consider the data from Example 1.3.2, reproduced in Table 1.29.

Height, h (inches)	62–63	64–65	66–67	68–71	72–75	76–79
Frequency	4	5	8	13	5	4

Table 1.29. Heights of people from the datafile 'Brain size'.

There are 0 observations less than 61.5.

There are 4 observations less than 63.5.

There are 4 + 5, or 9, observations less than 65.5.

There are 4 +5 + 8, or 17, observations less than 67.5.

⋮   ⋮   ⋮

There are 39 observations less than 79.5.

This results in Table 1.30, which shows the cumulative frequency.

Height, h (inches)	<61.5	<63.5	<65.5	<67.5	<71.5	<75.5	<79.5
Cumulative frequency	0	4	9	17	30	35	39

Table 1.30. Heights of people from the datafile 'Brain size'.

The points (61.5, 0), (63.5, 4), ..., (79.5, 39) are then plotted. The points are joined with straight lines, as shown in Fig. 1.31.

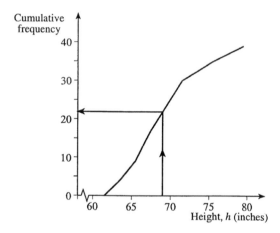

Fig. 1.31. Cumulative frequency graph for the data in Table 1.30.

You may also see cumulative frequency diagrams in which the points have been joined with a smooth curve. If you join the points with a straight line then you are making the assumption that the observations in each class are evenly spread throughout the range of values in that class. This is usually the most sensible procedure unless you know something extra about the distribution of the data which would suggest that a curve was more appropriate. You should not be surprised, however, if you encounter cumulative frequency graphs in which the points are joined by a curve.

You can also use the graph to read off other information. For example, you can estimate the proportion of the sample whose heights are under 69 inches. Read off the cumulative frequency corresponding to a height of 69 in Fig. 1.31. This is approximately 21.9. Therefore an estimate of the proportion of the sample whose heights were under 69 inches would be $\frac{21.9}{39} \approx 0.56$, or 56%.

Exercise 1C

1 The cumulative frequency diagram below illustrates data relating to the height (in cm) of 400 children at a certain school.

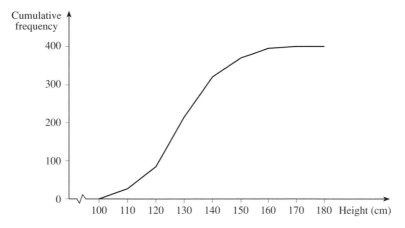

(a) Estimate how many children are

(i) less than 124 cm tall   (ii) more than 152 cm tall.

(b) Estimate the height that is exceeded by 50% of the children.

2 Draw a cumulative frequency diagram for the data in Question 1 of Exercise 1B. With the help of the diagram estimate

(a) the percentage of cars that were travelling at more than 65 m.p.h.,

(b) the speed below which 25% of the cars were travelling.

3 Draw a cumulative frequency diagram for the examination marks in Question 5 of Exercise 1B.

(a) Candidates with at least 44 marks received Grade A. Find the percentage of the students that received Grade A.

(b) It is known that 81.8% of these students gained Grade E or better. Find the lowest Grade E mark for these students.

4 Estimates of the age distribution of a European country for the year 2010 are given in the following table.

Age	under 16	16–39	40–64	65–79	80 and over
Percentage	14.3	33.1	35.3	11.9	5.4

(a) Draw a percentage cumulative frequency diagram.

(b) It is expected that people who have reached the age of 60 will be drawing a state pension in 2010. If the projected population of the country is 42.5 million, estimate the number who will then be drawing this pension.

5 The records of the sales in a small grocery store for the 360 days that it opened during the year 2003 are summarised in the following cumulative frequency table.

Sales, x (in £100s)	$x < 2$	$x < 3$	$x < 4$	$x < 5$
Number of days	15	42	106	178

Sales, x (in £100s)	$x < 6$	$x < 7$	$x < 8$	$x < 9$
Number of days	264	334	350	360

(a) Days for which sales fall below £325 are classified as 'poor' and those for which the sales exceed £775 are classified as 'good'. With the help of a cumulative frequency diagram estimate the number of poor days and the number of good days in 2003.

(b) Construct the corresponding frequency table.

6 A company has 132 employees who work in its city branch. The distances, x miles, that employees travel to work are summarised in the following grouped frequency table.

x	<5	5–9	10–14	15–19	20–24	>24
Frequency	12	29	63	13	12	3

Draw a cumulative frequency diagram and use it to find the number of miles below which

(a) one-quarter   (b) three-quarters

of the employees travel to work.

7 The lengths of 250 electronic components were measured very accurately. The results are summarised in the following table.

Length (cm)	<7.00	7.00–7.05	7.05–7.10	7.10–7.15	7.15–7.20	>7.20
Frequency	10	63	77	65	30	5

Given that 10% of the components are scrapped because they are too short and 8% are scrapped because they are too long, use a cumulative frequency diagram to estimate limits for the length of an acceptable component.

8 As part of a health study the blood glucose levels of 150 students were measured. The results, in mmol l^{-1} correct to 1 decimal place, are summarised in the following table.

Glucose level	<3.0	3.0–3.0	4.0–4.9	5.0–5.9	6.0–6.9	≥7.0
Frequency	7	55	72	10	4	2

Draw a cumulative frequency diagram and use it to find the percentage of students with blood glucose level greater than 5.2.

The number of students with blood glucose level greater than 5.2 is equal to the number with blood glucose level less than a. Find a.

1.5   Practical activities

1 **One-sidedness**   Investigate whether reaction times are different when you use only information from one 'side' of your body.

   (a) Choose a subject and instruct them to close their left eye. Against a wall hold a ruler pointing vertically downwards with the 0 cm mark at the bottom and ask the subject to place the index finger of their right hand aligned with this 0 cm mark. Explain that you will let go of the ruler without warning, and that the subject must try to pin it against the wall using the index finger of their right hand. Measure the distance dropped.

   (b) Repeat this for, say, 30 subjects.

   (c) Take a further 30 subjects and carry out the experiment again for each of these subjects, but for this second set of 30 make them close their right eye and use their left hand.

   (d) Draw a stem-and-leaf diagram for both sets of data and compare the distributions.

   (e) Draw two histograms and use these to compare the distributions.

   (f) Do subjects seem to react more quickly using their right side than they do using their left side? Are subjects more erratic when using their left side? How does the fact that some people are naturally left-handed affect the results? Would it be more appropriate to investigate 'dominant' side versus 'non-dominant' side rather than left versus right?

2 **High jump**   Find how high people can jump.

   (a) Pick a subject and ask them to stand against a wall and stretch their arm as far up the wall as possible. Make a mark at this point. Then ask the subject to jump as high as they can and make a second mark at this highest point. Measure the distance between the two marks. This is a measure of how high they jumped.

   (b) Take two samples, one of Year 11 students and another of Year 7 students, and plot a histogram of the results for each group.

   (c) Do Year 11 students jump higher than Year 7 students?

3 **Darts**

   (a) Throw four darts at a dart-board, aiming for the treble twenty, and record the total score. Get a sample of students to repeat this. Plot the results on a stem-and-leaf diagram.

   (b) Take a second sample of students and ask each of them to throw four darts at the dart-board, but this time tell each student to aim for the bull. Plot these results on a second stem-and-leaf diagram which is back-to-back with the first, for easy comparison. Is the strategy of aiming for the treble twenty more successful than that of aiming for the bull? Does one of the strategies result in a more variable total score?

Miscellaneous exercise 1

1 The following gives the scores of a cricketer in 40 consecutive innings.

$$\begin{array}{cccccccccc}
6 & 18 & 27 & 19 & 57 & 12 & 28 & 38 & 45 & 66 \\
72 & 85 & 25 & 84 & 43 & 31 & 63 & 0 & 26 & 17 \\
14 & 75 & 86 & 37 & 20 & 42 & 8 & 42 & 0 & 33 \\
21 & 11 & 36 & 11 & 29 & 34 & 55 & 62 & 16 & 82
\end{array}$$

Illustrate the data on a stem-and-leaf diagram. State an advantage that the diagram has over the data. What information is given by the data that does not appear in the diagram?

2 The service time, t seconds, was recorded for 120 customers at a supermarket till. The results are summarised in the following grouped frequency table.

t	<30	30–60	60–120	120–180	180–240	240–300	300–360	>360
Frequency	2	3	8	16	42	25	18	6

Draw a histogram of the data. Estimate the greatest service time that is exceeded by 30 customers.

3 At the start of a new school year, the heights of the 100 new pupils entering the school are measured. The results are summarised in the following table. The 10 pupils in the class 110– have heights not less than 110 cm but less than 120 cm.

Height (cm)	100–	110–	120–	130–	140–	150–	160–
Number of pupils	2	10	22	29	22	12	3

Use a cumulative frequency diagram to estimate the height of the tallest pupil of the 18 shortest pupils.

4 The following ordered set of numbers represents the salinity of 30 specimens of water taken from a stretch of the Irish Sea, near the mouth of a river.

$$\begin{array}{cccccccccc}
4.2 & 4.5 & 5.8 & 6.3 & 7.2 & 7.9 & 8.2 & 8.5 & 9.3 & 9.7 \\
10.2 & 10.3 & 10.4 & 10.7 & 11.1 & 11.6 & 11.6 & 11.7 & 11.8 & 11.8 \\
11.9 & 12.4 & 12.4 & 12.5 & 12.6 & 12.9 & 12.9 & 13.1 & 13.5 & 14.3
\end{array}$$

(a) Form a grouped frequency table for the data using 6 equal classes.

(b) Draw a cumulative frequency diagram. Estimate the 12th highest salinity level. Calculate the percentage error in this estimate.

5 The following are ignition times in seconds, correct to the nearest 0.1 s, of samples of 80 flammable materials. They are arranged in numerical order by rows.

1.2	1.4	1.4	1.5	1.5	1.6	1.7	1.8	1.8	1.9	2.1	2.2
2.3	2.5	2.5	2.5	2.5	2.6	2.7	2.8	3.1	3.2	3.5	3.6
3.7	3.8	3.8	3.9	3.9	4.0	4.1	4.2	4.3	4.5	4.5	4.6
4.7	4.7	4.8	4.9	5.1	5.1	5.1	5.2	5.2	5.3	5.4	5.5
5.6	5.8	5.9	5.9	6.0	6.3	6.4	6.4	6.4	6.4	6.7	6.8
6.8	6.9	7.3	7.4	7.4	7.6	7.9	8.0	8.6	8.8	8.8	9.2
9.4	9.6	9.7	9.8	10.6	11.2	11.8	12.8				

Group the data into 8 equal classes, starting with 1.0–2.4 and 2.5–3.9 and form a grouped frequency table. Draw a histogram. State what it indicates about the ignition times.

6 A company employs 2410 people whose annual salaries are summarised as follows.

Salary (in £1000s)	<5	5–10	10–15	15–20	20–25	25–30	30–40	40–50	>50
Number of staff	16	31	502	642	875	283	45	12	4

(a) Draw a cumulative frequency diagram for the grouped data.

(b) Estimate the percentage of staff with salaries between £13,000 and £26,000.

(c) If you were asked to draw a histogram of the data, what problem would arise and how would you overcome it?

7 Certain insects can cause small growths, called 'galls', on the leaves of trees. The numbers of galls found on 60 leaves of an oak tree are given below.

5	19	21	4	17	10	0	61	3	31	15	39	16	27	48
51	69	32	1	25	51	22	28	29	73	14	23	9	2	0
1	37	31	95	10	24	7	89	1	2	50	33	22	0	75
7	23	9	18	39	44	10	33	9	11	51	8	36	44	10

(a) Put the data into a grouped frequency table with classes 0–9, 10–19, ..., 70–99.

(b) Draw a histogram of the data.

(c) Draw a cumulative frequency diagram and use it to estimate the number of leaves with fewer than 34 galls.

(d) State an assumption required for your estimate in part (c), and briefly discuss its justification in this case.

8 The traffic noise levels on two city streets were measured one weekday, between 5.30 a.m. and 8.30 p.m. There were 92 measurements on each street, made at equal time intervals, and the results are summarised in the following grouped frequency table.

Noise level (dB)	<65	65–67	67–69	69–71	71–73	73–75	75–77	77–79	>79
Street 1 frequency	4	11	18	23	16	9	5	4	2
Street 2 frequency	2	3	7	12	27	16	10	8	7

(a) On the same axes, draw cumulative frequency diagrams for the two streets.

(b) Use them to estimate the highest noise levels exceeded on 50 occasions in each street.

(c) Write a brief comparison of the noise levels in the two streets.

9 The time intervals (in seconds) between which telephone calls are received at a solicitor's office were monitored on a particular day. The first 51 calls after 9.00 a.m. gave the following 50 intervals.

34	25	119	16	12	72	5	41	12	66
118	2	22	40	25	39	19	67	4	13
23	104	35	118	85	67	14	16	50	16
24	10	48	24	76	6	3	61	5	58
56	2	24	44	12	20	8	11	29	82

Illustrate the data with a stem-and-leaf diagram, and with a histogram, using 6 equal classes.

10 Construct a grouped frequency table for the following data.

19.12	21.43	20.57	16.97	14.82	19.61	19.35
20.02	12.76	20.40	21.38	20.27	20.21	16.53
21.04	17.71	20.69	15.61	19.41	21.25	19.72
21.13	20.34	20.52	17.30			

(a) Draw a histogram of the data.

(b) Draw a cumulative frequency diagram.

(c) Draw a stem-and-leaf diagram using leaves in hundredths, separated by commas.

2 Measures of location

This chapter describes three different measures of location and their method of calculation. When you have completed it you should

- know what the median is, and be able to calculate it
- know what the mean is, and be able to calculate it efficiently
- know what the mode and the modal class are, and be able to find them
- be able to choose which is the appropriate measure to use in a given situation.

2.1 Introduction

Suppose that you wanted to know the typical playing time for a compact disc (CD). You could start by taking a few CDs and finding out the playing time for each one. You might obtain a list of values such as

$$49, 56, 55, 68, 61, 57, 61, 52, 63$$

where the values have been given in minutes, to the nearest whole minute. You can see that the values are located roughly in the region of 1 hour (rather than, say, 2 hours or 10 minutes). It would be useful to have a single value which gave some idea of this location. A single value would condense the information contained in the data set into a 'typical' value, and would allow you to compare this data set with another one. Such a value is called a **measure of location**, or a **measure of central tendency**, or, in everyday language, an **average**.

2.2 The median

You can get a clearer picture of the central tendency of the playing times by arranging them in ascending order of size:

$$49, 52, 55, 56, 57, 61, 61, 63, 68.$$

A simple measure of central tendency is the middle value. There are equal numbers of values above and below it. In this case there are nine values and the middle one is 57. This value is called the **median**.

If there are an even number of values then there is no single 'middle' value. In the case of the six values

$$47, 49, 59, 62, 65, 68,$$

which are the playing times of another six CDs (in order), the median is taken to be halfway between the third and fourth values, which is $\frac{1}{2}(59 + 62)$, or 60.5. Again, there are equal numbers of values below and above this value: in this case, three.

> To find the median of a data set of n values, arrange the values in order of increasing size.
>
> If n is odd, the median is the $\frac{1}{2}(n+1)$th value. If n is even, the median is halfway between the $\frac{1}{2}n$th value and the following value.

A convenient way of sorting the values into order of increasing size is to draw an ordered stem-and-leaf diagram. Fig. 2.1 is a stem-and-leaf diagram of the masses of the female students from the 'Brain size' datafile in Chapter 1.

There are 20 students and so the median is calculated from the 10th and 11th values. These two values are shown in bold type in Fig. 2.1. The median is $\frac{1}{2}(138 + 139)$, or 138.5 pounds.

```
10 | 6                (1)
11 | 4 8 8            (3)
12 | 2 7 7            (3)
13 | 5 6 8 9          (4)
14 | 0 3 6 6 7        (5)
15 | 3 5 9            (3)
16 |                  (0)
17 | 5                (1)
```
Key: 12|2 means 122 pounds

Fig. 2.1. Stem-and-leaf diagram of the masses of female students.

2.3 Finding the median from a frequency table

Data sets are often much larger than the ones in the previous section and the values will often have been organised in some way, maybe in a frequency table. As an example, Table 2.2 gives the number of brothers and sisters of the children in Year 8 at a school.

Number of brothers and sisters	Frequency	Cumulative frequency
0	36	36
1	94	130
2	48	178
3	15	193
4	7	200
5	3	203
6	1	204
	Total: 204	

Table 2.2. Frequency distribution of the number of brothers and sisters of the children in Year 8 at a school.

One way of finding the median is to write out a list of all the individual values, starting with 36 '0's, then 94 '1's and so on, and find the $\frac{1}{2} \times 204$, or 102nd value and the 103rd value. A much easier method is to add a column of cumulative frequencies, as in Table 2.2. From this you can see that when you have come to the end of the '0's you have not yet reached the 102nd value but, by the end of the '1's, you have reached the 130th value. This means that the 102nd and 103rd values are both 1, so the median is also 1.

In this example the data had not been grouped, so it was possible to count to the median. Large data sets for continuous variables, however, are nearly always grouped, and the individual values are lost. This means that you cannot find the median exactly and you have to estimate it. Table 2.3 gives the frequency distribution for the playing time of a much larger selection of CDs.

Playing time, x (min)	Class boundaries	Frequency	Less than	Cumulative frequency
40–44	$39.5 \leq x < 44.5$	1	44.5	1
45–49	$44.5 \leq x < 49.5$	7	49.5	8
50–54	$49.5 \leq x < 54.5$	12	54.5	20
55–59	$54.5 \leq x < 59.5$	24	59.5	44
60–64	$59.5 \leq x < 64.5$	29	64.5	73
65–69	$64.5 \leq x < 69.5$	14	69.5	87
70–74	$69.5 \leq x < 74.5$	5	74.5	92
75–79	$74.5 \leq x < 79.5$	3	79.5	95
		Total: 95		

Table 2.3. Playing times of 95 CDs.

A column for cumulative frequency has been added to the table, and Fig. 2.4 shows a cumulative frequency graph for the data.

> Reminder: cumulative frequency is plotted against the upper class boundary of each class.

The cumulative frequency curve allows you to find the number of CDs with a playing time less than a given value. To obtain the median playing time from the cumulative frequency graph, you read off the value corresponding to a cumulative frequency equal to half the total frequency, in this case $\frac{1}{2} \times 95$, or 47.5. This gives a playing time of 60 minutes. This value is taken as an estimate of the median, because roughly half the playing times will be below it and so about half will be above it.

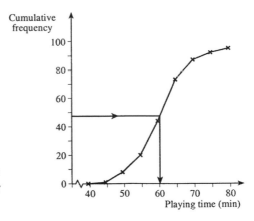

Fig. 2.4. Cumulative frequency graph for data in Table 2.3.

> To find the median value for grouped data from a cumulative frequency graph, read off the value of the variable corresponding to a cumulative frequency equal to half the total frequency.

> Some books suggest reading off the value from the cumulative frequency graph which corresponds to a cumulative frequency of $\frac{1}{2}(n+1)$ rather than $\frac{1}{2}n$. This will give a slightly different value but the difference is not important.

Sometimes discrete data are grouped into classes so that, once again, you cannot list the individual values. An example was given in Table 1.12. To estimate the median for such data, treat the variable as though it were continuous and find the median from the cumulative frequency graph.

Exercise 2A

1 Find the median mass of 6.6 kg, 3.2 kg, 4.8 kg, 7.6 kg, 5.4 kg, 7.1 kg, 2.0 kg, 6.3 kg and 4.3 kg.

  A mass of 6.0 kg is added to the set. What is the median of the 10 masses?

2 With the help of the stem-and-leaf diagram in Fig. 1.3, obtain the median cereal rating.

3 Using the stem-and-leaf diagrams from Exercise 1A Question 2 (which are given in the answers), obtain the medians of the two data sets.

4 Obtain the median of the haemoglobin levels in Exercise 1B Question 6.

5 Using your cumulative frequency diagram from Exercise 1C Question 5, obtain an estimate of the median value of the sales.

6 From the grouped frequency table obtained in Miscellaneous exercise 1 Question 5 (which is given in the answers), draw a cumulative frequency diagram and use it to estimate the median ignition time.

  Find the exact median from the data set, and account for any difference in your two answers.

7 The number of rejected CDs produced each day by a machine was monitored for 100 days. The results are summarised in the following table.

Number of rejects	0–9	10–19	20–29	30–39	40–49	50–59
Number of days	5	8	19	37	22	9

  Estimate the median number of rejects.

8 For the Brain size datafile of Table 1.5, find the median VIQ scores of

  (a) the men, (b) the women,

  and compare them.

2.4 The mean

The median does not use the actual values of the observations in a data set, apart from the middle value(s) when the data are arranged in order of increasing size. A measure of central tendency which does make use of the actual values of all the observations is the **mean**. This is the quantity which most people are referring to when they talk about the 'average'. The mean is found by adding all the values and dividing by the number of values. For the nine CDs in Section 2.1,

$$\text{mean} = \frac{49 + 56 + 55 + 68 + 61 + 57 + 61 + 52 + 63}{9} = \frac{522}{9} = 58 \text{ minutes.}$$

> The **mean** of a data set is equal to the sum of the values in the data set divided by the number of values.

2.5 Summation notation

It is possible to express the definition of the mean as a mathematical formula by introducing some new mathematical notation. Suppose you have n data values. The symbol x_i denotes the ith value in the data set. For the playing times of the nine CDs in the previous section, $x_1 = 49$, $x_2 = 56$, $x_3 = 55$ and so on. The sum of these values is

$$x_1 + x_2 + x_3 + x_4 + x_5 + x_6 + x_7 + x_8 + x_9.$$

The abbreviation for this sum is $\sum_{i=1}^{9} x_i$. The symbol $\sum$ (which is read as 'sigma') is a Greek capital S, standing for 'sum'. The '$i = 1$' at the bottom and the '9' at the top of the $\sum$ tell you that the sum starts at x_1 and finishes at x_9. Usually it is fairly obvious which values should be summed and so the sum may be written more simply as $\sum_i x_i$, $\sum x_i$ or $\sum x$. This notation for a sum is called Σ-**notation**. A symbol is also needed for the sample mean. This is $\bar{x}$ (which is read as 'x bar').

> The mean, $\bar{x}$, of a data set of n values is given by
>
> $$\bar{x} = \frac{x_1 + x_2 + \cdots + x_n}{n} = \frac{\sum x_i}{n}. \tag{2.1}$$

The following example illustrates some uses of Σ-notation which you will meet in this book.

Example 2.5.1
If $x_1 = 1$, $x_2 = 3$, $x_3 = 4$, $x_4 = 5$ and $y_1 = 7$, $y_2 = 12$, $y_3 = 14$, $y_4 = 20$, evaluate

(a) $\sum_{i=1}^{4} x_i$, (b) $\sum_{i=1}^{4} y_i$, (c) $\sum_{i=1}^{4} x_i^2$, (d) $\sum_{i=1}^{4} x_i y_i$, (e) $\bar{x}$, (f) $\sum_{i=1}^{4} (x_i - \bar{x})$, (g) $\sum_{i=1}^{4} (x_i - \bar{x})^2$.

(a) $\displaystyle\sum_{i=1}^{4} x_i = x_1 + x_2 + x_3 + x_4 = 1 + 3 + 4 + 5 = 13.$

(b) $\displaystyle\sum_{i=1}^{4} y_i = y_1 + y_2 + y_3 + y_4 = 7 + 12 + 14 + 20 = 53.$

(c) $\displaystyle\sum_{i=1}^{4} x_i^2 = x_1^2 + x_2^2 + x_3^2 + x_4^2 = 1^2 + 3^2 + 4^2 + 5^2 = 51.$

(d) $\displaystyle\sum_{i=1}^{4} x_i y_i = x_1 y_1 + x_2 y_2 + x_3 y_3 + x_4 y_4$

$$= (1 \times 7) + (3 \times 12) + (4 \times 14) + (5 \times 20) = 199.$$

(e) $\bar{x} = \dfrac{\sum x}{n} = \dfrac{13}{4} = 3.25.$

(f) $\displaystyle\sum_{i=1}^{4}(x_i - \bar{x}) = (x_1 - \bar{x}) + (x_2 - \bar{x}) + (x_3 - \bar{x}) + (x_4 - \bar{x})$

$$= (1 - 3.25) + (3 - 3.25) + (4 - 3.25) + (5 - 3.25)$$
$$= -2.25 - 0.25 + 0.75 + 1.75 = 0.$$

(g) $\displaystyle\sum_{i=1}^{4}(x_i - \bar{x})^2 = (x_1 - \bar{x})^2 + (x_2 - \bar{x})^2 + (x_3 - \bar{x})^2 + (x_4 - \bar{x})^2$

$$= (1 - 3.25)^2 + (3 - 3.25)^2 + (4 - 3.25)^2 + (5 - 3.25)^2$$
$$= (-2.25)^2 + (-0.25)^2 + 0.75^2 + 1.75^2 = 8.75.$$

2.6   Calculating the mean from a frequency table

Table 2.5 contains a copy of the data in Table 2.2, which was the frequency distribution of the number of brothers and sisters of the children in Year 8 at a school. Of the 204 values, 36 are '0's, 94 are '1's, 48 are '2's and so on. Their sum will be

$$(0 \times 36) + (1 \times 94) + (2 \times 48) + (3 \times 15) + (4 \times 7) + (5 \times 3) + (6 \times 1).$$

You can include this calculation in the table by adding a third column in which each value of the variable, x_i, is multiplied by its frequency, f_i.

Number of brothers and sisters, x_i	Frequency, f_i	$x_i f_i$
0	36	0
1	94	94
2	48	96
3	15	45
4	7	28
5	3	15
6	1	6
Totals: $\sum f_i = 204$		$\sum x_i f_i = 284$

Table 2.5. Calculating the mean for the data in Table 2.2.

The mean is equal to $\frac{284}{204} = 1.39$, correct to 3 significant figures.

> Although the number of brothers and sisters of each child must be a whole number, the mean of the data values need not be a whole number.

In this example the answer is a recurring decimal, and so the answer has been rounded to 3 significant figures. This degree of accuracy is suitable for the answers to most statistical calculations. However it is important to keep more significant figures when values are carried forward for use in further calculations.

The calculation of the mean can be expressed in Σ-notation as follows:

> The mean, $\bar{x}$, of a data set in which the variable takes the value x_1 with frequency f_1, x_2 with frequency f_2 and so on is given by
>
> $$\bar{x} = \frac{x_1 f_1 + x_2 f_2 + \cdots + x_n f_n}{f_1 + f_2 + \cdots + f_n} = \frac{\sum x_i f_i}{\sum f_i}.$$
>
> (2.2)

If the data in a frequency table are grouped, you need a single value to represent each class before you can calculate the mean using Equation 2.2. A reasonable choice is to take the value halfway between the class boundaries. This is called the **mid-class value**. Table 2.6 reproduces Table 2.3 for the playing times of 95 CDs. Two other columns have been included, one giving the mid-class value for each class and the other the product of this mid-class value and the frequency.

Playing time, x (min)	Class boundaries	Frequency, f_i	Mid-class value, x_i	$x_i f_i$
40–44	$39.5 \leq x < 44.5$	1	42	42
45–49	$44.5 \leq x < 49.5$	7	47	329
50–54	$49.5 \leq x < 54.5$	12	52	624
55–59	$54.5 \leq x < 59.5$	24	57	1368
60–64	$59.5 \leq x < 64.5$	29	62	1798
65–69	$64.5 \leq x < 69.5$	14	67	938
70–74	$69.5 \leq x < 74.5$	5	72	360
75–79	$74.5 \leq x < 79.5$	3	77	231
	Totals: $\sum f_i = 95$			$\sum x_i f_i = 5690$

Table 2.6. Calculation of the mean playing time for 95 CDs.

Thus the estimate of the mean is $\dfrac{\sum x_i f_i}{\sum f_i} = \dfrac{5690}{95} = 59.9$ minutes, correct to 3 significant figures.

> This value is only an estimate of the mean playing time for the CDs, because individual values have been replaced by mid-class values: some information has been lost by grouping the data.

2.7 Making the calculation of the mean easier

Most calculators will calculate $\bar{x}$ for you if you key in the values of x and f. You should check that you get the same answers to the calculations in the previous section when you use your calculator in this way.

You can see that the calculation of the mean involves quite large numbers. Even with a calculator the calculation can become tedious because of the amount of data-entry involved. There are ways in which you can simplify the calculation. Suppose you had to find the mean of the numbers 907, 908, 898, 902, 897. The direct method of calculation would be to add the numbers and divide by 5. You can check that this gives 902.4. Alternatively you could first make these numbers smaller by subtracting 900 from each of them, giving 7, 8, –2, 2 and –3. You can add these numbers in your head to give 12. Their mean is $\frac{12}{5}$, or 2.4. To find the mean of the original values you add 900 to give 902.4, as before.

The number which is subtracted from the data values, in this case 900, is sometimes called an **assumed mean** and the resulting values, in this case, 7, 8, –2, 2 and –3 are called **coded values**.

Example 2.7.1
The heights, x cm, of a sample of 80 female students are summarised by the equation $\sum(x - 160) = 240$. Find the mean height of a female student.

$$\bar{x} = \frac{\sum(x - 160)}{80} + 160 = \frac{240}{80} + 160 = 163.$$

The mean height of a female student is 163 cm.

The general result is:

$$\bar{x} = \frac{\sum(x - a)}{n} + a, \text{ where } a \text{ is a constant.}$$

Example 2.7.2
Given that $\sum(x - 40) = 34$ and $n = 50$, find $\sum x$.

$$\bar{x} = \frac{\sum(x - 40)}{50} + 40 = \frac{34}{50} + 40 = 40.68.$$

Now $\bar{x} = \frac{\sum x}{n}$, so

$$\sum x = n\bar{x} = 50 \times 40.48 = 2034.$$

Exercise 2B

1   The test marks of 8 students were 18, 2, 5, 0, 17, 15, 16 and 11. Find the mean score.

2   For the data set in Table 1.5, find the mean male height. The mean height of adult males is about 69 inches. Comment on your answer in the light of this information.

3   (a) Find $\bar{x}$ given that $\sum\limits_{i=1}^{20} x_i = 226$.   (b) Find $\bar{y}$ given that $\sum\limits_{i=1}^{12}(y_i - 100) = 66$.

4   The number of misprints on each page of the draft of a book containing 182 pages is summarised in the following table.

Number of misprints	0	1	2	3	4
Number of pages	144	24	10	2	2

Find the mean number of misprints on a page.

5 The following table gives the frequency distribution for the lengths of rallies (measured by the number of shots) in a tennis match.

Length of rally	1	2	3	4	5	6	7	8
Frequency	2	20	15	12	10	5	3	1

Find the mean length of a rally.

6 The table below gives the number of shoots produced by 50 plants in a botanical research laboratory.

No. of shoots	0–4	5–9	10–14	15–19	20–24	25–29	30–34	35–39	40–44
Frequency	1	1	1	6	17	16	4	2	2

Calculate the mean number of shoots per plant.

7 The speeds, in miles per hour, of 200 vehicles travelling on a motorway were measured using a radar device. The results are summarised in the following grouped frequency table.

Speed (m.p.h.)	30–40	40–50	50–60	60–70	70–80	over 80
Frequency	12	32	56	72	20	8

Estimate the mean speed.

8 Calls made by a telephone saleswoman were monitored. The lengths (in minutes, to the nearest minute) of 30 calls are summarised in the following table.

Length of call	0–2	3–5	6–8	9–11	12–15
Number of calls	17	6	4	2	1

(a) Write down the class boundaries.

(b) Estimate the mean length of the calls.

9 The volumes of the contents of 48 half-litre bottles of orangeade were measured, correct to the nearest millilitre. The results are summarised in the following table.

Volume (ml)	480–489	490–499	500–509	510–519	520–529	530–539
Frequency	8	11	15	8	4	2

Estimate the mean volume of the contents of the 48 bottles.

10 The price of a CD is denoted by £x. For 60 CDs bought in different stores it is found that $\sum(x - 12) = 53.40$. Calculate the mean price of these CDs. The mean price of a further 40 CDs is found to be £11.64. Find the mean price of the 100 CDs.

11* Given that $\sum(x - 10) = 212$ and $n = 20$, find $\sum x$.

2.8   The mode and the modal class

A third measure of central tendency is the **mode**, sometimes called the **modal value**. This is defined to be the most frequently occurring value. You can pick it out from a frequency table (if the data have not been grouped) by looking for the value with the highest frequency. If you look back to Table 2.2 you will see that the mode for the number of brothers and sisters is 1.

If the data have been grouped then it is only possible to estimate the mode. Alternatively, you can give the **modal class**, which is the class with the highest frequency density. For example, the modal class for the playing time in Table 2.3 is 60–64 minutes.

If you are given a small data set then you can find the mode just by looking at the data. For the first nine CDs in Section 2.2, with playing times

49, 52, 55, 56, 57, 61, 61, 63, 68

the mode is 61.

It is not uncommon for all the values to occur only once, so that there is no mode. For example, the next six CDs had playing times

47, 49, 59, 62, 65, 68,

and there is no modal value. Combining the two data sets gives

47, 49, 49, 52, 55, 56, 57, 59, 61, 61, 62, 63, 65, 68, 68.

Now there are three values which have a frequency of 2, giving three modes: 49, 61 and 68. One of these values is low, one high and the other is near the centre of the data set. In this case, the mode fails to provide only one measure of location to represent the data set. You can see that the mode is not a very useful measure of location for small data sets.

In contrast to the mean and median, the mode can be found for qualitative data. For example, for the datafile 'Cereals' in Table 1.1 the mode for the variable 'type' is C (standing for 'cold'), since there are 74 cereals of type C and only 3 of type H ('hot').

> The **mode** of a data set is the value which occurs with the highest frequency. A data set can have more than one mode if two or more values have the same maximum frequency. A data set has no mode if all the values have the same frequency.
>
> The **modal class** for a grouped frequency table is the class with the highest frequency density.

2.9   Comparison of the mean, median and mode

The examples in this chapter show that the mean, median and mode of a data set can differ from each other. For example, for the first nine CDs, the median was 57, the mean 58 and the mode 61. The question then arises as to why there are different ways of calculating the average of a data set. The answer is that an average describes a large amount of information with a single value, and there is no completely satisfactory way of doing this. Each average conveys different information and each has its advantages and disadvantages. You can see this by comparing the mean, median and mode for the following data set, which gives the monthly salaries of the thirteen employees in a small firm.

£1000 £1000 £1000 £1000 £1100 £1200 £1250
£1400 £1600 £1600 £1700 £2900 £4200

Median $= \frac{1}{2}(n+1)$th value $= \frac{1}{2}(13+1)$th value $=$ 7th value $=$ £1250.
Mean $=$ sum of the values $\div n = \frac{20\,950}{13} =$ £1612, correct to the nearest pound.
Mode $=$ value with the highest frequency $=$ £1000.

A new employee who had been told that the 'average' wage was £1612 (the mean) would probably be disappointed when he learnt his own salary, because 10 out of the 13 employees earn less than £1612. In this example the median would measure the centre of the distribution better because the median is not affected by the large distance of the last two salaries from the other salaries, whereas the mean is 'pulled up' by them. Normally the median is preferable to the mean as an average when there are values which are not typical. Such values are called **outliers**. The mode is not a very useful measure of the centre in this example, because it is £1000, the lowest salary: 9 of the 13 employees earn more than this.

You can see the same effect of a few high values on the mean for the data set in Table 2.5. The frequency distribution is illustrated in Fig. 2.8. The distribution is not symmetrical but is said to be **skewed**. The 'tail' of high values on the right of the distribution has the effect of making the mean (1.4) higher than the median (1).

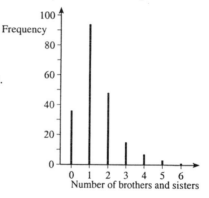

Fig. 2.8. Bar diagram of the data in Table 2.5.

A distribution which has a 'tail' of low values on the left will have a mean which is less than the median.

Distributions which are roughly symmetrical will have similar values for the mean and the median. The data for the CD playing times in Table 2.3 illustrate this. The histogram in Fig. 2.9, which illustrates this distribution, is approximately symmetrical; the estimates for the mean (59.9) and median (60) are nearly equal. For such a distribution the mean might be considered the 'best' average, because it uses all the information in the data set.

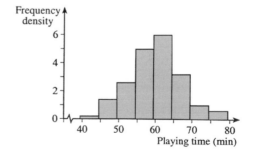

Fig. 2.9. Histogram of the data in Table 2.3.

From these examples it should be clear that the mean, median and mode often provide different information. When you are given an 'average' it is important to know whether it is the mean, the median or the mode. When you calculate an average, it is important to choose the average which is the most 'typical' value.

Example 2.9.1

A commuter who travels to work by car has a choice of two different routes, V and W. She decides to compare her journey times for each route. So she records the journey times, in minutes, for 10 consecutive working days, for each route. The results are:

Route V	53	52	48	51	49	47	42	48	57	53
Route W	43	41	39	108	52	42	38	45	39	51

Calculate the mean and median for route V, and the mean and median for route W. Which average do you think is more suitable for comparing the time taken on each route?

For route V, $\bar{v} = \dfrac{\sum v_i}{n} = \dfrac{500}{10} = 50.$ For route W, $\bar{w} = \dfrac{\sum w_i}{n} = \dfrac{498}{10} = 49.8.$

Arranging the values in order of increasing size gives:

Route V	42	47	48	48	49	51	52	53	53	57
Route W	38	39	39	41	42	43	45	51	52	108

For route V, median $= \frac{1}{2}(\text{5th} + \text{6th})$ values $= \frac{1}{2}(49 + 51) = 50.$

For route W, median $= \frac{1}{2}(\text{5th} + \text{6th})$ values $= \frac{1}{2}(42 + 43) = 42.5.$

For route V, the mean and the median are equal. For route W the mean is greater than the median, because the single high value of 108 pulls up the mean. This unusual value was probably due to bad weather or an accident and is not typical. So it is better to use the median as the average journey time, because it is not affected by such outliers. This suggests that route W, with a median of 42.5 minutes, is quicker than route V, with a median of 50 minutes.

2.10   Practical activities

1   **One–sidedness**   Calculate the mean and median for each set of data in Practical activity 1 in Section 1.5. Which average is more appropriate for comparing the reaction times? Give a reason for your choice.

2   **High jump**   Calculate the mean and median for each set of data in Practical activity 2 in Section 1.5. Which average is more appropriate for comparing the heights jumped? Give a reason for your choice.

3   **Newspapers**   Does the length of the sentences in a newspaper differ between broadsheet and tabloid newspapers?

   (a) For each type of newspaper count the number of words per sentence for at least 100 sentences. (You should ignore the headlines.)

   (b) Make a frequency table of the results for each newspaper.

   (c) Illustrate the results with diagrams and comment on the shape of the distributions.

(d) Calculate the mean and median for each distribution. Which would you use to compare the distributions and why?

4 **Age distribution** The Office for National Statistics publishes many statistics relating to the United Kingdom. From the website www.statistics.gov.uk/statbase/datasets.asp, or from its other publications obtain the most recent data for 'Population by gender and age.'

   (a) Illustrate the data in a way which allows you to compare the age distribution for males and females, and comment on the shape of the distributions.

   (b) Calculate the mean and median for the two distributions, explaining any assumptions which you may have to make.

   (c) Would you use the mean or the median to compare the average age of men and women? Explain your choice.

5 **Just a minute!** How well can people estimate time?

   (a) Ask at least 100 people to estimate a time interval of one minute. You will need to decide on a standard procedure for doing this. Record the value of the estimates to the nearest second. If possible have two distinct groups of at least 50, for example children in a particular age range and adults.

   (b) Calculate the mean and median for each group.

   (c) Assemble the results for each group into a frequency table and illustrate the distribution for each group with a histogram.

   (d) Comment on the shape of the distributions. Which would you use, mean or median, to compare the two groups? Give a reason for your choice.

Exercise 2C

1 For the following distributions state, where possible, the mode or the modal class.

(a)

x	0	1	2	3	4
f	7	4	2	5	1

(b)

x	70	75	80	85	90
f	5	5	5	5	5

(c)

x	2–3	4–5	6–7	8–9	10–11
f	7	4	4	4	1

(d)

Eye colour	Blue	Brown	Green
f	23	39	3

2 State, giving a reason, which of the mean, median or mode would be most useful in the following situations.

   (a) The manager of a shoe shop wishes to stock shoes of various sizes.

   (b) A City Council wishes to plan for a school to serve a new housing estate. In order to estimate the number of pupils, it studies family sizes on similar estates.

   (c) A person travels by car from York to Crewe regularly and has kept a record of the times taken. She wishes to make an estimate of the time that her next journey will take.

3 An estate agent makes the following statement.
'Over 60% of houses sold this month were sold for more than the average selling price.'
Consider the possible truth of this statement, and what is meant by 'average'.

4 State whether you would expect the following variables to have distributions which are skewed, or which are roughly symmetrical.

(a) The heights of female students in a university.

(b) The running times of competitors in a marathon race.

(c) The scores obtained by candidates in an easy examination.

(d) The numbers of pages in the books in a library.

5 A mental arithmetic test of 8 questions was given to a class of 32 pupils. The results are summarised in the following table.

Number of correct answers	0	1	2	3	4	5	6	7	8
Number of pupils		1	2	1	4	4	6	7	4	3

(a) Find the mean, median and mode of the number of correct answers. Interpret the median and mode in the context of this maths test.

(b) Describe the shape of the distribution.

Miscellaneous exercise 2

1 The number of times each week that a factory machine broke down was noted over a period of 50 consecutive weeks. The results are given in the following table.

Number of breakdowns	0	1	2	3	4	5	6
Number of weeks	2	12	14	8	8	4	2

(a) Find the mean number of breakdowns in this period. Is this value exact or an estimate?

(b) Give the mode and median of the number of breakdowns.

2 The costs, £x, of regional and national telephone calls costing over £0.40 made by a household over a period of three months are as follows.

$$
\begin{array}{ccccccccccc}
0.92 & 0.66 & 0.46 & 0.42 & 0.54 & 0.41 & 0.49 & 0.59 & 0.75 & 0.52 & 0.42 \\
0.40 & 0.49 & 0.52 & 0.64 & 0.48 & 0.57 & 0.46 & 0.49 & 0.42 & 0.65 & 0.73 \\
0.40 & 1.12 & 0.94 & 0.76 & 0.48 & 0.85 & 1.66 & 0.40 & 0.50
\end{array}
$$

$\sum x = 19.14$

(a) State why it is advisable to omit 1.66 from a stem-and-leaf diagram of these data.

(b) Draw an ordered stem-and-leaf diagram, with 1.66 omitted but noted as HI 1.66 next to the diagram. (HI is short for 'high'.)

(c) For the data obtain the median, the mean, and the mode.

(d) Which of the median, mean and mode would be best used to give the average cost of a phone call costing over £0.40? Give a reason for your answer.

(e) In the same period, the number of regional and national calls which cost £0.40 or under was 125, with mean cost £0.142. Find the mean cost of all the regional and national calls for the period.

3 The following table summarises the maximum daily temperatures in two holiday resorts in July and August 2003.

Temperature (°C)	18.0–19.9	20.0–21.9	22.0–23.9	24.0–25.9	26.0–27.9	28.0–29.9
Resort 1 frequency	9	13	18	10	7	5
Resort 2 frequency	6	21	23	8	3	1

(a) State the modal classes for the two resorts.

(b) A student analysed the data and came to the conclusion that, on average, Resort 1 was hotter than Resort 2 during July and August 2003. Is this conclusion supported by your answer to part (a)? If not, then obtain some evidence that does support the conclusion.

4 The following table shows data about the time taken (in seconds, to the nearest second) for each one of a series of 75 similar chemical experiments.

Time (s)	50–60	61–65	66–70	71–75	76–86
Number of experiments	4	13	26	22	10

(a) State the type of diagram appropriate for illustrating the data.

(b) A calculation using the data in the table gave an estimate of 69.64 seconds for the mean time of the experiments. Explain why this value is an estimate.

(c) Estimate the median of the times taken for completing the experiment.

(d) It was discovered later that the four experiments in the class 50–60 had actually taken 57, 59, 59 and 60 seconds. State, without more calculation, what effect (if any) there would be on the estimates of the median and mean if this information were taken into account.

(OCR, adapted)

5 The standardised marks received by 318 students who took a Mechanics examination are summarised in the following grouped frequency table.

Mark	0–29	30–39	40–49	50–59	60–69	70–79	80–89	90–100
Frequency	12	7	13	25	46	78	105	32

(a) Draw a histogram of these data, and describe the skewness of the distribution.

(b) Estimate the mean Mechanics mark.

(c) Estimate the median Mechanics mark by drawing a cumulative frequency diagram.

The same 318 students also took a Statistics examination during the same session. The mean and median of those marks were 71.5 and 70.0 respectively. Write a brief comparison of the students' performances in the two examinations.

6 Three hundred sixth-formers were asked to keep a record of the total time they spent watching television during the final week of their summer holiday. The times, to the nearest $\frac{1}{4}$ hour, are summarised in the following table.

Number of hours	$0–4\frac{3}{4}$	$5–9\frac{3}{4}$	$10–14\frac{3}{4}$	$15–19\frac{3}{4}$	$20–24\frac{3}{4}$	$25–29\frac{3}{4}$	$30–34\frac{3}{4}$	$35–39\frac{3}{4}$
Frequency	4	21	43	62	90	56	18	6

(a) Estimate the mean viewing time.

(b) State two sources of inaccuracy in your estimate of the mean.

(c) Find an estimate of the median viewing time.

(d) What do the values of the mean and median indicate about the skewness of the data?

7 It is sometimes said that for any set of quantitative data, the median (me), mode (mo) and mean ($\bar{x}$) are such that either $\bar{x} \leq$ me $\leq$ mo or mo $\leq$ me $\leq \bar{x}$. Check that this is true of the distribution in Question 2. Show that the statement is untrue for the following data.

x	1	2	3	4	5
f	2	1	11	9	7

8 The table gives the prices (in pence) of shares in 10 firms on Monday and Tuesday of a particular week. The Monday price is m, the Tuesday price is t, and $d = t - m$.

Firm	A	B	C	D	E	F	G	H	I	J
m	151	162	200	233	287	302	303	571	936	1394
t	144	179	182	252	273	322	260	544	990	1483
d	–7	17	–18	19	–14	20	–43	–27	54	89

(a) Calculate $\bar{m}$, $\bar{t}$ and $\bar{d}$. Does $\bar{d} = \bar{t} - \bar{m}$?

(b) Calculate the medians of m, t and d. Is it true that $\text{me}_d = \text{me}_t - \text{me}_m$?

9 The height, correct to the nearest metre, was recorded for each of the 59 birch trees in an area of woodland. The heights are summarised in the following table.

Height (m)	5–9	10–12	13–15	16–18	19–28
Number of trees	14	18	15	4	8

(a) A student was asked to draw a histogram to illustrate the data and produced the following diagram. Give two criticisms of this attempt at a histogram.

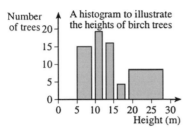

(b) Using graph paper, draw a correct histogram to illustrate the above data.

(c) Calculate an estimate of the mean height of the birch trees, giving your answer correct to 3 significant figures. (OCR)

10* An ordinary dice was thrown 50 times and the resulting scores were summarised in a frequency table. The mean score was calculated to be 3.42. It was later found that the frequencies 12 and 9, of two consecutive scores, had been swapped. What is the correct value of the mean?

3 Measures of spread

This chapter describes three different measures of spread and their methods of calculation. When you have completed it you should

- know what the range is, and be able to calculate it
- know what the quartiles are and how to find the interquartile range from them
- be able to construct a box plot from a set of data
- know what the variance and standard deviation are, and be able to calculate them
- be able to select an appropriate measure of spread to use in a given situation.

3.1 Introduction

You saw in Chapter 2 how a set of data could be summarised by choosing an appropriate typical value, or 'measure of location' as it is more correctly known. Three different measures of location, the mean, the median and the mode, were introduced.

Now consider the two sets of data A and B given below.

$$A: \quad 48 \quad 52 \quad 60 \quad 60 \quad 60 \quad 68 \quad 72$$
$$B: \quad 0 \quad 10 \quad 60 \quad 60 \quad 60 \quad 110 \quad 120$$

For both data sets A and B, mean = median = mode = 60. If you were just given a measure of location for each set you might be tempted to think that the two sets of data were similar. Yet if you look in detail at the two sets of data you can see that they are quite different. The most striking difference between the two data sets is that set B is much more spread out than set A. Measures of location do not give any indication of these differences in spread, so it is necessary to devise some new measures to summarise the spread of data. Measures of spread are also called **measures of dispersion**.

3.2 The range

The most obvious method of measuring spread is to calculate the difference between the lowest value and the highest value. This difference is called the **range**.

> The **range** of a set of data values is defined by the equation
>
> range = largest value − smallest value.

The range of data set A is $72 - 48 = 24$, whereas the range of data set B is $120 - 0 = 120$. Calculating the ranges shows clearly that data set B is more spread out than data set A.

> It is quite common for students to give the range as an interval. This would mean, for instance, that the range of data set A would be given as 48 to 72, or $48-72$, or $48 \rightarrow 72$. In statistics it is usually much more helpful to give the range as a single value, so the definition above is used.

If you are going to use the range as a measure of spread it is helpful to realise its limitations. If you consider the two further data sets C and D shown below, you will see that they both have the same range, 8.

$$
\begin{array}{llllll}
C: & 2 & 4 & 6 & 8 & 10 \\
D: & 2 & 6 & 6 & 6 & 10
\end{array}
$$

Although both data sets C and D have the same range, the patterns of their distributions are quite different from one another. Data set C is evenly spread within the interval 2 to 10 whereas dataset D has more of its values 'bunched' centrally. Because the range is calculated from extreme values it ignores the pattern of spread for the rest of the values. This is a major criticism of using the range as a measure of spread. Although the range is easy to calculate, it ignores the pattern of spread and considers only the extreme values.

3.3 The interquartile range

Since the range ignores the internal spread of the values in a data set, an alternative measure is needed. One possibility is to look at the spread between two values which are at some fixed, but interior, position. A sensible choice, which is associated naturally with the median, is to choose the values that are at the positions one-quarter and three-quarters of the way through the data when the values are arranged in order. These points are known as the **lower quartile** and the **upper quartile** respectively, and they are usually denoted by the symbols Q_1 and Q_3 respectively. The difference between these values is called the **interquartile range**.

> Interquartile range = upper quartile − lower quartile = $Q_3 - Q_1$.

The interquartile range is really just the range of the middle 50% of the distribution.

Notice that there is also a **middle quartile**, Q_2, which is the median.

To find the position of the quartiles for small data sets there are several possible methods that you might see in textbooks. The one suggested below is fairly easy to apply.

Finding the quartiles

First arrange the data in ascending order.

Case 1   An even number of data values

- Split the data into their upper half and lower half.
- Then the median of the upper half is Q_3, and the median of the lower half is Q_1.

Case 2   An odd number of data values

- Find the median, Q_2, and delete it from the list.
- Split the remaining data into their upper half and lower half.
- Then the median of the upper half is Q_3, and the median of the lower half is Q_1.

Example 3.3.1

Find the quartiles and the interquartile range for each of the two sets of data below.

(a) 7   9   12   13   8   11

(b) 7   8   22   20   15   18   19   13   11

(a) First, arrange the data in numerical order.

   7   8   9   11   12   13

The number of data values is even, so divide the data into its lower and upper halves:

   Lower half: 7   8   9   Upper half: 11   12   13

The lower quartile Q_1 is the median of the lower half, which is 8. The upper quartile Q_3 is the median of the upper half, which is 12. So

   interquartile range $= Q_3 - Q_1 = 12 - 8 = 4$.

(b) Arrange the data in numerical order.

   7   8   11   13   15   18   19   20   22

Since the number of data values (9) is odd, find the median $Q_2 = 15$ and delete it.

   7   8   11   13   18   19   20   22

This automatically divides the data into lower and upper halves.

The median of the lower half is the lower quartile, so $Q_1 = \frac{1}{2}(8 + 11) = 9.5$, and the median of the upper half is the upper quartile, so $Q_3 = \frac{1}{2}(19 + 20) = 19.5$.

The interquartile range is $Q_3 - Q_1 = 19.5 - 9.5 = 10$.

In Chapter 2 you saw how the median of the masses of female students taken from the 'Brain size' datafile could be found with the aid of the stem-and-leaf diagram in Fig. 2.1. The diagram is reproduced in Fig. 3.1.

Since there are 20 students, the upper and lower halves of the data set will contain 10 values each. The lower quartile is then at the position which is equivalent to the median of the lower half. This is half way between the 5th and 6th values (in ascending order). These are shown in bold type in Fig. 3.1.

10	6	(1)
11	4 8 8	(3)
12	**2 7** 7	(3)
13	5 6 8 9	(4)
14	0 3 6 **6 7**	(5)
15	3 5 9	(3)
16		(0)
17	5	(1)

Key: 12|4 means 124 pounds

Fig. 3.1. Stem-and-leaf diagram of the masses of female students.

Therefore $Q_1 = \frac{1}{2}(122 + 127) = 124.5$.

Similarly the upper quartile is at the position which is equivalent to the median of the upper half of the data set. This is halfway between the 15th and 16th values (in ascending order). These are also shown in bold type in Fig. 3.1.

Therefore $Q_3 = \frac{1}{2}(146 + 147) = 146.5$.

The interquartile range is therefore $Q_3 - Q_1 = 146.5 - 124.5 = 22$.

It is quite likely that the size of a data set will be much larger than the ones which have so far been considered. Larger data sets are usually organised into frequency tables and it is then necessary to think carefully about how to find the position of the quartiles. In Chapter 2 you saw how to find the median of a set of data which referred to the numbers of brothers and sisters of children in a year at a school. This was given in Table 2.2. Table 3.2 below reproduces Table 2.2.

Number of brothers and sisters	Frequency	Cumulative frequency
0	36	36
1	94	130
2	48	178
3	15	193
4	7	200
5	3	203
6	1	204
	Total: 204	

Table 3.2. Frequency distribution of the number of brothers and sisters of the children in Year 8 at a school.

There were 204 observations. This means that each half will have 102 data values.

The position of the lower quartile, Q_1, will be halfway between the 51st and 52nd values (in ascending order). From the cumulative frequency column you can see that both values are 1s, so $Q_1 = 1$. The position of the upper quartile, Q_3, will be halfway between the $(102 + 51)$th and $(102 + 52)$th values (in ascending order); that is, between the 153rd and 154th values. From the cumulative frequency column you can see that both values are 2s, so $Q_3 = 2$.

For continuous variables large data sets are usually grouped and so the individual values are lost. The quartiles are estimated from a cumulative frequency graph using a method similar to that described in Chapter 2 to find the median.

Table 3.3 gives the frequency distribution for the playing times of the selection of CDs which you first met in Table 2.3.

To obtain an estimate of the lower quartile of the playing times you read off the value corresponding to a cumulative frequency equal to one-quarter of the total frequency, which in this case is $\frac{1}{4} \times 95 = 23.75$. From the cumulative frequency graph in Fig. 3.4 you can see that $Q_1 \approx 55$ minutes. Similarly you find an estimate of the upper quartile by reading off the value corresponding to a cumulative frequency equal to three-quarters of the total frequency, which is $\frac{3}{4} \times 95 = 71.25$. From the cumulative frequency graph in Fig. 3.4 this gives $Q_3 \approx 64$ minutes.

Then the interquartile range is

$$Q_3 - Q_1 \approx 64 - 55 = 9,$$

so the interquartile range is approximately 9 minutes.

Playing time, x (min)	Class boundaries	Frequency	Less than	Cumulative frequency
40–44	$39.5 \leq x < 44.5$	1	44.5	1
45–49	$44.5 \leq x < 49.5$	7	49.5	8
50–54	$49.5 \leq x < 54.5$	12	54.5	20
55–59	$54.5 \leq x < 59.5$	24	59.5	44
60–64	$59.5 \leq x < 64.5$	29	64.5	73
65–69	$64.5 \leq x < 69.5$	14	69.5	87
70–74	$69.5 \leq x < 74.5$	5	74.5	92
75–79	$74.5 \leq x < 79.5$	3	79.5	95
		Total: 95		

Table 3.3. Playing times of 95 CDs.

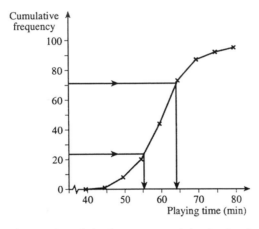

Fig. 3.4. Cumulative frequency graph for the data in Table 3.3.

You may be wondering how to interpret the interquartile range for a set of data. For example, is the value of 9 in the example above large or small? The answer is that you cannot tell without more information. Normally you would be comparing the spread of two or more data sets. You can then make a more sensible comment on whether a particular interquartile range is large or small by comparing its size with the other interquartile ranges. The following example illustrates this idea.

Example 3.3.2

Two people did separate traffic surveys at different locations. Each person noted down the speed of 50 cars which passed their observation point. The results are given in Table 3.5.

(a) Draw a cumulative frequency diagram for each set of data and use it to estimate the median speed and the interquartile range of speeds at each observation point.

(b) Use your results to part (a) to comment on the locations.

Speed, v (km h^{-1})	A frequency	B frequency
$0 \leq v < 20$	7	1
$20 \leq v < 40$	11	3
$40 \leq v < 60$	13	5
$60 \leq v < 80$	12	20
$80 \leq v < 100$	5	18
$100 \leq v < 120$	2	3
Totals:	50	50

Table 3.5. Table showing the speeds of 50 cars at each of two locations in a county.

(a)

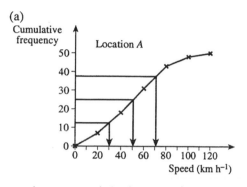

Fig. 3.6. Cumulative frequency diagram to show the distribution of speeds of 50 cars at location A.

Fig. 3.7. Cumulative frequency diagram to show the distribution of speeds of 50 cars at location B.

From Fig. 3.6, you can estimate the median and quartiles for the cars at location A. The median corresponds to a cumulative frequency of 25 and, from Fig. 3.6, it is approximately 51. The lower quartile corresponds to a cumulative frequency of 12.5, and it is approximately 30. The upper quartile corresponds to a cumulative frequency of 37.5, and it is approximately 71.

From Fig. 3.7, you can estimate the median and quartiles for the cars at location B. The equivalent values of the median and the quartiles are approximately 76, 64 and 89.

(b) You can now compare the medians and the interquartile ranges.

For A the median is 51 and the interquartile range is 41.

For B the median is 76 and the interquartile range is 25.

The median speed at A is lower than the median speed at B and the interquartile range at A is higher than the interquartile range at B. So at location A the cars go more slowly and there is a greater variation in their speeds. Perhaps B is on or near a motorway, and A may be in a town near some point of congestion. You cannot say for certain what types of location A and B are but the summary values do give you an idea of the type of road at each position.

3.4   Box plots

One helpful way of summarising data is to give values which provide essential information about the data set. One such summary is called the **five-number summary**. This summary gives the median, Q_2, the lower quartile Q_1, the upper quartile Q_3, the minimum value and the maximum value.

Example 3.4.1

The data below give the number of fish caught each day over a period of 11 days by an angler. Give a five-number summary of the data.

$$0 \quad 2 \quad 5 \quad 2 \quad 0 \quad 4 \quad 4 \quad 8 \quad 9 \quad 8 \quad 8$$

Rearranging the data in order gives:

$$0 \quad 0 \quad 2 \quad 2 \quad 4 \quad 4 \quad 5 \quad 8 \quad 8 \quad 8 \quad 9$$

The median value is $Q_2 = 4$. As the number of data values is odd, deleting the middle one and finding the medians of the lower and upper halves gives

$$Q_1 = 2 \quad \text{and} \quad Q_3 = 8.$$

The five-number summary is then the minimum value, 0, the lower quartile, 2, the median, 4, the upper quartile, 8, and the maximum value, 9.

You can convert this five-number summary into a useful diagram, called a **box plot** or a **box-and-whisker diagram**. To draw a box plot, first draw a scale, preferably using graph paper. You can draw the scale vertically or horizontally, but in this book, the scale and the diagram are always drawn horizontally. Above the scale draw a box (or rectangle) in which the left side is above the point corresponding to the lower quartile and the right side is

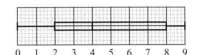

Fig. 3.8. Box plot to show the distribution of the numbers of fish caught by an angler.

above the point corresponding to the upper quartile. Then mark a third line inside the box above the point which corresponds to the median value. After this you draw the two whiskers. The left whisker extends from the lower quartile to the minimum value and the right whisker extends from the upper quartile to the maximum. Fig. 3.8 shows the box plot for the data in Example 3.4.1.

In a box plot the box itself indicates the location of the middle 50% of the data. The whiskers then show how the data is spread overall.

Another important feature of a set of data is its shape when represented as a frequency diagram. The three pictures in Fig. 3.9 show three different shapes which commonly occur when you draw frequency diagrams.

The distribution in Fig. 3.9a is symmetrical. If a distribution lacks symmetry it is said to be **skew**, or to have **skewness**. The distribution in Fig. 3.9a may therefore be said to have zero skewness. You were briefly introduced to the term 'skewness' in Section 2.9.

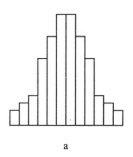
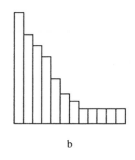
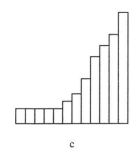

a   b   c

Fig. 3.9. Possible shapes of frequency distributions.

The distribution in Fig. 3.9b is certainly not symmetrical, and there is a 'tail' which stretches towards the higher values. This distribution is said to have **positive skew**, or to be **skewed positively**.

The distribution in Fig. 3.9c is also not symmetrical. There is a 'tail' which stretches towards the lower values. This distribution is said to have **negative skew**, or to be **skewed negatively**.

Another method of assessing the skewness of a distribution is to use the quartiles Q_1, Q_2 and Q_3. Remember that Q_2 denotes the median, and that Q_1 and Q_3 denote the lower and upper quartiles.

If $Q_3 - Q_2 \approx Q_2 - Q_1$ then the distribution is said to be (almost) symmetrical, and a box plot of such data, as in Fig. 3.10, would show a box in which the line corresponding to the median was in the centre of the box.

Fig. 3.10. Box plot for a set of data in which $Q_3 - Q_2 \approx Q_2 - Q_1$.

If $Q_3 - Q_2 > Q_2 - Q_1$, as in Fig. 3.11, then the data is said to have positive skew, and the line representing the median would be nearer to the left side of the box.

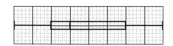

Fig. 3.11. Box plot for a set of data in which $Q_3 - Q_2 > Q_2 - Q_1$.

If $Q_3 - Q_2 < Q_2 - Q_1$, as in Fig. 3.12, then the data would be said to have negative skew, and the line representing the median would be nearer to the right side of the box.

For the data in Example 3.4.1, $Q_1 = 2$, $Q_2 = 4$ and $Q_3 = 8$, so $Q_3 - Q_2 = 8 - 4 = 4$ and $Q_2 - Q_1 = 4 - 2 = 2$. The set of data in Example 3.4.1 therefore has positive skew.

Fig. 3.12. Box plot for a set of data in which $Q_3 - Q_2 < Q_2 - Q_1$.

The length of the whiskers can also give some indication of skewness. If the left whisker is shorter than the right whisker then that would tend to indicate positive skew, whereas if the right whisker is shorter than the left whisker, negative skew would be implied.

It is possible for the data to give different results for skewness depending on what measure you use. For example, it is perfectly possible for a box plot to have $Q_3 - Q_2 > Q_2 - Q_1$, indicating positive skew, but for the left whisker to be longer than the right whisker, which would tend to suggest negative skew. In such cases you must make a judgement about which method of assessing skewness you think is the more important. Fortunately data of this sort does not occur commonly.

3.5* Outliers

The quartiles of a data set can also be used to assess whether the data set has any outliers. Outliers are unusual or 'freak' values which differ greatly in magnitude from the majority of the data values. But just how large or small does a value have to be to be an outlier? There is no simple answer to this question but one 'rule of thumb' developed by a statistician called John Tukey is to use 'fences'.

The upper fence is at a value 1.5 times the interquartile range above the upper quartile.

$$\text{Upper fence} = Q_3 + 1.5(Q_3 - Q_1).$$

The lower fence is at a value 1.5 times the interquartile range below the lower quartile.

$$\text{Lower fence} = Q_1 + 1.5(Q_3 - Q_1).$$

John Tukey then said that any value which is bigger than the upper fence or smaller than the lower fence is considered to be an outlier.

For the data of Example 3.4.1, $Q_1 = 2$ and $Q_3 = 8$, so

$$\text{upper fence} = Q_3 + 1.5(Q_3 - Q_1) = 8 + 1.5 \times (8 - 2) = 17,$$
$$\text{lower fence} = Q_1 - 1.5(Q_3 - Q_1) = 2 - 1.5(8 - 2) = -7.$$

In this case there is no value above 17 or below -7, so this data set does not contain any values which could be said to be outliers.

Exercise 3A

1 Find the range and interquartile range of each of the following data sets.

(a)   7   4   14   9   12   2   19   6   15
(b)   7.6   4.8   1.2   6.9   4.8   7.2   8.1   10.3   4.8   6.7

2 Find the interquartile range of the leaf lengths displayed in Question 1 of Exercise 1A.

3 The number of times a factory machine broke down was noted over a period of 50 consecutive weeks. The results are given in the following table.

Number of breakdowns	0	1	2	3	4	5	6
Number of weeks		2	12	14	8	8	4	2

Find the interquartile range of the number of breakdowns in a week.

4 For the data in Question 6 of Miscellaneous exercise 1, find the lower and upper quartiles of the annual salaries.

5 For the data in Question 8 of Miscellaneous exercise 1, find the median and interquartile traffic noise levels in the two streets. Use the statistics to compare the noise levels in the streets.

6 The audience size in a theatre performing a long-running detective play was monitored over a period of one year. The sizes for Monday and Wednesday nights are summarised in the following table.

Audience size	50–99	100–199	200–299	300–399	400–499	500–599
Number of Mondays	12	20	12	5	3	0
Number of Wednesdays	2	3	20	18	5	4

Compare the audience sizes on Mondays and Wednesdays.

7 The following back-to-back stem-and-leaf diagram refers to the datafile 'Cereals' in Chapter 1. It gives the ratings of the cereals with fat content 0 and with fat content 1.

	Fat content 0		Fat content 1	
(7)	9 8 8 7 4 3 2 2	2	3 4 7 8 8 9	(1)
(13)	9 9 9 9 8 7 6 6 6 2 1 1 0	3	1 3 5 6	(4)
(3)	9 7 0	4	1 1 1 2 2 4 6 7	(8)
(6)	9 5 2 2 0 0	5	3 3 3 5 8 9	(6)
(1)	8	6	0 1 3 5 8	(5)
(0)		7	3 4	(2)
(0)		8		(0)
(0)		9	4	(1)

Key: 4|7 means 47

Compare the two sets of ratings by finding the ranges, medians and quartiles.

8 Draw box plots for data which have the following five-number summaries, and in each case describe the shape of the distribution.

(a)   6.0 kg   10.2 kg   12.7 kg   13.2 kg   15.7 kg
(b)   −12 °C   −8 °C   −6 °C   3 °C   11 °C
(c)   37 m   48 m   60 m   72 m   82 m

9 State, with reasons, whether box plots or histograms are better for comparing two distributions.

10 The following figures are the amounts spent in a supermarket by a family for 13 weeks.
£48.25   £43.70   £52.83   £49.24   £58.28   £55.47   £47.29
£51.82   £58.42   £38.73   £42.76   £50.42   £40.85

(a) Obtain a five-number summary of the data.

(b) Construct a box plot of the data.

(c) Describe any skewness of the data.

3.6   Variance and standard deviation

One of the reasons for using the interquartile range in preference to the range as a measure of spread was that it took some account of how the more central values were spread rather than concentrating solely on the spread of the extreme values. The interquartile range, however, does not take account of the spread of all of the data values and so, in some sense, it is still an inadequate measure. An alternative measure of spread which does take into account the spread of all the values can be devised by finding how far each data value is from the mean. To do this you would calculate the quantities $x_i - \bar{x}$ for each x_i.

An example in Section 2.4 used the playing times, in minutes, of 9 CDs.

$$49 \quad 56 \quad 55 \quad 68 \quad 61 \quad 57 \quad 61 \quad 52 \quad 63$$

The mean of these times was found to be 58 minutes. If the mean is subtracted from each of the original values you get the following values.

$$-9 \quad -2 \quad -3 \quad 10 \quad 3 \quad -1 \quad 3 \quad -6 \quad 5$$

If you ignore the negative signs, then the resulting values give an idea of the distance of each of the original values from the mean. So these distances would be

$$9 \quad 2 \quad 3 \quad 10 \quad 3 \quad 1 \quad 3 \quad 6 \quad 5.$$

The mean of these distances would be a sensible measure of spread. It would represent the mean distance from the mean.

In this case the mean distance would be

$$\tfrac{1}{9}(9 + 2 + 3 + 10 + 3 + 1 + 3 + 6 + 5) = \tfrac{1}{9} \times 42 = 4.66\ldots$$

Unfortunately there are difficulties using this method. To represent it with a simple formula it is necessary to use the modulus symbol $|v|$, which denotes the magnitude, or numerical value, of v. It is now possible to write a precise formula for the mean distance:

$$\text{mean distance} = \frac{1}{n} \sum |x_i - \bar{x}|.$$

*The mean distance is also called the **mean absolute deviation from the mean**.

The simplest way to avoid the modulus is to square each of the quantities $(x_i - \bar{x})$.

This leads to the expression $\dfrac{1}{n}\sum(x_i - \bar{x})^2$ as a measure of spread.

This quantity is called the **variance** of the data values. It is the mean of the squared distances from the mean. For the data on playing times of CDs the calculation can be set out in a table as shown on the right.

$$\text{So variance} = \frac{1}{n}\sum(x - \bar{x})^2 = \frac{274}{9} = 30.4\ldots$$

If the data values $x_1, x_2, \ldots, x_n$ have units associated with them then the variance will be measured in unit^2. In the example the

x	$(x - \bar{x})$	$(x - \bar{x})^2$
49	−9	81
56	−2	4
55	−3	9
68	10	100
61	3	9
57	−1	1
61	3	9
52	−6	36
63	5	25
		Total: 274

data values were measured in minutes and therefore the variance would be measured in minutes^2. This is something which can be avoided by taking the positive square root of the variance. The positive square root of the variance is known as the **standard deviation**, often shortened to 'SD', and it always has the same units as the original data values. The formula for standard deviation is

$$\sqrt{\frac{1}{n}\sum(x_i - \bar{x})^2}.$$

The standard deviation of the playing times of the 9 CDs is $\sqrt{30.4\ldots} = 5.52$, correct to 3 significant figures.

The calculation of the variance can be quite tedious, particularly when the mean is not a whole number. Fortunately, there is an alternative formula which is easier to use:

$$\text{variance} = \frac{1}{n}\left(x_1^2 + x_2^2 + \cdots + x_n^2\right) - \bar{x}^2.$$

This can be written in Σ-notation as

$$\text{variance} = \frac{1}{n}\sum x_i^2 - \bar{x}^2.$$

The calculation of the variance of the playing times of CDs, using this alternative formula, can be set out in a table as shown on the right.

x	x^2
49	2401
56	3136
55	3025
68	4624
61	3721
57	3249
61	3721
52	2704
63	3969
	Total: 30 550

$$\text{Variance} = \frac{1}{n}\sum x_i^2 - \bar{x}^2$$

$$= \frac{1}{9} \times 30\,550 - 58^2 = 30.4\ldots$$

This is the same value as was found using the original formula. This does not, of course, prove that the two formulae are always equivalent to one another. A proof is given in the next section.

> The **variance** of a set of data values $x_1, x_2, \ldots, x_n$ whose mean is
> $$\bar{x} = \frac{x_1 + x_2 + \cdots + x_n}{n} = \frac{1}{n}\sum x_i$$
> is given by either of the two alternative formulae
> $$\text{variance} = \frac{1}{n}\sum(x_i - \bar{x})^2 \quad \text{or} \quad \text{variance} = \frac{1}{n}\sum x_i^2 - \bar{x}^2. \qquad (3.1), (3.2)$$
> The **standard deviation** is the square root of the variance.

It is important to note that errors can occur when formula (3.2) is used if the value of $\bar{x}$ has been rounded off. This can be avoided by having $\bar{x}^2$ in the form $\left(\dfrac{\sum x}{n}\right)^2$.

Example 3.6.1

There are 12 boys and 13 girls, in a class of 25 students, who were given a test. The mean mark for the 12 boys was 31 and the standard deviation of the boys' marks was 6.2. The mean mark of the girls was 36 and the standard deviation of the girls' marks was 4.3. Find the mean mark and standard deviation of the marks of the whole class of 25 students.

Let $x_1, x_2, \ldots, x_{12}$ be the marks of the 12 boys in the test and let $y_1, y_2, \ldots, y_{13}$ be the marks of the 13 girls in the test.

Since the mean of the boys' marks is 31, $\dfrac{\sum x}{12} = 31$, so $\sum x = 12 \times 31 = 372$.

As the standard deviation of the boys' marks is 6.2, the variance is $6.2^2 = 38.44$.

Therefore, using Equation 3.2,

$$38.44 = \frac{\sum x^2}{12} - 31^2, \text{ which gives } \sum x^2 = 12 \times (38.44 + 31^2) = 11\,993.28.$$

Similarly,

$$\sum y = 13 \times 36 = 468, \text{ and}$$

$$\sum y^2 = 13 \times (4.3^2 + 36^2) = 17\,088.37.$$

The overall mean is $\dfrac{\sum x + \sum y}{25} = \dfrac{372 + 468}{25} = \dfrac{840}{25} = 33.6$.

The overall variance is $\dfrac{\sum x^2 + \sum y^2}{25} - 33.6^2 = \dfrac{11\,993.28 + 17\,088.37}{25} - 33.6^2$

$$= 34.306.$$

The overall standard deviation is $\sqrt{34.306} = 5.86$, correct to 3 significant figures.

3.7* Proof of the equivalence of the variance formulae

You may omit this section if you wish.

First note that $\bar{x} = \dfrac{x_1 + x_2 + \cdots + x_n}{n}$, so $n\bar{x} = x_1 + x_2 + \cdots + x_n$.

Then variance $= \dfrac{1}{n}\sum(x_i - \bar{x})^2$

$$= \frac{1}{n}\left\{(x_1 - \bar{x})^2 + (x_2 - \bar{x})^2 + \cdots + (x_n - \bar{x})^2\right\}$$

$$= \frac{1}{n}\left\{(x_1^2 - 2x_1\bar{x} + \bar{x}^2) + (x_2^2 - 2x_2\bar{x} + \bar{x}^2) + \cdots + (x_n^2 - 2x_n\bar{x} + \bar{x}^2)\right\}$$

$$= \frac{1}{n}\left\{(x_1^2 + x_2^2 + \cdots + x_n^2) - 2\bar{x}(x_1 + x_2 + \cdots + x_n) + \left(\overbrace{\bar{x}^2 + \bar{x}^2 + \cdots + \bar{x}^2}^{n \text{ of these}}\right)\right\}$$

$$= \frac{1}{n}\left\{(x_1^2 + x_2^2 + \cdots + x_n^2) - 2\bar{x} \times n\bar{x} + n\bar{x}^2\right\}$$

$$= \frac{1}{n}\left\{(x_1^2 + x_2^2 + \cdots + x_n^2) - 2n\bar{x}^2 + n\bar{x}^2\right\}$$

$$= \frac{1}{n}\left\{(x_1^2 + x_2^2 + \cdots + x_n^2) - n\bar{x}^2\right\}$$

$$= \frac{1}{n}\sum x_i^2 - \bar{x}^2.$$

This shows that the two formulae for the variance are equivalent.

Exercise 3B

1 State or find the mean of

  (a) 1, 2, 3, 4, 5, 6, 7   (b) 4, 12, −2, 7, 0, 9.

  Using the formula $\sqrt{\frac{1}{n}\sum(x - \bar{x})^2}$, find the standard deviation of each data set.

2 Find the standard deviation of the following data sets, using the formula $\sqrt{\frac{1}{n}\sum(x - \bar{x})^2}$.

  (a) 2, 1, 5.3, −4.2, 6.7, 3.1   (b) 15.2, 12.3, 5.7, 4.3, 11.2, 2.5, 8.7

3 The masses, x grams, of the contents of 25 tins of Brand A anchovies are summarised by $\sum x = 1268.2$ and $\sum x^2 = 64\,585.16$. Find the mean and variance of the masses. What is the unit of measurement of the variance?

4 The standard deviation of 10 values of a variable is 2.8. The sum of the squares of the 10 values is 92.8. Find the mean of the 10 values.

5 The mean and standard deviation of the heights of 12 boys in a class are 148.8 cm and 5.4 cm respectively. A boy of height 153.4 cm joins the class. Find the mean and standard deviation of the heights of the 13 boys.

6 The runs made by two batsmen, Anwar and Brian, in 12 innings during the 2003 cricket season are shown in the following table.

Anwar	23	83	40	0	89	98	71	31	102	48	15	18
Brian	43	32	61	75	68	92	17	15	25	43	86	12

  (a) calculate the mean and standard deviation for each batsman.

  Giving your reasons, state which batsman you consider to be

  (b) better,   (c) more consistent.

7 The following stem-and-leaf diagrams are for the masses of 20 female students and 18 male students from the datafile 'Brain size' in Chapter 1.

Females   **Males**

10	6	(1)
11	4 8 8	(3)
12	2 7 7	(3)
13	5 6 8 9	(4)
14	0 3 6 6 7	(5)
15	3 5 9	(3)
16		(0)
17	5	(1)

13	2 4	(2)
14	3 4 8	(3)
15	1 5	(2)
16		(0)
17	1 2 2 8 9	(5)
18	0 1 6 7	(4)
19	1 2	(2)

Key: 13|3 means 133 pounds

Summary: $\sum f = 2744$, $\sum f^2 = 381\,938$, $\sum m = 2996$, $\sum m^2 = 505\,500$.

Compare the masses of the females and males by drawing box plots and calculating the means and standard deviations of the masses.

3.8   Calculating variance from a frequency table

Table 3.13 reproduces Table 2.5, which gave the frequency distribution of the numbers of brothers and sisters of children in Year 8 in a school.

Number of brothers and sisters, x_i	Frequency, f_i	$x_i f_i$
0	36	0
1	94	94
2	48	96
3	15	45
4	7	28
5	3	15
6	1	6
Totals: $\sum f_i = 204$		$\sum x_i f_i = 284$

Table 3.13. Frequency distribution of the number of brothers and sisters of Year 8 children.

In order to calculate the variance you need first to find the mean. This was done in Section 2.6, and the mean was $\frac{284}{204} = 1.39\ldots$ (using the totals in the table above).

Since the 204 values consist of 36 0s, 94 1s, 48 2s and so on,

$$x_1^2 + x_2^2 + \cdots + x_n^2 = \left(\overbrace{0^2 + 0^2 + \cdots + 0^2}^{36 \text{ of these}} \right) + \left(\overbrace{1^2 + 1^2 + \cdots + 1^2}^{94 \text{ of these}} \right) + \cdots$$

$$+ \left(\overbrace{4^2 + 4^2 + \cdots + 4^2}^{7 \text{ of these}} \right) + \left(\overbrace{5^2 + 5^2 + \cdots + 5^2}^{3 \text{ of these}} \right) + 6^2$$

$$= (0^2 \times 36) + (1^2 \times 94) + (2^2 \times 48)$$
$$+ (3^2 \times 15) + (4^2 \times 7) + (5^2 \times 3) + (6^2 \times 1)$$
$$= 0 + 94 + 192 + 135 + 112 + 75 + 36 = 644.$$

You can include this calculation in the table by adding a fourth column for $x_i^2 \times f_i$.

Number of brothers and sisters, x_i	Frequency, f_i	$x_i f_i$	$x_i^2 f_i$
0	36	0	0
1	94	94	94
2	48	96	192
3	15	45	135
4	7	28	112
5	3	15	75
6	1	6	36
Totals: $\sum f_i = 204$		$\sum x_i f_i = 284$	$\sum x_i^2 f_i = 644$

Table 3.14. Calculating the variance for the data in Table 2.5.

So the variance is $\frac{644}{204} - (1.39\ldots)^2 = 1.218\ldots = 1.22$ correct to 3 significant figures.

The standard deviation is then $= \sqrt{1.218\ldots} = 1.10$ correct to 3 significant figures.

To summarise the method used to find the variance:

> The variance of data given in a frequency table in which the variable takes the value x_1 with frequency f_1, the value x_2 with frequency f_2 and so on is given by the two formulae
>
> $$\text{variance} = \frac{\sum (x_i - \bar{x})^2 f_i}{\sum f_i} \quad \text{or} \quad \text{variance} = \frac{\sum x_i^2 f_i}{\sum f_i} - \bar{x}^2. \qquad (3.3), (3.4)$$

The second formula is usually easier to use.

If the data are grouped you need a single value to represent each class. In Section 2.6 you saw that the most reasonable choice was the mid-class value. After you have made this simplifying assumption, then the calculation proceeds in the same way as in Table 3.14.

Example 3.8.1
Calculate an estimate of the variance of the data given in Table 2.6.

Table 3.15 reproduces Table 2.6 with an extra column representing $x_i^2 f_i$.

Using the totals from Table 3.15 and the formula $\text{variance} = \dfrac{\sum x_i^2 f_i}{\sum f_i} - \bar{x}^2$,

$$\text{variance} = \frac{345\,680}{95} - \left(\frac{5690}{95}\right)^2 = 51.4, \text{ correct to 3 significant figures.}$$

The variance is therefore 51.4 minutes^2, correct to 3 significant figures.

Playing time, x (min)	Class boundaries	Frequency, f_i	Mid-class value, x_i	$x_i f_i$	$x_i^2 f_i$
40–44	$39.5 \leq x < 44.5$	1	42	42	1764
45–49	$44.5 \leq x < 49.5$	7	47	329	15 463
50–54	$49.5 \leq x < 54.5$	12	52	624	32 448
55–59	$54.5 \leq x < 59.5$	24	57	1 368	77 976
60–64	$59.5 \leq x < 64.5$	29	62	1 798	111 476
65–69	$64.5 \leq x < 69.5$	14	67	938	62 846
70–74	$69.5 \leq x < 74.5$	5	72	360	25 920
75–79	$74.5 \leq x < 79.5$	3	77	231	17 787
	Totals: $\sum f_i = 95$			$\sum x_i f_i = 5\,690$	$\sum x_i^2 f_i = 345\,680$

Table 3.15. Calculating the variance of the playing times for 95 CDs.

You should remember that, just as with the mean calculation in Section 2.6, this value is only an estimate, because the individual values have been replaced by mid-class values.

3.9 Making the calculation of variance easier

You saw in Section 2.7 that you could simplify the calculation of the mean. To find the mean of 907, 908, 898, 902 and 897 you subtracted 900 from each of the numbers, giving 7, 8, −2, 2 and −3. You then found the mean of these numbers, which was 2.4. To recover the mean of the original five numbers 907, 908, 898, 902 and 897 you simply added 900 to 2.4 to give a mean for the original numbers of 902.4. You can also use this idea of simplifying the numbers when calculating variance, but the details are slightly different.

To find the variance of 907, 908, 898, 902 and 897, subtract 900 as before to give 7, 8, −2, 2 and −3. The dispersion of the two sets of numbers will be identical, so the variance of 907, 908, 898, 902 and 897 will be the same as the variance of 7, 8, −2, 2 and −3.

The variance of 7, 8, −2, 2 and −3 is given by

$$\tfrac{1}{5}(7^2 + 8^2 + (-2)^2 + 2^2 + (-3)^2) - 2.4^2 = 20.24.$$

This value will also represent the variance of the original numbers. Notice also that the standard deviation will be $\sqrt{20.24} = 4.498\ldots$ for both sets of data. After you found the mean of the new numbers it was necessary to add 900 to the new mean to recover the mean of the original set of numbers. Notice that you do *not* need to add anything to the variance of the new numbers to recover the variance of the original set of numbers. This is because the amount of dispersion is the same for both sets of data.

Example 3.9.1
The heights of a sample of 80 female students are summarised by the equations

$$\sum(x - 160) = 240 \quad \text{and} \quad \sum(x - 160)^2 = 8720.$$

Find the mean and standard deviation of the heights of the 80 female students.

Let $y = x - 160$ and then $\sum y = 240$ and $\sum y^2 = 8720$.

The mean of the y-values is given by

$$\bar{y} = \frac{\sum y}{n} = \frac{240}{80} = 3.$$

Therefore the mean of the x-values is given by

$$\bar{x} = 3 + 160 = 163.$$

The variance of the y-values is given by

$$\text{variance} = \frac{\sum y^2}{n} - \bar{y}^2 = \frac{8720}{80} - \left(\frac{240}{80}\right)^2 = 109 - 3^2 = 100.$$

Therefore the standard deviation of the y-values is 10.

But the standard deviation of the x-values will be the same as the standard deviation of the y-values. Therefore the standard deviation of the girls' heights will also be 10.

3.10   Practical activities

1 One-sidedness

(a) Calculate the variance for each set of data in Practical activity 1 in Section 1.5. Does one 'side' show more variability than the other?

(b) Find estimates for the interquartile range of each set of data by drawing two cumulative frequency diagrams. What conclusions can you draw from these two values?

2 High jump

(a) Calculate the variance for each set of data in Practical activity 2 in Section 1.5. Does one group show more variability than the other?

(b) Find estimates for the interquartile range of each set of data by drawing two cumulative frequency diagrams. What conclusions can you draw from these two values?

3 Waste paper

(a) Select a student and ask them to try to throw a ball of paper into a waste paper bin 10 metres away with their 'natural' or stronger throwing arm. Repeat this until the student is successful and record the total number of attempts needed by the student. Repeat this experiment with about 30 students.

(b) Select a second group of students and ask them to throw the paper ball into the bin with their 'weaker' arm. Record the number of attempts needed for each student.

(c) Select an appropriate measure of spread and find it for each of the two sets of data. Does the weaker arm give more variable results than the stronger arm?

4 Newspapers   Calculate the variance and the interquartile range for each set of data in Practical activity 3 in Section 2.10. Which paper shows greater variability in sentence length? Which measure of spread is more appropriate for these data?

5 Just a minute!   Calculate the variance and the interquartile range for each set of data in Practical activity 5 in Section 2.10. Which group shows greater variability in estimation of time? Which measure of spread is more appropriate for these data?

Exercise 3C

1 The number of absences by employees in an office was recorded over a period of 96 days, with the following results.

Number of employees absent	0	1	2	3	4	5
Number of days		54	24	11	4	2	1

Calculate the mean and variance of the number of daily absences, setting out your work in a table similar to Table 3.14.

2 Plates of a certain design are painted by a particular factory employee. At the end of each day the plates are inspected and some are rejected. The table shows the number of plates rejected over a period of 30 days.

Number of rejects	0	1	2	3	4	5	6
Number of days	18	5	3	1	1	1	1

Show that the standard deviation of the daily number of rejects is approximately equal to one quarter of the range.

3 The times taken in a 20 km race were noted for 80 people. The results are summarised in the following table.

Time (minutes)	60–80	80–100	100–120	120–140	140–160	160–180	180–200
No. of people	1	4	26	24	10	7	8

Estimate the variance of the times of the 80 people in the race.

4 The mass of coffee in each of 80 packets of a certain brand was measured correct to the nearest gram. The results are shown in the following table.

Mass (grams)	244–246	247–249	250–252	253–255	256–258
Number of packets	10	20	24	18	8

Estimate the mean and standard deviation of the masses, setting out your work in a table similar to Table 3.15.

State two ways in which the accuracy of these estimates could be improved.

5 (a) Given that $n = 10$, $\sum(x - 30) = 410$ and $\sum(x - 30)^2 = 16\,930$, find the mean and variance of x.

(b) Given that $n = 5$, $\sum(y - 20) = 74$ and $\sum(y - 20)^2 = 1116.2$, find the mean and variance of y.

6 Here are 10 values of a variable x. Find the variance using the coded values $u = x - 20$.

18.9   20.7   19.3   20.1   21.3   19.6   20.5   20.9   18.8   20.8

7 The coded values $u = x + 20$ are used to find the standard deviation of the values of x given in a frequency table. It is found that $\sum f_i = 40$, $\sum u_i f_i = 112$ and $\sum u_i^2 f_i = 10\,208$. Find the mean and variance of the values of x.

8 At the start of a new school year, the heights of the 100 new pupils entering the school are measured. The results are summarised in the following table. The 10 pupils in the 110– group have heights not less than 110 cm but less than 120 cm.

Height (h cm)	100–	110–	120–	130–	140–	150–	160–
Number of pupils	2	10	22	29	22	12	3

By using the coded values $u = h - 135$, obtain estimates of the mean and variance of the heights of the 100 pupils.

9 The ages, in completed years, of the 104 workers in a company are summarised as follows.

Age (years)	16–20	21–25	26–30	31–35	36–40	41–50	51–60	61–70
Frequency	5	12	18	14	25	16	8	6

Estimate the mean and standard deviation of the workers' ages.

In another company, with a similar number of workers, the mean age is 28.4 years and the standard deviation is 9.9 years. Briefly compare the age distribution in the two companies.

Miscellaneous exercise 3

1 Seven mature robins (*Erithacus rubecula*) were caught and their wingspans were measured. The results, in centimetres, were as follows.

    23.1   22.7   22.1   24.2   23.9   20.9   25.2

Here are the corresponding figures for seven mature house sparrows (*Passer domesticos*).

    22.6   24.1   23.5   21.8   21.0   24.4   22.8

Find the mean and standard deviation of each species' wingspan, and use these statistics to compare the two sets of figures.

2 The following histograms are of two sets of 100 masses.

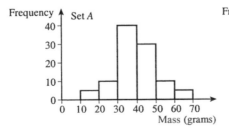 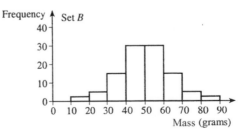

(a) Which set has the greater mean?   (b) Which set has the greater variance?

(c) Estimate the mean and variance of Set A.   (d) Why are your answers to (c) estimates?

3 The lengths of 120 nails of nominal length 3 cm were measured, each correct to the nearest 0.05 cm. The results are summarised in the following table.

Length (cm)	2.85	2.90	2.95	3.00	3.05	3.10	3.15
Frequency	1	11	27	41	26	12	2

(a) Draw a box plot of these results, taking the extremes as 2.825 cm and 3.175 cm.

(b) Estimate the standard deviation.

(c) It is claimed that for a roughly symmetrical distribution the statistic obtained by dividing the interquartile range by the standard deviation is approximately 1.3. Calculate the value of this statistic for these data, and comment.

4 Three statistics students, Ali, Les and Sam, spent the day fishing. They caught three different types of fish and recorded the type and mass (correct to the nearest 0.01 kg) of each fish caught. At 4 p.m. they summarised the results as follows.

	Number of fish by type			All fish caught	
	Perch	Tench	Roach	Mean mass (kg)	Standard deviation (kg)
Ali	2	3	7	1.07	0.42
Les	6	2	8	0.76	0.27
Sam	1	0	1	1.00	0

(a) State how you can deduce that the mass of each fish caught by Sam was 1.00 kg.

(b) The winner was the person who had caught the greatest total mass of fish by 4 p.m. Determine who was the winner, showing your working.

(c) Before leaving the waterside, Sam catches one more fish and weighs it. He then announces that if this extra fish is included with the other two fish he caught, the standard deviation is 1.00 kg. Find the mass of this extra fish.   (OCR)

5 The heights of 94 policemen based at a city police station were measured, and the results (in metres) are summarised in the following table.

Height (m)	1.65–1.69	1.70–1.74	1.75–1.79	1.80–1.84	1.85–1.89
Frequency	2	4	11	23	38

Height (m)	1.90–1.94	1.95–1.99	2.00–2.04	2.05–2.09
Frequency	9	4	2	1

(a) Draw a cumulative frequency diagram and estimate the median and quartiles.

(b) What do the values found in part (a) indicate about the shape of the distribution?

(c) Estimate the mean and standard deviation of the heights.

6 The depth of water in a lake was measured at 50 different points on the surface of the lake. The depths, x metres, are summarised by $\sum x = 934.5$ and $\sum x^2 = 19\,275.81$.

(a) Find the mean and variance of the depths.

(b) Some weeks later the water level in the lake rose by 0.23 m. What would be the mean and variance of the depths taken at the same points on the lake as before?

7 The following table gives the ages in completed years of the 141 persons convicted of shop-lifting in a town during a particular year.

Age (years)	12–15	16–20	21–25	26–30	31–40	41–50	51–70
Frequency	15	48	28	17	14	7	12

Working in years, and giving your answers to 1 decimal place, calculate estimates of

(a) the mean and standard deviation of the ages,

(b) the median age.

Which do you consider to be the better representative average of the distribution, the mean or the median? Give a reason for your answer.

8 The diagram shows a cumulative frequency curve for the lengths of telephone calls from a house during the first six months of last year.

(a) Find the median and interquartile range.

(b) Construct a histogram with six equal intervals to illustrate the data.

(c) Use the frequency distribution associated with your histogram to estimate the mean length of call.

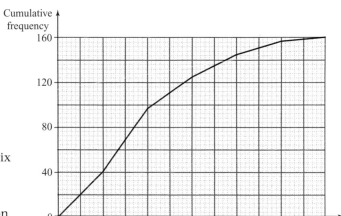

(d) State whether each of the following is true or false.

(i) The distribution of these call times is skewed.

(ii) The majority of the calls last longer than 6 minutes.

(iii) The majority of the calls last between 5 and 10 minutes.

(iv) The majority of the calls are shorter than the mean length.

4 Probability

This chapter is about calculating with probabilities. When you have completed it you should

- know what a 'sample space' is
- know the difference between an 'outcome' and an 'event' and be able to calculate the probability of an event from the probabilities of the outcomes in the sample space
- be able to use the addition law for mutually exclusive events
- know the multiplication law of conditional probability, and be able to use tree diagrams
- know the multiplication law for independent events.

4.1 Assigning probability

You will frequently have been unsure of the outcome of some activity or experiment, but have known what the possible outcomes were. For example, you do not know whether you will win the National Lottery next time you buy a ticket, but you do know that you will either win or not win. You know that if you toss a coin twice, then the possible outcomes are (H, H), (H, T), (T, H) and (T, T). If you are testing a transistor to see if it is defective, then the possible outcomes are 'defective' and 'not defective'.

The list of all the possible outcomes is called the **sample space** of the experiment. The list is usually written in curly brackets, { }.

Thus the sample space for buying a ticket for the National Lottery is {win, not win}, the sample space for tossing a coin twice is $\{(H, H), (H, T), (T, H), (T, T)\}$, and the sample space for testing a transistor is {defective, not defective}.

> Notice that it is conventional when writing pairs of things like H, H to put them in brackets, like coordinates.

Each of the outcomes of an experiment has a probability assigned to it. Sometimes you can assign the probability using symmetry. For example the sample space for throwing a dice is $\{1, 2, 3, 4, 5, 6\}$, and you would assign each outcome the probability $\frac{1}{6}$, in the belief that the dice was fair, and that each outcome was equally likely. This is the usual method for calculations about games of chance.

Now suppose that the dice is not fair, so that you cannot use the method of symmetry for assigning probabilities. In this case you will have to carry out an experiment and throw the dice a large number of times. Suppose that you threw the dice 1000 times and the frequencies of the six possible outcomes in the sample space were as in Table 4.1.

Outcome	1	2	3	4	5	6
Frequency	100	216	182	135	170	197

Table 4.1. Frequencies for the outcomes when rolling a dice 1000 times.

The probabilities you would assign would then be $\frac{100}{1000}, \frac{216}{1000}, \frac{182}{1000}, \frac{135}{1000}, \frac{170}{1000}$ and $\frac{197}{1000}$ for the outcomes 1, 2, 3, 4, 5 and 6 respectively. These are called the **relative frequencies** of the outcomes, and you can use them as estimates of the probabilities. You should realise that if you were to roll the dice another 1000 times, the results would probably not be exactly the same, but you would hope that they would not be too different. You could roll the dice more times and hope to improve the relative frequency as an approximation to the probability.

Sometimes you cannot assign a probability by using symmetry or by carrying out an experiment. For example, there is a probability that my house will be struck by lightning next year, and I could insure against this happening. The insurance company will have to have a probability in mind when it calculates the premium I have to pay, but it cannot calculate it by symmetry, or carry out an experiment for a few years. It will assign its probability using its experience of such matters and its records.

If an event cannot possibly occur, then its probability is 0. If an event is certain to occur then its probability is 1. For example, the probability of throwing a 7 on a single throw of an ordinary dice is 0 and the probability of throwing less than 7 is 1.

> When **probabilities** are assigned to the outcomes of a sample space,
>
> - each probability must lie between 0 and 1 inclusive, and
> - the sum of all the probabilities assigned must be equal to 1.

Example 4.1.1
How would you assign probabilities to the following experiments or activities?

(a) Choosing a playing card from a standard pack of cards.

(b) The combined experiment of tossing a coin and rolling a dice.

(c) Tossing a drawing pin on to a table to see whether it lands point down or point up.

(d) Four international football teams, Denmark, England, France and Germany (D, E, F and G), play a knockout tournament. Who will be the winner?

(a) The sample space would consist of the list of the 52 playing cards $\{AC, 2C, 3C, \ldots, KS\}$ in some order. (Here A means ace, C means clubs, and so on.) Assuming that these cards are equally likely to be picked, the probability assigned to each of them is $\frac{1}{52}$.

(b) The sample space is $\begin{Bmatrix} (H, 1), (H, 2), (H, 3), (H, 4), (H, 5), (H, 6), \\ (T, 1), (T, 2), (T, 3), (T, 4), (T, 5), (T, 6) \end{Bmatrix}$, and each of the outcomes would be assigned a probability of $\frac{1}{12}$.

(c) The sample space is {point down, point up}. You would need to carry out an experiment to assign probabilities.

(d) The sample space is $\{D \text{ wins}, E \text{ wins}, F \text{ wins}, G \text{ wins}\}$. You have to assign probabilities subjectively, according to your knowledge of the game. The probabilities p_D, p_E, p_F and p_G must all be non-negative and satisfy $p_D + p_E + p_F + p_G = 1$.

4.2 Probabilities of events

Sometimes you may be interested not in one particular outcome, but in two or three or more of them. For example, suppose you toss a coin twice. You might be interested in whether the result is the same both times. The list of outcomes in which you are interested is called an **event**, and is written in brackets. The event that both tosses of the coin give the same result is $\{(H, H), (T, T)\}$. Events are often denoted by capital letters. Thus if A denotes this event, then $A = \{(H, H), (T, T)\}$. An event can be just one outcome, or a list of outcomes or even no outcomes at all.

You can find the probability of an event by looking at the sample space and adding the probabilities of the outcomes which make up the event. For example, if you were tossing a coin twice, the sample space would be $\{(H, H), (H, T)\,(T, H), (T, T)\}$. There are four outcomes, each equally likely, so they each have probability $\frac{1}{4}$. The event A consists of the two outcomes (H, H) and (T, T), so the probability of A is $\frac{1}{4} + \frac{1}{4}$, or $\frac{1}{2}$.

This is an example of a general rule.

> The probability, $P(A)$, of an event, A, is the sum of the probabilities of the outcomes which make up A.

Often a list of outcomes can be constructed in such a way that all of them are equally likely. If all the outcomes are equally likely then the probability of any event A can be found by finding the number of outcomes which make up event A and dividing by the total number of outcomes. When the outcomes are not equally likely then the probability of any event has to be found by adding the individual probabilities of all the outcomes which make up event A.

Example 4.2.1

In the USA, a roulette wheel consists of 38 sections of equal area; 18 are black, 18 are red and 2 are green. The wheel is spun and a ball is thrown onto the wheel. The ball will eventually land on one of the 38 sections.

(a) Find the probability of landing on a black colour.

Let A be the event that the ball does not land on a black section.

(b) Find the probability of A.

(a) The probabilities of each section are equally likely, so each of them has probability $\frac{1}{38}$. There are 18 black sections, each with probability $\frac{1}{38}$, so

$$P(\text{black}) = \tfrac{18}{38} = \tfrac{9}{19}.$$

(b) $P(A) = P(\text{red or green}) = P(\text{red}) + P(\text{green}) = \tfrac{18}{38} + \tfrac{2}{38} = \tfrac{20}{38} = \tfrac{10}{19}.$

Example 4.2.2
The numbers 1, 2, ..., 9 are written on separate cards. The cards are shuffled and the top one is turned over. Calculate the probability that the number on this card is prime.

The sample space for this situation is {1, 2, 3, 4, 5, 6, 7, 8, 9}. As each outcome is equally likely it has probability $\frac{1}{9}$.

Let B be the event that the card turned over is prime. Then $B = \{2, 3, 5, 7\}$.

$P(B) =$ sum of the probabilities of the outcomes in $B = \frac{4}{9}$.

Example 4.2.3
A circular wheel is divided into three equal sectors, numbered 1, 2 and 3, as shown in Fig. 4.2. The wheel is spun twice. Each time, the score is the number to which the black arrow points. Calculate the probabilities of the following events:

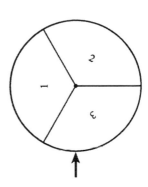

(a) both scores are the same as each other,

(b) neither score is a 2,

(c) at least one of the scores is a 3,

(d) neither score is a 2 and both scores are the same,

(e) neither score is a 2 or both scores are the same.

Fig. 4.2.

Start by writing down the sample space.

{(1, 1), (1 2), (1, 3), (2, 1), (2, 2), (2, 3), (3, 1), (3, 2), (3, 3)}

Each outcome has probability $\frac{1}{9}$.

(a) Let A be the event that both scores are the same, so $A = \{(1, 1), (2, 2), (3, 3)\}$.

$P(A) =$ sum of the probabilities of the outcomes in $A = \frac{3}{9} = \frac{1}{3}$.

(b) Let B be the event that neither score is a 2, so $B = \{(1, 1), (1, 3), (3, 1), (3, 3)\}$.

$P(B) =$ sum of the probabilities of the outcomes in $B = \frac{4}{9}$.

(c) Let C be the event that at least one of the scores is a 3, so

$C = \{(1, 3), (2, 3), (3, 1), (3, 2), (3, 3)\}$. Then $P(C) = \frac{5}{9}$.

(d) Let D be the event that neither score is a 2 *and* both scores are the same, so

$D = \{(1, 1), (3, 3)\}$. Then $P(D) = \frac{2}{9}$.

(e) Let E be the event that neither score is a 2 *or* both scores are the same, so

$E = \{(1, 1), (1, 3), (3, 1), (3, 3), (2, 2)\}$, and $P(E) = \frac{5}{9}$.

Example 4.2.4

Jason has three playing cards, two queens and a king. Anya selects one of the cards at random, and returns it to Jason, who shuffles the cards. Anya then selects a second card. Anya wins if both cards selected are kings. Find the probability that Anya wins.

Imagine that the queens are different, and call them Q_1 and Q_2, and call the king K. Then the sample space is:

$$\{(Q_1, Q_1), (Q_1, Q_2), (Q_1, K), (Q_2, Q_1), (Q_2, Q_2), (Q_2, K), (K, Q_1), (K, Q_2), (K, K)\}.$$

Each outcome has probability $\frac{1}{9}$.

Let A be the event that Anya wins. Then $A = \{(K, K)\}$ and

$$P(A) = \text{sum of the probabilities of the outcomes in } A = \tfrac{1}{9}.$$

The probability that Anya wins a prize is $\frac{1}{9}$.

> Although the event that Anya won is just a single outcome, it is still listed in curly brackets.

Example 4.2.5

What is the probability of getting a total score of more than 7 when two fair dice are rolled together?

Here the sample space is most easily constructed in a grid, as below, which shows the score on the individual dice and the totals.

		Score on first dice				
	1	2	3	4	5	6
1	2	3	4	5	6	7
2	3	4	5	6	7	8
3	4	5	6	7	8	9
4	5	6	7	8	9	10
5	6	7	8	9	10	11
6	7	8	9	10	11	12

(Score on second dice)

Each of the 36 equally likely outcomes has a probability of $\frac{1}{36}$. There are 12 outcomes which are greater than 7. If A is the outcome that the score is more than 7, then

$$P(A) = 12 \times \tfrac{1}{36} = \tfrac{1}{3}.$$

Example 4.2.6

A dice with six faces has been made from brass and aluminium, and is not fair. The probability of a 6 is $\frac{1}{4}$, the probabilities of 2, 3, 4, and 5 are each $\frac{1}{6}$, and the probability of 1 is $\frac{1}{12}$. The dice is rolled. Find the probability of   (a) a 1 or a 6,   (b) an even number.

(a) $P(1 \text{ or } 6) = P(1) + P(6) = \tfrac{1}{12} + \tfrac{1}{4} = \tfrac{1}{3}.$

(b) $P(\text{an even number}) = P(2 \text{ or } 4 \text{ or } 6) = P(2) + P(4) + P(6) = \tfrac{1}{6} + \tfrac{1}{6} + \tfrac{1}{4} = \tfrac{7}{12}.$

Sometimes it is worth using a different approach to calculating the probability of an event.

Example 4.2.7

You draw two cards from an ordinary pack. Find the probability that they are not both kings.

The problem is that the sample space has a large number of outcomes. In fact there are 52 ways of picking the first card, and then 51 ways of picking the second, so there are $52 \times 51 = 2652$ possibilities. The sample space therefore consists of 2652 outcomes, each of which is assigned a probability $\frac{1}{2652}$.

To avoid counting all the outcomes which are not both kings, it is easier to look at the number of outcomes which *are* both kings.

Writing the first card to be drawn as the first of the pair, these outcomes are (KC, KD), (KD, KC), (KC, KH), (KH, KC), (KC, KS), (KS, KC), (KD, KH), (KH, KD), (KD, KS), (KS, KD), (KH, KS), and (KS, KH).

There are thus 12 outcomes that are both kings. So the number which are not both kings is $2652 - 12 = 2640$. All 2640 of these outcomes have probability $\frac{1}{2652}$, so P(not both kings) $= \frac{2640}{2652} = \frac{220}{221}$.

It is always worth looking out for this short cut, and it is also useful to have some language for it. If A is an event, the event 'not A' is the event consisting of those outcomes in the sample space which are not in A. Since the sum of the probabilities assigned to outcomes in the sample space is 1,

$$P(A) + P(\text{not } A) = 1.$$

The event 'not A' is called the **complement** of the event A. The symbol A' is used to denote the complement of A.

> If A is an event, then A' is the complement of A, and
> $$P(A) + P(A') = 1. \qquad (4.1)$$

4.3 Addition of probabilities

Consider a game in which a fair cubical dice with faces numbered 1 to 6 is rolled twice. A prize is won if the total score on the two rolls is 4 or if both individual scores are over 4.

You can write the sample space of all possible outcomes as 36 equally likely pairs,

$$\left\{ \begin{array}{cccccc} (1,1) & (1,2) & (1,3) & (1,4) & (1,5) & (1,6) \\ (2,1) & (2,2) & & \cdots & & (2,6) \\ \vdots & \vdots & & & & \vdots \\ (6,1) & (6,2) & & \cdots & & (6,6) \end{array} \right\},$$

each having probability $\frac{1}{36}$.

Let A be the event that the total score is 4 and let B be the event that both rolls of the dice give a score over 4.

Then $A = \{(1, 3), (2, 2), (3, 1)\}$, and $B = \{(5, 5), (5, 6), (6, 5), (6, 6)\}$, so

$$P(A) = \tfrac{3}{36} = \tfrac{1}{12} \quad \text{and} \quad P(B) = \tfrac{4}{36} = \tfrac{1}{9}.$$

A prize is won if A happens *or* if B happens, so P(a prize is won) $= P(A \text{ or } B)$.

This means that a prize will be won if any of the outcomes in $\{(1, 3), (2, 2), (3, 1), (5, 5), (5, 6), (6, 5), (6, 6)\}$ occurs. Therefore

$$P(\text{a prize is won}) = P(A \text{ or } B) = \tfrac{7}{36}.$$

The key point is that $P(A \text{ or } B) = P(A) + P(B)$. The word 'or' is important. Whenever you see it, it should suggest to you the idea of adding probabilities. Notice, however, that A and B have no outcomes which are common to both events. Two events which have no outcomes common to both are called **mutually exclusive** events. So the result $P(A \text{ or } B) = P(A) + P(B)$ is known as the **addition law of mutually exclusive events**.

The law of mutually exclusive events can be extended to apply to more than two events provided that none of the events has any outcome in common with any of the other events.

> If $A_1, A_2, \ldots, A_n$ are n mutually exclusive events then
> $$P(A_1 \text{ or } A_2 \text{ or } \ldots \text{ or } A_n) = P(A_1) + P(A_2) + \cdots + P(A_n). \qquad (4.2)$$

Example 4.3.1

A box contains 5 red, 6 green and 8 blue beads. A bead is drawn at random. What is the probability that it is blue or red?

Let B be the event that the bead is blue and R be the event that the bead is red.

Then $P(B) = \tfrac{8}{19}$ and $P(R) = \tfrac{5}{19}$.

The events B and R are mutually exclusive since a bead cannot be both red and blue.

Therefore $P(B \text{ or } R) = P(B) + P(R) = \tfrac{8}{19} + \tfrac{5}{19} = \tfrac{13}{19}$.

The addition law needs to be modified when the events are not mutually exclusive. Here is an example.

Example 4.3.2

Two fair dice are thrown. A prize is won if the total is 10 or if each individual score is over 4.

The sample space is the same set of 36 pairs listed at the beginning of this section.

Let C be the event that the total score is 10, so $C = \{(5, 5), (4, 6), (6, 4)\}$.

Let B be the event that each roll of the dice results in a score over 4, as before, so $B = \{5, 5), (5, 6), (6, 5), (6, 6)\}$.

Therefore $P(C) = \tfrac{3}{36} = \tfrac{1}{12}$ and $P(B) = \tfrac{4}{36} = \tfrac{1}{9}$.

A prize is won if B or C occurs, and the possible outcomes which comprise this event are $\{(5, 5), (4, 6), (6, 4), (5, 6), (6, 5), (6, 6)\}$.

Therefore $P(B \text{ or } C) = \frac{6}{36} = \frac{1}{6}$. But $P(B) + P(C) = \frac{1}{12} + \frac{1}{9} = \frac{7}{36}$, so in this case $P(B \text{ or } C) \neq P(B) + P(C)$.

For events such as B and C which are not mutually exclusive, the addition rule, Equation (4.2), is not valid.

> There is a way of modifying the rule so that it applies to any two events. This will be studied later in the course in S4. Can you see how to modify the rule?

Exercise 4A

1 A fair dice is thrown once. Find the probabilities that the score is
   (a) bigger than 3,   (b) bigger than or equal to 3,
   (c) an odd number,   (d) a prime number,
   (e) bigger than 3 and a prime number,   (f) bigger than 3 or a prime number or both,
   (g) bigger than 3 or a prime number, but not both.

2 A card is chosen at random from an ordinary pack. Find the probability that it is
   (a) red,   (b) a picture card (K, Q, J),
   (c) an honour ($A, K, Q, J, 10$),   (d) a red honour,
   (e) red, or an honour, or both.

3 Two fair dice are thrown simultaneously. Find the probability that
   (a) the total is 7,   (b) the total is at least 8,
   (c) the total is a prime number,   (d) neither of the scores is a 6,
   (e) at least one of the scores is a 6,   (f) exactly one of the scores is a 6,
   (g) the two scores are the same,
   (h) the difference between the scores is an odd number.

4 A fair dice is thrown twice. If the second score is the same as the first, the second throw does not count, and the dice is thrown again until a different score is obtained. The two different scores are added to give a total.

   List the possible outcomes.

   Find the probability that
   (a) the total is 7,   (b) the total is at least 8,
   (c) at least one of the two scores is a 6, (d) the first score is higher than the last.

5 Draw a bar-chart to illustrate the probabilities of the various total scores when two fair dice are thrown simultaneously.

4.4   Conditional probability and the multiplication law

Consider a class of thirty pupils, of whom seventeen are girls and thirteen are boys. Suppose further that five of the girls and six of the boys are left-handed, and all of the remaining pupils are right-handed. If a pupil is selected at random from the whole class then the chance that he or she is left-handed is $\frac{6+5}{30} = \frac{11}{30}$. However, suppose now that a pupil is selected at random from the girls in the class. The chance that this girl will be left-handed is $\frac{5}{17}$. So being told that the selected pupil is a girl alters the chance that the pupil will be left-handed. This is an example of **conditional probability**. The probability has been calculated on the basis of an extra 'condition' which you have been given.

There is some notation which is used for conditional probability. Let L be the event that a left-handed person is chosen, and let G be the event that a girl is chosen. The symbol $P(L \mid G)$ stands for the probability that the pupil chosen is left-handed *given* that the pupil chosen is a girl. So in this case $P(L \mid G) = \frac{5}{17}$, although $P(L) = \frac{11}{30}$.

It is useful to find a connection between conditional probabilities (where some extra information is known) and probabilities where you have no extra information. Notice that the probability $P(L \mid G)$ can be written as

$$P(L \mid G) = \frac{5}{17} = \frac{5/30}{17/30}.$$

The fraction in the numerator is the probability of choosing a left-handed girl if you were selecting from the whole class, and the denominator is the probability of choosing a girl if you were selecting from the whole class. In symbols this could be written as

$$P(L \mid G) = \frac{P(L \text{ and } G)}{P(G)}.$$

This can be generalised to any two events A and B for which $P(A) > 0$.

> If A and B are two events and $P(A) > 0$, then the **conditional probability** of B given A is
>
> $$P(B \mid A) = \frac{P(A \text{ and } B)}{P(A)}. \qquad (4.3)$$
>
> Also $P(A \mid B) = \dfrac{P(A \text{ and } B)}{P(B)}.$
>
> Rewriting these equations gives
>
> $$P(A \text{ and } B) = P(A) \times P(B \mid A) = P(B) \times P(A \mid B) \qquad (4.4)$$
>
> which is known as the **multiplication law of probability**.

Suppose a jar contains 7 red discs and 4 white discs. Two discs are selected without replacement. ('Without replacement' means that the first disc is not put back in the jar before the second disc is selected.) Let R_1 be the event {the first disc is red}, let R_2 be the event {the second disc is red}, let W_1 be the event {the first disc is white} and let W_2 be the event {the second disc is white}. To find the probability that both of the discs are red you want to find $P(R_1 \text{ and } R_2)$.

Using the multiplication law, Equation 4.4, to find this probability,

$$P(R_1 \text{ and } R_2) = P(R_1) \times P(R_2 \mid R_1).$$

Now $P(R_1) = \frac{7}{11}$, since there are 7 red discs in the jar and 11 discs altogether. The probability $P(R_2 \mid R_1)$ appears more complicated, but it represents the probability that the second disc selected is red *given* that the first disc was red. To find this just imagine that one red disc has already been removed from the jar. The jar now contains 6 red discs and 4 white discs. The probability *now* of getting a red disc is $P(R_2 \mid R_1) = \frac{6}{10}$.

Therefore, using the multiplication rule,

$$P(R_1 \text{ and } R_2) = P(R_1) \times P(R_2 \mid R_1) = \frac{7}{11} \times \frac{6}{10}.$$

You can represent all the possible outcomes when two discs are selected from the jar in a **tree diagram**, as in Fig. 4.3.

Notice that probabilities on the first 'layer' of branches give the chances of getting a red disc or a white disc when the first disc is selected. The probabilities on the second 'layer' are the conditional probabilities. You can use the tree diagram to calculate the probability of any of the four possibilities, R_1 and R_2, R_1 and W_2, W_1 and R_2 and W_1 and W_2.

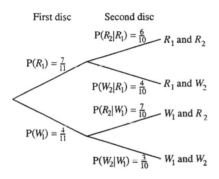

Fig. 4.3. Tree diagram to show the outcomes when two discs are drawn from a jar.

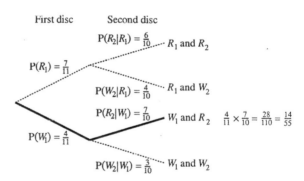

Fig. 4.4. Tree diagram to show the outcomes when two discs are drawn from a jar.

To do this you move along the appropriate route, multiplying the probabilities, as shown in Fig. 4.4. For example, to find the probability of getting a white disc followed by a red disc, $P(W_1 \text{ and } R_2)$, trace that route on the tree diagram and multiply the relevant probabilities.

You could also have found $P(W_1 \text{ and } R_2)$ by using the multiplication rule.

$$P(W_1 \text{ and } R_2) = P(W_1) \times P(R_2 \mid W_1) = \frac{4}{11} \times \frac{7}{10} = \frac{14}{55}.$$

You can now use the addition and multiplication rules together to find the probability of more complex events. For example,

$$P(\text{both discs are the same colour}) = P((R_1 \text{ and } R_2) \text{ or } (W_1 \text{ and } W_2)).$$

The event R_1 and R_2 is the event that both discs are red, and the event W_1 and W_2 is the event that both discs are white. These events cannot both be satisfied at the same time, so they must be mutually exclusive. Therefore you can use the addition rule, giving

$$P((R_1 \text{ and } R_2) \text{ or } (W_1 \text{ and } W_2)) = P(R_1 \text{ and } R_2) + P(W_1 \text{ and } W_2)$$
$$= P(R_1) \times P(R_2 \mid R_1) + P(W_1) \times P(W_2 \mid W_1)$$
$$= \tfrac{7}{10} \times \tfrac{6}{10} + \tfrac{4}{11} \times \tfrac{3}{10} = \tfrac{42}{110} + \tfrac{12}{110} = \tfrac{54}{110} = \tfrac{27}{55}.$$

You can also use the tree diagram for this calculation. This time there is more than one route through the tree diagram which satisfies the event whose probability is to be found. As before, you follow the appropriate routes and multiply the probabilities. You then add all the resulting products, as in Fig. 4.5.

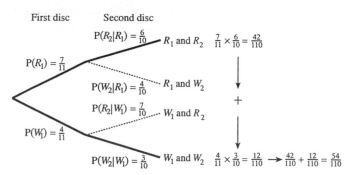

Fig. 4.5. Tree diagram to show the outcomes when two discs are drawn from a jar.

You can use tree diagrams in any problem in which there is a clear sequence to the outcomes, including problems which are not necessarily to do with selection of objects.

Example 4.4.1

Weather records indicate that the probability that a particular day is dry is $\tfrac{3}{10}$. Liverton Villa is a football team whose record of success is better on dry days than on wet days. The probability that Liverton win on a dry day is $\tfrac{3}{8}$, whereas the probability that they win on a wet day is $\tfrac{3}{11}$. Liverton are due to play their next match on Saturday.

(a)   What is the probability that Liverton will win?

(b)* Three Saturdays ago Liverton won their match. What is the probability that it was a dry day?

Here the sequence involves first the type of weather and then the result of the football match. The tree diagram in Fig. 4.6 illustrates the information.

Notice that the probabilities in blue type were not given in the statement of the question. They have been calculated by using equations like $P(\text{wet}) + P(\text{dry}) = 1$.

(a) $P(\text{win}) = P((\text{dry and win}) \text{ or } (\text{wet and win}))$
$$= P(\text{dry and win}) + P(\text{wet and win})$$
$$= P(\text{dry}) \times P(\text{win} \mid \text{dry}) + P(\text{wet}) \times P(\text{win} \mid \text{wet})$$
$$= \tfrac{3}{10} \times \tfrac{3}{8} + \tfrac{7}{10} \times \tfrac{3}{11} = \tfrac{9}{80} + \tfrac{21}{110} = \tfrac{267}{880}.$$

(b)* In this case you have been asked to calculate a conditional probability. However, here the sequence of events has been reversed and you want to find $P(\text{dry} \mid \text{win})$.

$$P(\text{dry} \mid \text{win}) = \frac{P(\text{dry and win})}{P(\text{win})} = \frac{9/80}{267/880} = \frac{99}{267}.$$

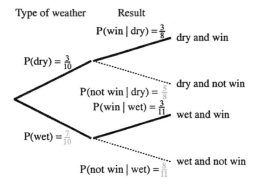

Fig. 4.6. Tree diagram for football results.

You can think of P(dry | win) as being the proportion of times that the weather is dry out of all the times that Liverton win.

4.5 Independent events

Consider again a jar containing 7 red discs and 4 white discs. Two discs are selected, but this time with replacement. This means that the first disc is returned to the jar before the second disc is selected.

Let R_1 be the event that the first disc is red, R_2 be the event that the second disc is red, W_1 be the event that the first disc is white and W_2 be the event that the second disc is white. You can represent the selection of the two discs with Fig. 4.7, a tree diagram similar to Fig. 4.3 but with different probabilities on the second 'layer'.

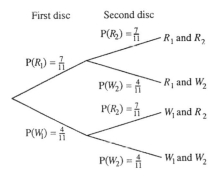

Fig. 4.7. Tree diagram to show the outcomes when two discs are drawn with replacement from a jar.

The probability $P(R_2)$ that the second disc is red can also be found using the addition and multiplication laws.

$$P(R_2) = P((R_1 \text{ and } R_2) \text{ or } P(W_1 \text{ and } R_2))$$
$$= P(R_1 \text{ and } R_2) + P(W_1 \text{ and } R_2) = \tfrac{7}{11} \times \tfrac{7}{11} + \tfrac{4}{11} \times \tfrac{7}{11} = \tfrac{7}{11}.$$

In this case $P(R_2) = P(R_2 \mid R_1)$, which means that the first disc's being red has no effect on the chance of the second disc being red. This is what you would expect, since the first disc was replaced before the second was removed. Two events A and B for which $P(B \mid A) = P(B)$ are called **independent**. Independent events have no effect upon one another.

Recall also that, from the definition of conditional probability, $P(B \mid A) = \dfrac{P(A \text{ and } B)}{P(A)}$. So when you equate the two expressions for $P(B \mid A)$ for independent events, you get $\dfrac{P(A \text{ and } B)}{P(A)} = P(B)$, which when rearranged gives $P(A \text{ and } B) = P(A) \times P(B)$.

Independent events are events which have no effect on one another. For two independents events A and B,

$$P(A \text{ and } B) = P(A) \times P(B). \tag{4.5}$$

This result is called the **multiplication law for independent events**.

Example 4.5.1

In a game at a fête, a contestant has to first spin a fair coin and then roll a fair cubical dice whose faces are numbered 1 to 6. The contestant wins a prize if the coin shows heads and the dice score is below 3. Find the probability that a contestant wins a prize.

P(prize won) = P((coin turns up heads) and (dice score is lower than 3)).

The event that the coin shows heads and the event that the dice score is lower than 3 are independent, because the result of the spin of the coin can have no effect on the score on the dice. Therefore the multiplication law for independent events can be used.

P(prize won) = P((coin shows heads) and (dice score is lower than 3))
= P((coin shows heads) × P(dice score is lower than 3) = $\frac{1}{2} \times \frac{2}{6} = \frac{1}{6}$.

The law of multiplication for independent events can be extended to more than two events, provided they are all independent of one another.

If $A_1, A_2, \ldots, A_n$ are n independent events then

$$P(A_1 \text{ and } A_2 \text{ and } \ldots \text{ and } A_n) = P(A_1) \times P(A_2) \times \cdots \times P(A_n).$$

Example 4.5.2

A fair cubical dice with faces numbered 1 to 6 is thrown four times. Find the probability that three of the four throws result in a 6.

One way of tackling this problem is by drawing a tree diagram, but it would not be very easy to draw as it has four sets of 'branches'. An alternative method is to use the addition law of mutually exclusive events and the multiplication law of independent events to break the event that 'three of the four scores are 6' down into smaller sub-events whose probabilities you can easily determine:

$$P(\text{three of the scores are 6s}) = P \begin{pmatrix} (6_1 \text{ and } 6_2 \text{ and } 6_3 \text{ and } N_4) \text{ or} \\ (6_1 \text{ and } 6_2 \text{ and } N_3 \text{ and } 6_4) \text{ or} \\ (6_1 \text{ and } N_2 \text{ and } 6_3 \text{ and } 6_4) \text{ or} \\ (N_1 \text{ and } 6_2 \text{ and } 6_3 \text{ and } 6_4) \end{pmatrix}$$

where, for example, 6_1 means that the first score was a six and N_3 means that the third score was not a six.

Using the addition and multiplication laws,

$$P(\text{three of the scores are 6s}) = P\begin{pmatrix} (6_1 \text{ and } 6_2 \text{ and } 6_3 \text{ and } N_4) \text{ or} \\ (6_1 \text{ and } 6_2 \text{ and } N_3 \text{ and } 6_4) \text{ or} \\ (6_1 \text{ and } N_2 \text{ and } 6_3 \text{ and } 6_4) \text{ or} \\ (N_1 \text{ and } 6_2 \text{ and } 6_3 \text{ and } 6_4) \end{pmatrix}$$

$$= P(6_1 \text{ and } 6_2 \text{ and } 6_3 \text{ and } N_4)$$
$$+ P(6_1 \text{ and } 6_2 \text{ and } N_3 \text{ and } 6_4)$$
$$+ P(6_1 \text{ and } N_2 \text{ and } 6_3 \text{ and } 6_4)$$
$$+ P(N_1 \text{ and } 6_2 \text{ and } 6_3 \text{ and } 6_4)$$
$$= P(6_1) \times P(6_2) \times P(6_3) \times P(N_4)$$
$$+ P(6_1) \times P(6_2) \times P(N_3) \times P(6_4)$$
$$+ P(6_1) \times P(N_2) \times P(6_3) \times P(6_4)$$
$$+ P(N_1) \times P(6_2) \times P(6_3) \times P(6_4)$$
$$= \left(\tfrac{1}{6} \times \tfrac{1}{6} \times \tfrac{1}{6} \times \tfrac{5}{6}\right) + \left(\tfrac{1}{6} \times \tfrac{1}{6} \times \tfrac{5}{6} \times \tfrac{1}{6}\right)$$
$$+ \left(\tfrac{1}{6} \times \tfrac{5}{6} \times \tfrac{1}{6} \times \tfrac{1}{6}\right) + \left(\tfrac{5}{6} \times \tfrac{1}{6} \times \tfrac{1}{6} \times \tfrac{1}{6}\right)$$
$$= 4 \times \left(\tfrac{1}{6}\right)^3 \times \tfrac{5}{6} = \tfrac{5}{324}.$$

4.6   Practical activities

1 **Cylinder**   When you throw a coin it is very unlikely to land on its edge (or curved surface). However, if you were to drop a baked-beans can on the floor there is quite a good chance that it will land on its curved surface. Both the coin and the baked-beans can are (nearly) cylindrical in shape.

   (a) Find several cylinders for which the ratio of the height to the radius is different, and investigate how the ratio of height to radius affects the chance of a cylinder landing on its curved surface.

   (b) Throw each cylinder 50 times and work out the experimental probability that the cylinder lands on its curved surface. Plot a graph of this experimental probability against the ratio of height to radius.

   (c) For what ratio of height to radius would you estimate that the cylinder was equally likely to land on its curved surface as it was to land on one of its plane faces?

2 **Darts 1**   Throw 100 darts at a dart-board but try not to aim for any particular section. Find the experimental probability of the dart landing in the 20 sector. Compare this with the percentage of the dart-board's area which is made up by the 20 sector.

3 **Darts 2**   Cut out an irregular-shaped piece of paper and stick it on the dart-board. Throw 100 darts at the dart-board again trying not to aim at any particular point and find the experimental probability of the dart landing on the piece of paper. Use this to get an estimate of the area of the piece of paper.

4 Cards

(a) Shuffle a pack of cards and pick a card. Record the identity of the card. Repeat this to give 50 selections in all, replacing the card and shuffling after every selection. From your data calculate the experimental probabilities of

(i) a red card,   (ii) an even score {2, 4, 6, 8, 10},   (iii) a picture card {J, Q, K}.

Check whether the following statements are true for your experimental probabilities:

(b) P(even or picture) = P(even) + P(picture),

(c) P(even or red) = P(even) + P(red),

(d) P(even and red) = P(even) × P(red).

Compare with what you would expect theoretically.

Exercise 4B

1 Two cards are drawn one after another, without replacement, from a well-shuffled pack. What is the probability that the second card is an ace, given that the first card was

(a) an ace,   (b) a king?

2 A box contains four pink and five blue beads. Three beads are drawn at random from the box, one after another, without replacement. What is the probability that

(a) the second bead is pink, given that the first bead was blue;

(b) the third bead is blue, given that the first two beads were pink;

(c) the third bead is pink, given that the first two beads were of different colours?

3 A bag contains ten counters, of which six are red and four are green. A counter is chosen at random; its colour is noted and it is replaced in the bag. A second counter is then chosen at random. Find the probabilities that

(a) both counters are red,   (b) both counters are green,

(c) exactly one counter is red,   (d) at least one counter is red,

(e) the second counter is red.

4 A bag contains six red and four green counters. Two counters are drawn, without replacement. Use a carefully labelled tree diagram to find the probabilities that

(a) both counters are red,   (b) both counters are green,   (c) just one counter is red,

(d) at least one counter is red,   (e) the second counter is red.

Compare your answers with those in Question 1.

Does it make any difference to your answers to parts (a), (b), (c) and (d) if the two counters are drawn simultaneously rather than one after the other?

5 Two cards are drawn, without replacement, from an ordinary pack. Find the probabilities

(a) that both are picture cards (K, Q, J),   (b) that neither is a picture card,

(c) that at least one is a picture card,   (d) that at least one is red.

6 Events A, B and C satisfy these conditions:

$$P(A) = 0.6, \quad P(B) = 0.8, \quad P(B \mid A) = 0.45, \quad P(B \text{ and } C) = 0.28.$$

Calculate

(a) P(A and B),   (b) P($C \mid B$)   (c) P($A \mid B$).

7 A class consists of seven boys and nine girls. Two different members of the class are chosen at random. A is the event {the first person is a girl}, and B is the event {the second person is a girl}. Find the probabilities of

(a) $B \mid A$,   (b) $B' \mid A$,   (c) $B \mid A'$,

(d) $B' \mid A'$,   (e) B.

Is it true that

(f) P($B \mid A$) + P($B' \mid A$) = 1,   (g) P($B \mid A$) + P($B \mid A'$) = 1?

8 A weather forecaster classifies all days as wet or dry. She estimates that the probability that 1 June next year is wet is 0.4. If any particular day in June is wet, the probability that the next day is wet is 0.6; otherwise the probability that the next day is wet is 0.3. Find the probability that, next year,

(a) the first two days of June are both wet,

(b) June 2nd is wet,

(c) at least one of the first three days of June is wet.

9 Two Russian chess players, K1 and K2, are playing each other in a series of games. The probability that K1 wins the first game is 0.3. If K1 wins any game, the probability that he wins the next is 0.4; otherwise the probability is 0.2. Find the probability that K1 wins

(a) the first two games,   (b) at least one of the first two games,

(c) the first three games,   (d) exactly one of the first three games.

The result of any game can be a win for K1, a win for K2, or a draw. The probability that any one game is drawn is 0.5, independent of the result of all previous games. Find the probability that, after two games,

(e) K1 won the first and K2 the second,   (f) each won one game,

(g) each has won the same number of games.

10 A fair cubical dice is thrown four times. Find the probability that

(a) all four scores are 4 or more,   (b) at least one score is less than 4,

(c) at least one of the scores is a six.

11 The Chevalier de Méré's Problem. A seventeenth-century French gambler, the Chevalier de Méré, had run out of takers for his bet that, when a fair cubical dice was thrown four times, at least one six would be scored. (See Question 10 part (c).) He therefore changed the game to throwing a pair of fair dice 24 times. What is the probability that, out of these 24 throws, at least one is a double six?

12* The Birthday Problem. What is the probability that, out of 23 randomly chosen people, at least two share a birthday? Assume that all 365 days of the year are equally likely and ignore leap years. (Hint: find the probabilities that two people have different birthdays, that three people have different birthdays, and so on.)

13 Given that $P(A) = 0.75$, $P(B \mid A) = 0.8$ and $P(B \mid A') = 0.6$, calculate $P(B)$.

14* The Doctor's Dilemma. It is known that, among all patients displaying a certain set of symptoms, the probability that they have a particular rare disease is 0.001. A test for the disease has been developed. The test shows a positive result on 98% of the patients who have the disease and on 3% of patients who do not have the disease.

The test is given to a particular patient displaying the symptoms, and it records a positive result. Find the probability that the patient has the disease. Comment on your answer.

Miscellaneous exercise 4

1 A box of sweets contains 6 toffees and 8 mints. Tia takes sweets out of the box at random, one at a time and without replacement, until she obtains a mint. Find the probability that Tia gets a mint on her third selection.

2 There are 10 yoghurts in a refrigerator. Three are strawberry flavoured, two raspberry flavoured and the remainder chocolate flavoured. Two yoghurts are chosen at random, one after the other without replacement. By drawing a tree diagram, or otherwise, find the probability that they are

(a) both strawberry flavoured,   (b) both chocolate flavoured,

(c) both the same flavour,   (d) of different flavours.

If three yoghurts are chosen at random without replacement, find the probability that they are all strawberry flavoured.

3 Bag A contains 1 red ball and 1 black ball, and bag B contains 2 red balls; all four balls are indistinguishable apart from their colour. One ball is chosen at random from A and is transferred to B. One ball is then chosen at random from B and is transferred to A.

(a) Draw a tree diagram to illustrate the possibilities for the colours of the balls transferred from A to B and then from B to A.

(b) Find the probability that, after both transfers, the black ball is in bag A.   (OCR)

4 The probability that an event A occurs is $P(A) = 0.3$. The event B is independent of A and $P(B) = 0.4$. Calculate $P(A \text{ or } B \text{ or both occur})$.

5 Two cubical fair dice are thrown, one red and one blue. The scores on their faces are added together. Determine which, if either, is greater:

(a) the probability that the total score will be 10 or more given that the red dice shows a 6,

(b) the probability that the total score will be 10 or more given that at least one of the dice shows a 6.   (OCR)

6 Half of the A-level students in a community college study science and 30% study mathematics. Of those who study science, 40% study mathematics.

(a) What proportion of the A-level students study both mathematics and science?

(b) Calculate the proportion of those students who study mathematics but do not study science. (OCR)

7 Three friends, Ahmed, Benjamin and Chi, live in a town where there are only three cafés. They arrange to meet at a café one evening but do not specify the name of the café. The probabilities that they will each choose a particular café are independent. Ahmed lives close to Café Expresso and so the probability that he will choose to go there is $\frac{5}{9}$ whereas Café Kola and Café Pepi have equal chances of being visited by him.

Benjamin lives a long distance from Café Kola and the probability that he will choose this one is $\frac{1}{7}$, but he will choose either of the other two cafés with equal probability.

Each café has an equal chance of being visited by Chi.

(a) Show that the probability that the three friends meet at Café Expresso is $\frac{5}{63}$.

(b) Calculate the probability that

   (i) the three friends will meet at the same café,

   (ii) at most two friends will meet at the same café. (OCR)

8 Two events A and B are such that $P(A) = \frac{3}{4}$, $P(B \mid A) = \frac{1}{5}$ and $P(B' \mid A') = \frac{4}{7}$. By use of a tree diagram, or otherwise, find

(a) $P(A \text{ and } B)$,   (b) $P(B)$,   (c) $P(A \mid B)$. (OCR, adapted)

9 Students have to pass a test before they are allowed to work in a laboratory. Students do not retake the test once they have passed it. For a randomly chosen student, the probability of passing the test at the first attempt is $\frac{1}{3}$. On any subsequent attempt, the probability of failing is half the probability of failing on the previous attempt. By drawing a tree diagram, or otherwise, show that the probability of a student passing the test in 3 attempts or fewer is $\frac{26}{27}$. (OCR, adapted)

10 A game is played using a regular 12-faced fair dice, with faces labelled 1 to 12, a coin and a simple board with nine squares as shown in the diagram.

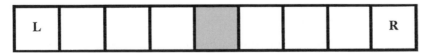

Initially, the coin is placed on the shaded rectangle. The game consists of rolling the dice and then moving the coin one rectangle towards **L** or **R** according to the outcome on the dice. If the outcome is a prime number (2, 3, 5, 7 or 11) the move is towards **R**, otherwise it is towards **L**. The game stops when the coin reaches either **L** or **R**. Find, giving your answers correct to 3 decimal places, the probability that the game

(a) ends on the fourth move at **R**,

(b) ends on the fourth move,

(c) ends on the fifth move. (OCR, adapted)

11 The probability that an event A occurs is $P(A) = 0.4$. B is an event independent of A and $P(A$ or B or both$) = 0.7$. Find $P(B)$.

12 A batch of forty tickets for an event at a stadium consists of ten tickets for the North stand, fourteen tickets for the East stand and sixteen tickets for the West stand. A ticket is taken from the batch at random and issued to a person, X. Write down the probability that X has a ticket for the North stand.

A second ticket is taken from the batch at random and issued to Y. Subsequently a third ticket is taken from the batch at random and issued to Z. Calculate the probability that

(a) both X and Y have tickets for the North stand,

(b) X, Y and Z all have tickets for the same stand,

(c) two of X, Y and Z have tickets for one stand and the other of X, Y and Z has a ticket for a different stand.   (OCR)

13 In a lottery there are 24 prizes allocated at random to 24 prize-winners. Ann, Ben and Cal are three of the prize-winners. Of the prizes, 4 are cars, 8 are bicycles and 12 are watches. Show that the probability that Ann gets a car and Ben gets a bicycle or a watch is $\frac{10}{69}$. Giving each answer either as a fraction or as a decimal correct to 3 significant figures, find

(a) the probability that either Ann or Cal (or both) gets a car,

(b) the probability that Ann gets a car and Ben gets a car or a bicycle.   (OCR, adapted)

14 In a certain part of the world there are more wet days than dry days. If a given day is wet, the probability that the following day will also be wet is 0.8. If a given day is dry, the probability that the following day will also be dry is 0.6.

Given that Wednesday of a particular week is dry, calculate the probability that

(a) Thursday and Friday of the same week are both wet days,

(b) Friday of the same week is a wet day.   (OCR, adapted)

15 A study of the numbers of male and female children in families in a certain population is being carried out.

(a) A simple model is that each child in any family is equally likely to be male or female, and that the sex of each child is independent of the sex of any previous children in the family. Using this model calculate the probability that, in a randomly chosen family of 4 children, there will be 2 males and 2 females.

(b) An alternative model is that the first child in any family is equally likely to be male or female, but that, for any subsequent children, the probability that they will be of the same sex as the previous child is $\frac{3}{5}$. Using this model, calculate the probability that, in a randomly chosen family of 4 children,

(i) all four will be of the same sex,

(ii) no two consecutive children will be of the same sex,

(iii) there will be 2 males and 2 females.   (OCR, adapted)

16 A dice is known to be biased in such a way that, when it is thrown, the probability of a 6 showing is $\frac{1}{4}$. This biased dice and an ordinary fair dice are thrown. Find the probability that

(a) the fair dice shows a 6 and the biased dice does not show a 6,

(b) at least one of the two dice shows a 6,

(c) exactly one of the two dice shows a 6, given that at least one of them shows a 6. (OCR)

17 Spares of a particular component are produced by two firms, Bestbits and Lesserprod. Tests show that, on average, 1 in 200 components produced by Bestbits fail within one year of fitting, and 1 in 50 components produced by Lesserprod fail within one year of fitting. Given that 20 per cent of the components sold and fitted are made by Bestbits and 80 per cent by Lesserprod, what is the probability that a component chosen at random from those sold and fitted will fail within a year of fitting?   (OCR, adapted)

18 The probability of event A occurring is $P(A) = \frac{13}{25}$. The probability of event B occurring is $P(B) = \frac{9}{25}$. The conditional probability of A occurring given that B has occurred is $P(A \mid B) = \frac{5}{9}$.

(a) Determine the following probabilities.

   (i) $P(A \text{ and } B)$ (ii) $P(B \mid A)$ (iii) $P(A \text{ or } B \text{ or both})$ (iv) $P(A' \mid B')$.

(b) Determine P (A occurs or B does not occur) showing your working.   (OCR, adapted)

5 Permutations and combinations

This chapter is about numbers of arrangements of different objects, and the number of ways you can choose different objects. When you have completed it you should

- know what a permutation is, and be able to calculate with permutations
- know what a combination is, and be able to calculate with combinations
- be able to apply permutations and combinations to probability.

5.1 Permutations

In the last chapter you often had to count the number of outcomes in a sample space. When the number of outcomes is fairly small, this is quite straightforward, but suppose, for example, that you were to deal hands of 5 playing cards from a standard pack of 52 cards. The number of different hands which you might receive is very large and it would not be sensible to try to list all of them. It is necessary to find a method of counting the number of possible hands which avoids writing out a complete list.

It is useful to start with an easier situation. Suppose that you have the three letters A, B and C, one on each of three separate cards, and that you are going to arrange them in a line to form 'words'. How many three-letter words are there?

In this case the number of words is small enough for you to write them out in full.

$$ABC \quad BAC \quad CAB \quad ACB \quad BCA \quad CBA$$

You could also show the possible choices by using a tree diagram, as in Fig. 5.1.

You have 3 choices for the first letter:

either A, B or C.

Having chosen the first letter, you then have just two choices for the second letter:

 B or C if A has been used,
 C or A if B has been used,
 A or B if C has been used.

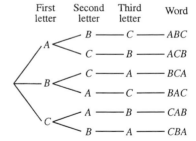

Fig. 5.1. Possible words made from the letters A, B and C.

Having chosen the first two letters, you then have only one choice for the third letter:

 only C is left if A and B have been used,
 only B is left if C and A have been used,
 only A is left if B and C have been used.

So altogether there are $3 \times 2 \times 1 = 6$ possible words you can make with three letters.

Using a similar argument you can find the number of words which you can make from 4 letters *A, B, C* and *D*.

> You have 4 possibilities for the first letter.
> Having chosen the first letter, you then have 3 possibilities for the second letter.
> Having chosen the first two letters, you then have 2 possibilities for the third letter.
> You then have only 1 possibility for the last letter.

Therefore there are $4 \times 3 \times 2 \times 1 = 24$ possible words.

Each of these 24 possibilities is listed in Fig. 5.2.

ABCD	*BACD*	*CABD*	*DABC*
ABDC	*BADC*	*CADB*	*DACB*
ACBD	*BCAD*	*CBAD*	*DBAC*
ACDB	*BCDA*	*CBDA*	*DBCA*
ADBC	*BDAC*	*CDAB*	*DCAB*
ADCB	*BDCA*	*CDBA*	*DCBA*

Fig. 5.2. All possible arrangements of the letters *A, B, C* and *D*.

You can now generalise this result to the case where there are *n* distinct letters.

> When you arrange *n* distinct letters in a line, the number of different 'words' you can make is
> $$n \times (n-1) \times (n-2) \times \cdots \times 2 \times 1.$$

The argument and the result given above apply whenever *n* distinct objects are arranged in a line. The objects need not be letters. The different arrangements of the objects are called **permutations**.

It is useful to have a concise way of writing the expression

$$n \times (n-1) \times (n-2) \times \cdots \times 2 \times 1.$$

The expression $n \times (n-1) \times (n-2) \times \cdots \times 2 \times 1$ is called *n* **factorial** and written as *n*!.

> The number of permutations of *n* distinct objects is *n*!, where
> $$n! = n \times (n-1) \times (n-2) \times \cdots \times 2 \times 1. \tag{5.1}$$

Table 5.3 shows how the number of permutations increases as the number of objects being arranged gets larger.

As you can see the number of permutations increases very rapidly as the number of objects being arranged gets larger. For example

$$8! = 8 \times 7 \times 6 \times 5 \times 4 \times 3 \times 2 \times 1 = 40\,320.$$

Your calculator will probably give you values of *n*!, but it can only approximate by using standard index form as *n* gets larger.

Number of objects	Number of permutations
1	$1 = 1$
2	$2 \times 1 = 2$
3	$3 \times 2 \times 1 = 6$
4	$4 \times 3 \times 2 \times 1 = 24$
5	$5 \times 4 \times 3 \times 2 \times 1 = 120$

Table 5.3. Number of permutations as n increases.

Suppose now that you have more letters than you need to make a word. For example, suppose that you have the 7 letters A, B, C, D, E, F and G but that you want to make a four-letter word.

> You have 7 choices for the first letter.
> Having chosen the first letter, you have 6 choices for the second letter.
> Having chosen the first two letters, you have 5 choices for the third letter.
> Having chosen the first three letters, you have 4 choices for the fourth (and last) letter.

The number of permutations of 4 letters chosen from 7 letters (that is, the number of four-letter words) is therefore $7 \times 6 \times 5 \times 4$.

This result can be written concisely in terms of factorials.

$$7 \times 6 \times 5 \times 4 = \frac{7 \times 6 \times 5 \times 4 \times 3 \times 2 \times 1}{3 \times 2 \times 1} = \frac{7!}{3!} = \frac{7!}{(7-4)!}.$$

This is an illustration of a general rule.

The number of different permutations of r objects which can be made from n distinct objects is $\dfrac{n!}{(n-r)!}$. This number is usually given the special symbol ^nP_r.

> The number ^nP_r of different permutations of r objects which can be made from n distinct objects, is given by $^nP_r = \dfrac{n!}{(n-r)!}$. $\qquad$ (5.2)

On some calculators, this is written as $_nP_r$.

Example 5.1.1

Eight runners are hoping to take part in a race, but the track has only six lanes. In how many ways can six of the eight runners be assigned to lanes?

Using Equation 5.2, the number of permutations is

$$^8P_6 = \frac{8!}{(8-6)!} = \frac{8!}{2!} = \frac{8 \times 7 \times 6 \times 5 \times 4 \times 3 \times 2 \times 1}{2 \times 1} = 20\,160.$$

Notice that, if you try to use the formula $^nP_r = \dfrac{n!}{(n-r)!}$ to find the number of permutations of the eight letters $A, B, C, \ldots, H$, you find that

$$^8P_8 = \frac{8!}{(8-8)!} = \frac{8!}{0!}.$$

But $0!$ cannot be defined using the relationship $n! = n \times (n-1) \times (n-2) \times \cdots \times 2 \times 1$, so what does $0!$ mean? The answer is that it can be defined to be any convenient value. Recall that $^8P_8$ denotes the number of permutations of 8 objects when you have selected them from 8 distinct objects. But this has already been shown to be $8!$.

Therefore $\dfrac{8!}{0!}$ should equal $8!$.

This will only be true if $0! = 1$. The value of $0!$ is defined to be 1 to make the formula for ^nP_r consistent when $r = n$.

Example 5.1.2
Eight people, $A, B, \ldots, H$ are arranged randomly in a line. What is the probability that (a) A and B are next to each other, (b) A and B are not next to each other?

(a) There is a neat trick which helps to solve this problem. Imagine that A and B are stuck together in the order AB. There are then $7!$ ways to arrange the people in line. There are also another $7!$ ways to arrange them if A and B are stuck together in the order BA. There are therefore $2 \times 7!$ ways of arranging the eight people in line with A and B next to each other.

However, there are $8!$ ways of arranging the eight people in line if there are no restrictions.

The required probability is therefore

$$\frac{2 \times 7!}{8!} = \frac{2 \times 7 \times 6 \times 5 \times 4 \times 3 \times 2 \times 1}{8 \times 7 \times 6 \times 5 \times 4 \times 3 \times 2 \times 1} = \frac{2}{8} = \frac{1}{4}.$$

(b) $P(A \text{ and } B \text{ are not together}) = 1 - P(A \text{ and } B \text{ are together})$, so $P(A \text{ and } B \text{ are not together}) = 1 - \frac{1}{4} = \frac{3}{4}$.

> If you need to find the probability that two objects are not together it is usually a good idea to find first the probability that they are together.

You will have noticed that in this section emphasis was placed on the fact that the objects being arranged had to be distinct. That is, you had to be able to identify each object uniquely. The next section shows how to tackle this problem when the objects are not distinct.

5.2 Permutations when the objects are not distinct

Recall that there were $4! = 24$ permutations of the letters A, B, C and D. These were listed earlier in Fig. 5.2. Imagine that the A remains but that the letters B, C and D are all replaced by the letter Z. How many permutations will there be now?

Suppose that B is temporarily replaced by Z_1, C is replaced by Z_2 and D is replaced by Z_3 so that you can tell the Zs apart. Fig. 5.4 shows the permutations of A, Z_1, Z_2 and Z_3 using a different procedure from that used to write out Fig. 5.2.

Write the first permutation of A, Z_1, Z_2 and Z_3 at the top of the first column. Any permutation can be the first permutation. Leave A in the same position, but write the other permutations of Z_1, Z_2 and Z_3 underneath. Write a permutation not already used at the top of the next column, and repeat writing the other permutations of Z_1, Z_2 and Z_3 underneath. Keep going until you have written all the permutations of A, Z_1, Z_2 and Z_3.

$AZ_1Z_2Z_3$	$Z_1AZ_2Z_3$	$Z_1Z_2AZ_3$	$Z_1Z_2Z_3A$
$AZ_1Z_3Z_2$	$Z_1AZ_3Z_2$	$Z_1Z_3AZ_2$	$Z_1Z_3Z_2A$
$AZ_2Z_1Z_3$	$Z_2AZ_1Z_3$	$Z_2Z_1AZ_3$	$Z_2Z_1Z_3A$
$AZ_2Z_3Z_1$	$Z_2AZ_3Z_1$	$Z_2Z_3AZ_1$	$Z_2Z_3Z_1A$
$AZ_3Z_1Z_2$	$Z_3AZ_1Z_2$	$Z_3Z_1AZ_2$	$Z_3Z_1Z_2A$
$AZ_3Z_2Z_1$	$Z_3AZ_2Z_1$	$Z_3Z_2AZ_1$	$Z_3Z_2Z_1A$

Fig. 5.4. Permutations of the letters A, Z_1, Z_2 and Z_3.

There are 4! arrangements in Fig. 5.4. Each column has all the permutations of Z_1, Z_2 and Z_3, 3! in all, so there must be $\dfrac{4!}{3!} = 4$ columns altogether. Now replace Z_1, Z_2 and Z_3 by Z and you have the permutations of A, Z, Z and Z in the top row. These are

$$AZZZ, \quad ZAZZ, \quad ZZAZ, \quad ZZZA.$$

You can generalise this result. Suppose that you have n objects and r of them are identical. Then the number of arrangements in the table equivalent to Fig. 5.4 will be $n!$. When you write down the permutations in the columns corresponding to the arrangement at the top of the column, you find that there are $r!$ of them, so the table will have $r!$ rows. The number of columns (that is, the number of distinct permutations) is therefore $\dfrac{n!}{r!}$.

This result also generalises.

> The number of distinct permutations of n objects, of which p are identical to each other, and then q of the remainder are identical, and r of the remainder are identical, and so on is
> $$\frac{n!}{p! \times q! \times r! \times \cdots} \quad \text{where} \quad p + q + r + \cdots = n.$$

Example 5.2.1
Find the number of distinct permutations of the letters of the word *MISSISSIPPI*.

The number of letters is 11, of which there are 4 Ss, 4 Is, 2 Ps and 1 M. The number of permutations of the letters is therefore

$$\frac{11!}{4! \times 4! \times 2! \times 1!} = 34\,650.$$

Exercise 5A

1 Without using a calculator, find the values of

(a) $5!$ (b) $\dfrac{8!}{6!}$ (c) $\dfrac{7!}{3!}$ (d) $\dfrac{6!}{4!\,2!}$ (e) $\dfrac{8!}{2!\,2!\,2!}$

2 Seven different cars are to be loaded on to a transporter truck. In how many different ways can the cars be arranged?

3 How many numbers are there between 1245 and 5421 inclusive which contain each of the digits 1, 2, 4 and 5 once and once only? One of these numbers is chosen at random. Find the probability that it is

(a) divisible by 5, (b) greater than 3000.

4 An artist is going to arrange five paintings in a row on a wall. In how many ways can this be done?

5 Ten athletes are running in a 100 metre race. In how many different ways can the first three places be filled?

6 By writing out all the possible arrangements of $D_1E_1E_2D_2$, show that there are $\dfrac{4!}{2!2!} = 6$ different arrangements of the letters of the word *DEED*.

7 A four-digit number is to be formed from the digits 1, 2, 3 and 4.

(a) How many different numbers can be formed if repetition is not allowed?

(b) How many odd numbers greater than 3000 can be formed if repetition is not allowed?

One of the numbers in (a) is chosen at random.

(c) What is the probability that it is an odd number greater than 3000?

8 A typist has five letters and five addressed envelopes. In how many different ways can the letters be placed in each envelope without getting every letter in the right envelope? If the letters are placed in the envelopes at random what is the probability that each letter is in its correct envelope?

9 How many different arrangements can be made of the letters in the word *MISSISSIPPI*?

10 (a) Calculate the number of arrangements of the letters in the word *NUMBER*.

(b) One of the arrangements in part (a) is chosen at random. What is the probability that it begins and ends with a vowel?

11 How many different numbers can be formed by taking one, two, three and four digits from the digits 1, 2, 7 and 8, if repetitions are not allowed?

One of these numbers is chosen at random. What is the probability that it is greater than 200?

12 How many four-digit numbers can be formed from the digits 1 and 2 if repetitions are allowed?

5.3   Combinations

In the last section you considered permutations (arrangements) for which the order of the objects was significant in counting the number of different possibilities. In some circumstances, however, the order of selection is irrelevant. For example, if you were dealt a hand of 13 cards from a standard pack of 52 playing cards, you would not be interested in the order in which you received the cards. When a selection is made from a set of objects and the order of selection is unimportant it is called a **combination**.

To see the difference between combinations and permutations consider what happens when you select 3 cards from the 4 cards A, B, C and D.

Here is a procedure for finding all the combinations. It starts by considering permutations, and gives you a method of counting the combinations.

Start with any permutation of three letters from A, B, C and D, and write it at the top of the first column. Write the other permutations of the letters at the top of the first column underneath it. Write a permutation not already used at the top of the next column, and repeat writing the other permutations of the letters underneath. Keep on until you have used all the permutations of three letters from A, B, C and D. Each column will then correspond to a single combination.

The results are shown in Fig. 5.5.

ABC	ABD	ACD	BCD
ACB	ADB	ADC	BDC
BAC	BAD	CAD	CBD
BCA	BDA	CDA	CDB
CAB	DAB	DAC	DBC
CBA	DBA	DCA	DCB

Fig. 5.5. Procedure for finding the number of combinations.

Look at the elements in any one column. The permutations are all different, but they all give rise to the same combination at the head of the column. To count the combinations, it is sufficient to count the columns.

Notice that there are ${}^4P_3$ permutations of 3 objects from 4 objects, so there are ${}^4P_3$ elements in total in Fig. 5.5.

In each column there are 3! elements, so, dividing, you find that there must be $\dfrac{{}^4P_3}{3!}$ columns, which means $\dfrac{{}^4P_3}{3!}$ combinations. As ${}^4P_3 = \dfrac{4!}{(4-3)!}$, there are $\dfrac{4!}{(4-3)! \times 3!}$ combinations of three cards from the four cards A, B, C and D. But

$$\frac{4!}{(4-3)! \times 3!} = \frac{4!}{1! \times 3!} = \frac{4 \times 3 \times 2 \times 1}{1 \times (3 \times 2 \times 1)} = 4,$$

so there are 4 combinations of three cards from the four cards A, B, C and D.

You can apply this reasoning and this calculation to finding the number of combinations of r objects taken from n objects. In the table which corresponds to Fig. 5.5, there would be $^{n}P_{r}$ permutations in total, and each column would have $r!$ objects. There would therefore be $\dfrac{^{n}P_{r}}{r!}$ columns, which corresponds to $\dfrac{^{n}P_{r}}{r!}$ combinations of r objects taken from n objects.

Writing $^{n}P_{r}$ in factorials as $\dfrac{n!}{(n-r)!}$ leads to a simpler expression to remember: the number of combinations of r objects taken from n objects is $\dfrac{n!}{(n-r)! \times r!}$.

The number of combinations of r objects chosen from n distinct objects is given the symbol $\dbinom{n}{r}$, which is often read as 'n choose r'. The older symbols, $_{n}C_{r}$ and $^{n}C_{r}$ are also used, and your calculator probably uses one of them.

> A **combination** is a selection in which the order of the objects selected is unimportant.
>
> The number of different combinations of r objects selected from n distinct objects is $\dbinom{n}{r}$ where $\dbinom{n}{r} = \dfrac{n!}{(n-r)! \times r!}$.

Example 5.3.1

The manager of a football team has a squad of 16 players. He needs to choose 11 to play in a match. How many possible teams can be chosen?

> This example is not entirely realistic because players will not be equally capable of playing in every position but it does show how many possible teams there are. It is important to decide whether this question is about permutations or combinations. Clearly the important issue here is the people in the team and not their order of selection. Therefore this question is about combinations rather than permutations.

$$\text{The number of teams is } \binom{16}{11} = \frac{16!}{(16-11)! \times 11!} = \frac{16!}{5! \times 11!} = 4368.$$

The number of teams is surprisingly large.

You may notice in Example 5.3.1 that if you had chosen the 5 players to drop out of the squad of 16 players, you would in effect be selecting the 11 by another method. You can select the 5 players in $\dbinom{16}{5}$ ways, and

$$\binom{16}{5} = \frac{16!}{(16-5)! \times 5!} = \frac{16!}{11! \times 5!},$$

which is clearly equal to $\dbinom{16}{11}$.

When you come to calculate a number like $\binom{16}{11}$ or $\binom{16}{5}$, you can take a short cut. Since

$$16! = 16 \times 15 \times \cdots \times 12 \times 11 \times 10 \times \cdots \times 2 \times 1,$$

you can cancel the $11 \times 10 \times \cdots \times 2 \times 1$ in the numerator with the 11! in the denominator.

Therefore you can write down immediately that

$$\binom{16}{5} = \frac{16 \times 15 \times \cdots \times 12}{5!},$$

where you need to make sure that you multiply 5 numbers in the numerator if the denominator is 5!.

In general,

$$\binom{n}{r} = \frac{\overbrace{n \times (n-1) \times \cdots \times (n-r+1)}^{r \text{ factors}}}{r!}.$$

Example 5.3.2

A team of 5 people is chosen from 8 men and 7 women. How many different teams can be selected if the team must contain   (a) 3 men and 2 women,   (b) at least 3 men?

(a) The number of different teams of 3 men which can be selected from 8 is $\binom{8}{3}$.

The number of different teams of 2 women which can be selected from 7 is $\binom{7}{2}$.

Any of the $\binom{8}{3}$ men's teams can join up with any of the $\binom{7}{2}$ women's teams to make an acceptable team of 5. Therefore you need to multiply these two quantities together to find the number of different teams possible.

The number of possible teams is

$$\binom{8}{3} \times \binom{7}{2} = \frac{8 \times 7 \times 6}{1 \times 2 \times 3} \times \frac{7 \times 6}{1 \times 2} = 56 \times 21 = 1176.$$

(b) There are three possible types of team with at least 3 men.

First, the teams can have 3 men and 2 women as in part (a). The number of possible teams of this type is 1176.

Second, you can have teams with 4 men and 1 woman. The number of ways in which the 4 men can be selected is $\binom{8}{4} = 70$ and the number of ways in which the woman can be selected is $\binom{7}{1} = 7$. So the number of possible teams with 4 men and 1 woman is $70 \times 7 = 490$.

Finally, you can have all-male teams. The number of possible teams of 5 men is $\binom{8}{5} = 56$.

Altogether the number of possible teams with at least 3 men is

$$1176 + 490 + 56 = 1722.$$

You can now apply some of these counting methods to probability examples.

Example 5.3.3

Five cards are dealt without replacement from a standard pack of 52 cards. Find the probability that exactly 3 of the 5 cards are hearts.

The sample space is very large. It would consist of a list of all possible sets of 5 cards which you could choose from the 52 cards in the pack. You do not need a list. All that you need to know is how many different sets of cards the sample space contains. You are choosing 5 objects from 52, so the number of unrestricted choices is $\binom{52}{5}$, because the order of selection is irrelevant.

Let A be the event that exactly three cards of the five dealt out are hearts. The method used to find the number of outcomes in the event A is very similar to the technique used in Example 5.3.2.

There are $\binom{13}{3}$ 'teams' of 3 hearts.

There are $\binom{39}{2}$ 'teams' of 'non-hearts'.

Therefore the number of sets of 5 cards with 3 hearts is $\binom{13}{3} \times \binom{39}{2}$.

The probability that event A happens is $\dfrac{\binom{13}{3} \times \binom{39}{2}}{\binom{52}{5}} = 0.0815$, correct to 3 significant figures.

> To find the probability of an event E using permutations or combinations, find
>
> (a) the total number of possible outcomes
> (b) the number of outcomes which result in E.
>
> Then $P(E) = \dfrac{\text{number of outcomes which result in } E}{\text{total number of possible outcomes}}$.

Exercise 5B

1   How many different three-card hands can be dealt from a pack of 52 cards?

2   From a sixth form of 30 boys and 32 girls, two girls and two boys are to be chosen to represent their school. How many possible selections are there?

3   A history exam paper contains eight questions, four in Part A and four in Part B. Candidates are required to attempt five questions. In how many ways can this be done if

   (a) there are no restrictions,

   (b) at least two questions from Part A and at least two questions from Part B must be attempted?

4* A committee of 3 is to be selected from 4 women and 5 men. The rules state that there must be at least one man and one woman on the committee. In how many different ways can the committee be chosen?

   Subsequently one of the men and one of the women marry each other. The rules also state that a married couple may not both serve on the committee. In how many ways can the committee be chosen now?

5   A box of one dozen eggs contains one that is bad. If three eggs are chosen at random, what is the probability that one of them will be bad?

6   In a game of bridge the pack of 52 cards is shared equally between all four players. What is the probability that one particular player has no hearts?

7   A bag contains 20 chocolates, 15 toffees and 12 peppermints. If three sweets are chosen at random what is the probability that they are

   (a) all different,   (b) all chocolates,

   (c) all the same,   (d) all not chocolates?

8* Show that $\binom{n}{r} = \binom{n}{n-r}$.

9* Show that the number of permutations of n objects of which r are of one kind and $n-r$ are of another kind is $\binom{n}{r}$.

5.4   Applications of permutations and combinations

In Example 5.1.2 you were asked to find the number of ways that eight people could stand in a line when two people had to stand next to each other. This was an example in which you were asked to find the number of permutations or combinations of a set of objects with some extra condition included. This section will show you how to answer such questions.

Example 5.4.1

Find the number of ways of arranging 6 women and 3 men to stand in a row so that all three men are standing together.

You can make this problem simpler by thinking of the 3 men as a single unit. Imagine tying them together for example! You would then have 7 items (or units), the 6 individual women and the block of 3 men.

So one possible arrangement would be

$$W_1 \quad W_3 \quad W_5 \quad W_6 \quad W_2 \quad W_4 \quad M_1 M_3 M_2,$$

where W_3, for example, represents the third woman.

The number of permutations of these 7 units is 7!. However, for each of these permutations the men could be arranged (inside the rope) in 3! different ways. Therefore the total number of permutations in which the 6 women and 3 men can be arranged so that the 3 men are standing together is $7! \times 3! = 30\,240$.

Example 5.4.2

Find the number of ways of arranging 6 women and 3 men in a row so that no two men are standing next to one another.

You can ensure that no two men stand next to one another in the following way.

Arrange the 6 women to stand in a line with a space between each of them and two extra spaces, one at each end of the row. One such arrangement is

Space 1 Space 2 Space 3 Space 4 Space 5 Space 6 Space 7
W_1 W_2 W_5 W_4 W_6 W_3

There are 6! arrangements of the 6 women. For any of these 6! arrangements you can now pick a space in which to place the first man M_1. This can be done in 7 ways.

Here is the arrangement above with one of the men, M_1, placed in Space 2.

Space 1 Space 3 Space 4 Space 5 Space 6 Space 7
W_1 M_1 W_2 W_5 W_4 W_6 W_3

By using a similar argument you can see that there will be 6 choices for the position of M_2 and 5 choices for the position of M_3. Once the three men have been placed the remaining spaces can be 'closed up' or simply ignored. By using this method you can guarantee that no two men can stand next to one another. Also all possible arrangements will be counted using this method.

Therefore the number of permutations in which no two men stand next to one another is $6! \times 7 \times 6 \times 5 = 151\,200$.

It should be clear that you multiply 6! by 7, 6 and 5 because for every one of the 6! arrangements of the women there will be 7 spaces to choose for M_1, and then 6 places to choose for M_2, and then 5 places to choose for M_3.

It is also worth noting that the answers to Examples 5.4.1 and 5.4.2 when added together do not give 9!, which is the total number of arrangements of 9 people without any restriction at all. This is because there is a third possibility. If two men were standing together and the third man was separated from these two by some women then it would not be the case that all the men were together but neither would it be the case that the three men were all apart from one another.

Example 5.4.3
A group of 12 people consisting of 6 married couples is arranged at random in a line for a photograph. Find the probability that each wife is standing next to her husband.

The number of unrestricted arrangements is 12!. Each of them is equally likely.

If each husband and wife 'couple' is to stand together, then you can consider each couple as a unit. There are therefore 6 such units.

The number of permutations of these units is 6!.

But the first couple $H_1 W_1$ can be arranged in 2! ways, either $H_1 W_1$ or $W_1 H_1$. This applies equally to couples 2, 3, 4, 5 and 6. Therefore the number of arrangements in which each couple stands together is $6! \times (2!)^6$.

Hence P(each couple stands together) $= \dfrac{6! \times (2!)^6}{12!} = \dfrac{1}{10\,395} = 9.62 \times 10^{-5}$ correct to 3 significant figures.

Example 5.4.4
Three different Chemistry books and four different Physics books are placed on a shelf. In how many ways can the books be arranged if

(a) any order is allowed,

(b) all the Chemistry books are together,

(c) all the Chemistry books are together and all the Physics books are together?

(a) The number of possible arrangements if there are no restrictions is $7! = 5040$.

(b) Imagine that the Chemistry books are tied together to form one object. Then there are $4 + 1 = 5$ objects to be arranged. This can be done in $5! = 120$ ways.

However the Chemistry books can be arranged in their bundle in $3! = 6$ ways.

So the total number of different arrangements is $120 \times 6 = 720$ ways.

(c) Now imagine that the Physics books are also tied together.

The two objects, the bundle of Chemistry books and the bundle of Physics books, can be arranged in $2! = 2$ ways.

The Physics books can be arranged in $4! = 24$ ways in their bundle.

The Chemistry books can be arranged in 6 ways in their bundle, as before.

So the total number of arrangements is $2 \times 24 \times 6 = 288$ ways.

Example 5.4.5*

Four letters are to be selected from the letters in the word *RIGIDITY*. How many different combinations are there?

The problem here is that the letters are not all distinct since there are three *I*s. Therefore the answer is not $\binom{8}{4}$. In order to deal with this problem a useful strategy is to split it into different cases depending on the number of *I*s chosen.

Case 1   Combinations with no *I*s

In this case you are selecting 4 letters from the 5 letters *R, G, D, T, Y*, so the number of combinations is $\binom{5}{4} = 5$.

These are the combinations with no *I*. Remember that since this is a problem about combinations you are not interested in the order. All that matters here is which 'team' of letters you choose. The possible teams are

  RGDT   RGDY   RGTY   RDTY   GDTY.

Case 2   Combinations with one *I*

In this case you are selecting 3 letters from the 5 letters *R, G, D, T, Y* together with one *I*, so the number of combinations is $\binom{5}{3} = 10$. Here are the combinations with one *I*:

  RGDI   RGTI   RGYI   RDTI   RDYI
  RTYI   GDTI   GDYI   GTYI   DTYI.

Case 3   Combinations with two *I*s

In this case you are selecting 2 letters from the 5 letters *R, G, D, T, Y* together with two *I*s, so the number of combinations is $\binom{5}{2} = 10$. Here they are:

  RGII   RDII   RTII   RYII   GDII
  GTII   GYII   DTII   DYII   TYII.

Case 4   Combinations with three *I*s.

In this case you are selecting 1 letter from the 5 letters *R, G, D, T, Y* together with three *I*s, so the number of combinations is $\binom{5}{1} = 5$. Here they are:

  RIII   GIII   DIII   TIII   YIII.

The total number of distinct combinations of 4 letters selected from the letters of the word *RIGIDITY* is $5 + 10 + 10 + 5 = 30$. All 30 combinations have been listed above.

Exercise 5C

1 The letters of the word *CONSTANTINOPLE* are written on 14 cards, one on each card. The cards are shuffled and then arranged in a straight line.

(a) How many different possible arrangements are there?

(b) How many arrangements begin with *P*?

(c) How many arrangements start and end with *O*?

(d)* How many arrangements are there where no two vowels are next to each other?

2 A coin is tossed 10 times.

(a) How many different sequences of heads and tails are possible?

(b) How many different sequences containing 6 heads and 4 tails are possible?

(c) What is the probability of getting 6 heads and 4 tails?

3 Eight cards are selected with replacement from a standard pack of 52 playing cards, with 12 picture cards, 20 odd cards and 20 even cards.

(a) How many different sequences of 8 cards are possible?

(b) How many of the sequences in part (a) will contain 3 picture cards, 3 odd-numbered cards and 2 even-numbered cards?

(c) Use parts (a) and (b) to determine the probability of getting 3 picture cards, 3 odd-numbered cards and 2 even-numbered cards if 8 cards are selected with replacement from a standard pack of 52 playing cards.

4 Eight women and five men are standing in a line.

(a) How many arrangements are possible if any individual can stand in any position?

(b) In how many arrangements will all 5 men be standing next to one another?

(c) In how many of the arrangements will no two men be standing next to one another?

5 Each of the digits 1, 1, 2, 3, 3, 4, 6 is written on a separate card. The seven cards are then laid out in a row to form a 7-digit number.

(a) How many distinct 7-digit numbers are there?

(b) How many of these 7-digit numbers are even?

(c) How many of these 7-digit numbers are divisible by 4?

(d) How many of these 7-digit numbers start and end with the same digit?

6 Three families, the Mehtas, the Campbells and the Lams, go to the cinema together to watch a film. Mr and Mrs Mehta take their daughter Indira, Mr and Mrs Campbell take their sons Paul and Mark, and Mrs Lam takes her children Susi, Kim and Lee. The families occupy a single row with eleven seats.

(a) In how many ways could the eleven people be seated if there were no restriction?

(b) In how many ways could the eleven people sit down so that the members of each family were all sitting together?

(c) In how many of the arrangements will no two adults be sitting next to one another?

7* The letters of the word *POSSESSES* are written on 9 cards, one on each card. The cards are shuffled and four of them are selected and arranged in a straight line.

(a) How many possible selections are there of 4 letters?

(b) How many arrangements are there of 4 letters?

Miscellaneous exercise 5

1 The judges in a 'Beautiful Baby' competition have to arrange 10 babies in order of merit. In how many different ways could this be done? Two babies are to be selected to be photographed. In how many ways can this selection be made?

2 In how many ways can a committee of four men and four women be seated in a row if

(a) they can sit in any position,

(b) no one is seated next to a person of the same sex?

3 How many distinct arrangements are there of the letters in the word *ABRACADABRA*?

4 Six people are going to travel in a six-seater minibus but only three of them can drive. In how many different ways can they seat themselves?

5 There are eight different books on a bookshelf: three of them are hardbacks and the rest are paperbacks.

(a) In how many different ways can the books be arranged if all the paperbacks are together and all the hardbacks are together?

(b) In how many different ways can the books be arranged if all the paperbacks are together?

6 Four boys and two girls sit in a line on stools in front of a coffee bar.

(a) In how many ways can they arrange themselves so that the two girls are together?

(b) In how many ways can they sit if the two girls are not together?   (OCR)

7 Ten people travel in two cars, a saloon and a Mini. If the saloon has seats for six and the Mini has seats for four, find the number of different ways in which the party can travel, assuming that the order of seating in each car does not matter and all the people can drive.   (OCR)

8 I have 7 yoghurts to last the week. Two are strawberry, three raspberry and two peach. I select one yoghurt each day. In how many different orders can I eat the yoghurts? If I select a yoghurt at random each day, what is the probability that I eat the two strawberry ones on consecutive days?

9 A class contains 30 children, 18 girls and 12 boys. Four complimentary theatre tickets are distributed at random to the children in the class. What is the probability that

(a) all four tickets go to girls,

(b) two boys and two girls receive tickets?   (OCR)

10 (a) How many different 7-digit numbers can be formed from the digits 0, 1, 2, 2, 3, 3, 3 assuming that a number cannot start with 0?

(b) How many of these numbers will end in 0?   (OCR)

11 Calculate the number of ways in which three girls and four boys can be seated on a row of seven chairs if each arrangement is to be symmetrical.   (OCR)

12 Find the number of ways in which

(a) 3 people can be arranged in 4 seats,

(b) 5 people can be arranged in 5 seats.   (OCR, adapted)

13 Eight different cards, of which four are red and four are black, are dealt to two players so that each receives a hand of four cards.

Calculate

(a) the total number of different hands which a given player could receive,

(b) the probability that each player receives a hand consisting of four cards all of the same colour.   (OCR)

14* A piece of wood of length 10 cm is to be divided into 3 pieces so that the length of each piece is a whole number of cm, for example 2 cm, 3 cm and 5 cm.

(a) List all the different sets of lengths which could be obtained.

(b) If one of these sets is selected at random, what is the probability that the lengths of the pieces could be lengths of the sides of a triangle?   (OCR)

15* Nine persons are to be seated at three tables holding 2, 3 and 4 persons respectively. In how many ways can the groups sitting at the tables be selected, assuming that the order of sitting at the tables does not matter?   (OCR)

16* A 'hand' of 5 cards is dealt from an ordinary pack of 52 playing cards. Show that there are nearly 2.6 million distinct hands and that, of these, 575 757 contain no card from the heart suit.

On three successive occasions a card player is dealt a hand containing no heart. What is the probability of this happening? What conclusion might the player justifiably reach?   (OCR)

6 Probability distributions

This chapter introduces the idea of a random variable. When you have completed it you should

- understand what a random variable is
- know the properties of a random variable
- be able to construct a probability distribution table for a random variable.

6.1 Random variables

Most people have played board games at some time. Here is an example.

Game A A turn consists of throwing a dice and then moving a number of squares equal to the score on the dice.

'The number of squares moved in a turn' is a variable because it can take different values, namely 1, 2, 3, 4, 5 and 6. However, the value taken at any one turn cannot be predicted, but depends on chance. For these reasons 'the number of squares moved in a turn' is called a 'random variable'.

> A **random variable** is a quantity whose value depends on chance.

Although you cannot predict the result of the next throw of the dice, you do know that, if the dice is fair, the probability of getting each value is $\frac{1}{6}$. A convenient way of expressing this information is to let X stand for 'the number of squares moved in a turn'. Then, for example, $P(X = 3) = \frac{1}{6}$ means 'the probability that X takes the value 3 is $\frac{1}{6}$'. Generalising, $P(X = x)$ means 'the probability that the variable X takes the value x'.

> Note how the capital letter stands for the variable itself and the small letter stands for the value which the variable takes.

This notation is used in Table 6.1 to give the possible values for the number of squares moved and the probability of each value. This table is called the 'probability distribution' of X.

x	1	2	3	4	5	6	Total
$P(X=x)$	$\frac{1}{6}$	$\frac{1}{6}$	$\frac{1}{6}$	$\frac{1}{6}$	$\frac{1}{6}$	$\frac{1}{6}$	1

Table 6.1. Probability distribution of X, the number of squares moved in a turn for a single throw of a dice.

> The **probability distribution** of a random variable is a listing of the possible values of the variable and the corresponding probabilities.

In some board games, a dice is used in a more complicated way in order to decide how many squares a person should move. Here are two different examples.

Game B A person is allowed a second throw of the dice if a 6 is thrown, and, in this case, moves a number Y of squares equal to the sum of the two scores obtained.

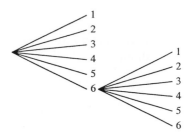

Fig. 6.2. Tree diagram for Game B.

Fig. 6.2 is a tree diagram illustrating Game B. As Y is the number of squares moved in a turn, it can take the values 1, 2, 3, 4, 5, 7, 8, 9, 10, 11 and 12. The probability of the first five values is $\frac{1}{6}$, as in the previous game. In order to score 7, you have to score 6 followed by 1. Since the two events are independent, the probability of scoring a 6 followed by a 1 is found by multiplying the two probabilities:

$$P(Y = 7) = P(6 \text{ on first throw}) \times P(1 \text{ on second throw})$$
$$= \tfrac{1}{6} \times \tfrac{1}{6} = \tfrac{1}{36}.$$

The probability that Y takes each of the values 8, 9, 10, 11 and 12 will also be $\frac{1}{36}$. Table 6.3 gives the probability distribution of Y.

Y	1	2	3	4	5	7	8	9	10	11	12	Total
$P(Y=y)$	$\frac{1}{6}$	$\frac{1}{6}$	$\frac{1}{6}$	$\frac{1}{6}$	$\frac{1}{6}$	$\frac{1}{36}$	$\frac{1}{36}$	$\frac{1}{36}$	$\frac{1}{36}$	$\frac{1}{36}$	$\frac{1}{36}$	1

Table 6.3. Probability distribution of Y, the number of squares moved in Game B.

Game C The dice is thrown twice and the number, W, of squares moved is the sum of the two scores.

The possible values of W in Game C can be found by constructing a table as shown in Fig. 6.4.

		First throw					
		1	2	3	4	5	6
Second throw	1	2	3	4	5	6	7
	2	3	4	5	6	7	8
	3	4	5	6	7	8	9
	4	5	6	7	8	9	10
	5	6	7	8	9	10	11
	6	7	8	9	10	11	12

Fig. 6.4. Possible total scores when two individual scores are added in Game C.

There are 36 outcomes in the table and they are all equally likely, so, for example, $P(W = 6) = \frac{5}{36}$ and $P(W = 7) = \frac{6}{36}$. Table 6.5 gives the probability distribution of W.

The fractions could have been cancelled but in their present forms it is easier to see the shape of the distribution.

w	2	3	4	5	6	7	8	9	10	11	12	Total
$P(W=w)$	$\frac{1}{36}$	$\frac{2}{36}$	$\frac{3}{36}$	$\frac{4}{36}$	$\frac{5}{36}$	$\frac{6}{36}$	$\frac{5}{36}$	$\frac{4}{36}$	$\frac{3}{36}$	$\frac{2}{36}$	$\frac{1}{36}$	1

Table 6.5. Probability distribution of W, the number of squares moved in Game C.

Fig. 6.6 allows you to compare the probability distributions of X, Y and W.

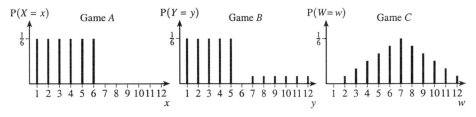

Fig. 6.6. Comparing the probability distributions of Games A, B and C.

Looking at Fig. 6.6, which method of scoring will take you round the board most quickly and which most slowly? (A method for finding the answer to this question by calculation using probabilities is given in Example 8.1.1.)

Examples 6.1.1 and 6.1.2 illustrate some other probability distributions.

Example 6.1.1
A bag contains two red and three blue marbles. Two marbles are selected at random without replacement and the number, X, of blue marbles is counted. Find the probability distribution of X.

Fig. 6.7 is a tree diagram illustrating this situation. R_1 denotes the event that the first marble is red and R_2 the event that the second marble is red. Similarly B_1 and B_2 stand for the events that the first and second marbles respectively are blue. X can take the values 0, 1 and 2.

$$P(R_2|R_1) = \tfrac{1}{4} \quad R_1 \text{ and } R_2$$
$$P(R_1) = \tfrac{2}{5}$$
$$P(B_2|R_1) = \tfrac{3}{4} \quad R_1 \text{ and } B_2$$
$$P(R_2|B_1) = \tfrac{2}{4} \quad B_1 \text{ and } R_2$$
$$P(B_1) = \tfrac{3}{5}$$
$$P(B_2|B_1) = \tfrac{2}{4} \quad B_1 \text{ and } B_2$$

$$P(X=0) = P(R_1 \text{ and } R_2)$$
$$= P(R_1) \times P(R_2 \mid R_1)$$
$$= \tfrac{2}{5} \times \tfrac{1}{4} = \tfrac{2}{20} = \tfrac{1}{10}.$$
$$P(X=1) = P(B_1 \text{ and } R_2) + P(R_1 \text{ and } B_2)$$
$$= P(B_1) \times P(R_2 \mid B_1) + P(R_1) \times P(B_2 \mid R_1)$$
$$= \tfrac{3}{5} \times \tfrac{2}{4} + \tfrac{2}{5} \times \tfrac{3}{4} = \tfrac{12}{20} = \tfrac{3}{5}.$$
$$P(X=2) = P(B_1 \text{ and } B_2)$$
$$= P(B_1) \times P(B_2 \mid B_1)$$
$$= \tfrac{3}{5} \times \tfrac{2}{4} = \tfrac{6}{20} = \tfrac{3}{10}.$$

Fig. 6.7. Tree diagram for Example 6.1.1.

Here is the probability distribution of X.

X	0	1	2	Total
$P(X=x)$	$\frac{1}{10}$	$\frac{3}{5}$	$\frac{3}{10}$	1

Example 6.1.2

A random variable, X has the probability distribution shown below.

x	1	2	3	4
$P(X=x)$	0.1	0.2	0.3	0.4

Two observations are made of X and the random variable Y is equal to the larger minus the smaller; if the two observations are equal, Y takes the value 0. Find the probability distribution of Y. Which value of Y is most likely?

The following table gives the values for X and the corresponding value of Y. Since the two observations of X are independent, you find the probability of each pair by multiplying the probabilities for the two X values, as shown in the last column of the table.

First value of X	Second value of X	Y	Probability
1	1	0	$0.1 \times 0.1 = 0.01$
1	2	1	$0.1 \times 0.2 = 0.02$
1	3	2	$0.1 \times 0.3 = 0.03$
1	4	3	$0.1 \times 0.4 = 0.04$
2	1	1	$0.2 \times 0.1 = 0.02$
2	2	0	$0.2 \times 0.2 = 0.04$
2	3	1	$0.2 \times 0.3 = 0.06$
2	4	2	$0.2 \times 0.4 = 0.08$
3	1	2	$0.3 \times 0.1 = 0.03$
3	2	1	$0.3 \times 0.2 = 0.06$
3	3	0	$0.3 \times 0.3 = 0.09$
3	4	1	$0.3 \times 0.4 = 0.12$
4	1	3	$0.4 \times 0.1 = 0.04$
4	2	2	$0.4 \times 0.2 = 0.08$
4	3	1	$0.4 \times 0.3 = 0.12$
4	4	0	$0.4 \times 0.4 = 0.16$

This table shows that Y takes the values 0, 1, 2 and 3. You can find the total probability for each value of Y by adding the individual probabilities:

$$P(Y = 0) = 0.01 + 0.04 + 0.09 + 0.16 = 0.30,$$
$$P(Y = 1) = 0.02 + 0.02 + 0.06 + 0.06 + 0.12 + 0.12 = 0.40,$$
$$P(Y = 2) = 0.03 + 0.08 + 0.03 + 0.08 = 0.22,$$
$$P(Y = 3) = 0.04 + 0.04 = 0.08.$$

So Y has the probability distribution shown below.

y	0	1	2	3	Total
$P(Y=y)$	0.30	0.40	0.22	0.08	1

The most likely value of Y is 1, because it has the highest probability.

Exercise 6A

1 A fair coin is thrown four times. The random variable X is the number of heads obtained. Tabulate the probability distribution of X.

2 Two fair dice are thrown simultaneously. The random variable D is the difference between the smaller and the larger score, or zero if they are the same. Tabulate the probability distribution of D.

3 A fair dice is thrown once. The random variable X is related to the number N thrown on the dice as follows. If N is even then X is half N; otherwise X is double N. Tabulate the probability distribution of X.

4 Two fair dice are thrown simultaneously. The random variable H is the highest common factor of the two scores. Tabulate the probability distribution of H, combining together all the possible ways of obtaining the same value.

5 When a four-sided dice is thrown, the score is the number on the bottom face. Two fair four-sided dice, each with faces numbered 1 to 4, are thrown simultaneously. The random variable M is the product of the two scores multiplied together. Tabulate the probability distribution of M, combining together all the possible ways of obtaining the same value.

6 A bag contains six red and three green counters. Two counters are drawn from the bag, without replacement. Tabulate the probability distribution of the number of green counters obtained.

7 Tim picks a card at random from an ordinary pack. If the card is an ace, he stops; if not, he continues to pick cards at random, without replacement, until either an ace is picked, or four cards have been drawn. The random variable C is the total number of cards drawn. Construct a tree diagram to illustrate the possible outcomes of the experiment, and use it to calculate the probability distribution of C.

8* Obtain the probability distribution of the total score when three cubical dice are thrown simultaneously.

9 If you have access to a spreadsheet, use it to draw diagrams to illustrate the probability distributions of the total number of heads obtained when 3, 4, 5, ... fair coins are thrown.

6.2   An important property of a probability distribution

You have probably noticed that, in all the probability distributions considered so far, the sum of the probabilities is 1. This must always be the case, because one of the outcomes must happen. This is an important property of a probability distribution and a useful check that you have found the probabilities correctly.

> For any random variable, X, the sum of the probabilities is 1; that is,
> $$\sum P(X = x) = 1.$$
>
> This can be abbreviated to $\sum p = 1$.

Example 6.2.1

The table below gives the probability distribution of the random variable T.

Find   (a) the value of c,   (b) $P(T \le 3)$,   (c) $P(T > 3)$.

t	1	2	3	4	5
$P(T = t)$	c	$2c$	$2c$	$2c$	c

(a) Since the probabilities must sum to 1,
$$c + 2c + 2c + 2c + c = 1, \quad \text{so} \quad 8c = 1, \quad \text{giving} \quad c = \tfrac{1}{8}.$$

(b) $P(T \le 3) = P(T = 1) + P(T = 2) + P(T = 3) = c + 2c + 2c = 5c = \tfrac{5}{8}$

(c) $P(T > 3) = P(T = 4) + P(T = 5) = 2c + c = 3c = \tfrac{3}{8}.$

Example 6.2.2

A computer is programmed to give single-digit numbers X between 0 and 9 inclusive in such a way that the probability of getting an odd digit (1, 3, 5, 7, 9) is half the probability of getting an even digit (0, 2, 4, 6, 8). Find the probability distribution of X.

Let the probability of getting an even digit be c. Then the probability of getting an odd digit is $\tfrac{1}{2}c$.

Since the probabilities must sum to 1,
$$\sum P(X = x) = \tfrac{1}{2}c + c + \tfrac{1}{2}c + c + \tfrac{1}{2}c + c + \tfrac{1}{2}c + c + \tfrac{1}{2}c + c = 1,$$

which gives $\tfrac{15}{2}c = 1$; that is, $c = \tfrac{2}{15}$.

The probability distribution of X is $P(X = x) = \tfrac{1}{15}$ for $x = 1, 3, 5, 7$ and 9 and $P(X = x) = \tfrac{2}{15}$ for $x = 0, 2, 4, 6$ and 8.

Exercise 6B

1 In the following probability distribution, c is a constant. Find the value of c.

X	0	1	2	3
P(X = x)	$\frac{1}{4}$	$\frac{1}{5}$	$\frac{1}{2}$	c

2 In the following probability distribution, d is a constant. Find the value of d.

X	0	1	2	3
P(X = x)	d	0.1	0.2	0.4

3 In the following probability distribution, d is a constant. Find the value of d.

x	0	1	2	3	4
P(X = x)	d	0.2	0.15	0.2	2d

4 The score S on a spinner is a random variable with distribution given by $P(S = s) = k$ (s = 1, 2, 3, 4, 5, 6, 7, 8), where k is a constant. Find the value of k.

5 A cubical dice is biased so that the probability of an odd number is three times the probability of an even number. Find the probability distribution of the score.

6 A cubical dice is biased so that the probability of any particular score between 1 and 6 (inclusive) being obtained is proportional to that score. Find the probability of scoring a 1.

7 For a biased cubical dice the probability of any particular score between 1 and 6 (inclusive) being obtained is inversely proportional to that score. Find the probability of scoring a 1.

8 In the following probability distribution, c is a constant. Find the value of c.

x	0	1	2	3
P(X = x)	0.6	0.16	c	c^2

6.3 Using a probability distribution as a model

So far, the discussion of probability distributions in this chapter has been very mathematical. At this point it may be helpful to point out the practical application of probability distributions. Probability distributions are useful because they provide models for experiments. Consider again the random variable X, the score on a dice, whose probability distribution was given in Table 6.1. Suppose you actually threw a dice 360 times. Since the values 1, 2, 3, 4, 5 and 6 have equal probabilities, you would expect them to occur with approximately equal frequencies of, in this case, $\frac{1}{6} \times 360 = 60$. It is very unlikely that all the observed frequencies will be exactly equal to 60. However, if the model is a suitable one, the observed frequencies should be close to the expected values.

What conclusion would you draw about the dice if the observed frequencies were not close to the expected values?

Now look at the random variable Y, whose probability distribution was given in Table 6.3 on page 104. For this variable the values are not equally likely and so you would not expect to observe approximately equal frequencies. In Chapter 4 you met the idea that

$$\text{relative frequency} = \frac{\text{frequency}}{\text{total frequency}} \approx \text{probability}.$$

You can rearrange this equation to give an expression for the frequencies you would expect to observe:

$$\text{frequency} \approx \text{total frequency} \times \text{probability}.$$

For 360 observations of Y, the expected frequencies will be about $360 \times \frac{1}{6} = 60$ for $y = 1, 2, 3, 4, 5$ and $360 \times \frac{1}{36} = 10$ for $y = 7, 8, 9, 10, 11$ and 12.

What will the expected frequencies be for 360 observations of the random variable W, whose probability distribution is given in Table 6.5?

Exercise 6C

1   A card is chosen at random from a pack and replaced. This experiment is carried out 520 times. State the expected number of times on which the card is

(a) a club,   (b) an ace,

(c) a picture card (K, Q, J) (d) either an ace or a club or both,

(e) neither an ace nor a club.

2   The biased dice of Exercise 6B, Question 5, is rolled 420 times. State how many times you would expect to obtain

(a) a one,   (b) an even number,   (c) a prime number.

3   The table below gives the cumulative probability distribution for a random variable R. 'Cumulative' means that the probability given is $P(R \le r)$, not $P(R = r)$.

r	0	1	2	3	4	5
$P(R \le r)$	0.116	0.428	0.765	0.946	0.995	1.000

One hundred observations of R are made. Calculate the expected frequencies of each outcome, giving each to the nearest whole number.

4* A random variable G has a probability distribution given by the following formulae:

$$P(G = g) = \begin{cases} 0.3 \times (0.7)^g & (g = 1, 2, 3, 4) \\ k & (g = 5) \\ 0 & \text{(all other values of } g\text{)}. \end{cases}$$

Find the value of k, and find the expected frequency of the result $G = 3$ when 1000 independent observations of G are made.

Miscellaneous exercise 6

1   Three cards are selected at random, without replacement, from a shuffled pack of 52 playing cards. Using a tree diagram, find the probability distribution of the number of honours $(A, K, Q, J, 10)$ obtained.

2   An electronic device produces an output of 0, 1 or 3 volts, each time it is operated, with probabilities $\frac{1}{2}$, $\frac{1}{3}$ and $\frac{1}{6}$ respectively. The random variable X denotes the result of adding the outputs for two such devices which act independently.

(a) Tabulate the possible values of X with their corresponding probabilities.

(b) In 360 independent operations of the device, state on how many occasions you would expect the outcome to be 1 volt.   (OCR, adapted)

3   The probabilities of the scores on a biased dice are shown in the table below.

Score	1	2	3	4	5	6
Probability	k	$\frac{1}{9}$	$\frac{1}{9}$	$\frac{1}{9}$	$\frac{1}{9}$	$\frac{1}{2}$

(a) Find the value of k.

Two players, Hazel and Ross, play a game with this biased dice and a fair dice. Hazel chooses one of the two dice at random and rolls it. If the score is 5 or 6 she wins a point.

(b) Calculate the probability that Hazel wins a point.

(c)* Hazel chooses a dice, rolls it and wins a point. Find the probability that she chose the biased dice.   (OCR)

4   In an experiment, a fair cubical dice was rolled repeatedly until a six resulted, and the number of rolls was recorded. The experiment was conducted 60 times.

(a) Show that you would expect to get a six on the first roll ten times out of the 60 repetitions of the experiment.

(b) Find the expected frequency for two rolls correct to one decimal place. (OCR, adapted)

5   The probability distribution of the random variable Y is given in the following table, where c is a constant.

y	1	2	3	4	5
$P(Y=y)$	c	$3c$	c^2	c^2	$\frac{15}{32}$

Prove that there is only one possible value of c, and state this value.

7 The binomial and geometric distributions

This chapter introduces you to two probability distributions, the binomial distribution and the geometric distribution. When you have completed it you should

- know the conditions for a random variable to have a binomial distribution
- be able to calculate the probabilities for the binomial distribution
- be able to use cumulative binomial tables
- know what the parameters of a binomial distribution are
- know the conditions necessary for a variable to have a geometric distribution
- be able to calculate probabilities for a geometric distribution
- know what the parameter of a geometric distribution is.

7.1 The binomial distribution

The spinner in Fig. 7.1 is an equilateral triangle. When it is spun it comes to rest on one of its three edges. Two of the edges are white and one is black. In Fig. 7.1 the spinner is resting on the black edge. This will be described as 'showing black'.

The spinner is fair, so the probability that the spinner shows black is $\frac{1}{3}$ and the probability that it shows white is $\frac{2}{3}$.

Suppose now that the spinner is spun on 5 separate occasions. Let the random variable X be the number of times out of 5 that the spinner shows black.

Fig. 7.1. A triangular spinner.

To derive the probability distribution of X, it is helpful to define some terms. The act of spinning the spinner once is called a **trial**. A simple way of describing the result of each trial is to call it a **success** (s) when the spinner shows black, and a **failure** (f) when the spinner shows white. So X could now be defined as the number of successes in the 5 trials.

It would be possible to draw a tree diagram to show the outcomes but it would be very large. So a different approach will be used here to calculate the probabilities of the different outcomes.

The event $\{X = 0\}$ would mean that the spinner did not show black on any of its 5 spins. The notation f_1 will be used to mean that the first trial resulted in a failure, f_2 will mean that the second trial resulted in a failure, and so on, giving

$$P(X = 0) = P(\text{there are 5 failures}) = P(f_1 \, f_2 \, f_3 \, f_4 \, f_5).$$

Since the outcomes of the trials are independent,

$$P(f_1 f_2 f_3 f_4 f_5) = P(f_1) \times P(f_2) \times P(f_3) \times P(f_4) \times P(f_5)$$
$$= \tfrac{2}{3} \times \tfrac{2}{3} \times \tfrac{2}{3} \times \tfrac{2}{3} \times \tfrac{2}{3} = \tfrac{32}{243}.$$

The probability $P(X = 1)$ is more complicated to calculate. The event $\{X = 1\}$ means that there is one success and also four failures. One possible sequence of a success and four failures is $s_1 f_2 f_3 f_4 f_5$ (where s_1 denotes the event that the first trial was a success).

The probability that the first trial is a success and the other four trials are failures is

$$P(s_1 f_2 f_3 f_4 f_5) = P(s_1) \times P(f_2) \times P(f_3) \times P(f_4) \times P(f_5)$$
$$= \tfrac{1}{3} \times \tfrac{2}{3} \times \tfrac{2}{3} \times \tfrac{2}{3} \times \tfrac{2}{3}$$
$$= \left(\tfrac{1}{3}\right)\left(\tfrac{2}{3}\right)^4 = \tfrac{16}{243}.$$

However there are four other possible sequences for the event $\{X = 1\}$. They are

$$f_1 s_2 f_3 f_4 f_5 \quad f_1 f_2 s_3 f_4 f_5 \quad f_1 f_2 f_3 s_4 f_5 \quad f_1 f_2 f_3 f_4 s_5.$$

Now

$$P(s_1 f_2 f_3 f_4 f_5) = \left(\tfrac{1}{3}\right) \times \left(\tfrac{2}{3}\right)^4$$
$$P(f_1 s_2 f_3 f_4 f_5) = \left(\tfrac{2}{3}\right) \times \left(\tfrac{1}{3}\right) \times \left(\tfrac{2}{3}\right)^3 = \left(\tfrac{1}{3}\right) \times \left(\tfrac{2}{3}\right)^4$$
$$P(f_1 f_2 s_3 f_4 f_5) = \left(\tfrac{2}{3}\right)^2 \times \left(\tfrac{1}{3}\right) \times \left(\tfrac{2}{3}\right)^2 = \left(\tfrac{1}{3}\right) \times \left(\tfrac{2}{3}\right)^4$$
$$P(f_1 f_2 f_3 s_4 f_5) = \left(\tfrac{2}{3}\right)^3 \times \left(\tfrac{1}{3}\right) \times \left(\tfrac{2}{3}\right) = \left(\tfrac{1}{3}\right) \times \left(\tfrac{2}{3}\right)^4$$
$$P(f_1 f_2 f_3 f_4 s_5) = \left(\tfrac{2}{3}\right)^4 \times \left(\tfrac{1}{3}\right) = \left(\tfrac{1}{3}\right) \times \left(\tfrac{2}{3}\right)^4$$

Therefore, summing, $P(X = 1) = 5 \times \left(\tfrac{1}{3}\right) \times \left(\tfrac{2}{3}\right)^4 = \tfrac{80}{243}.$

Notice that the probability for each individual sequence is the same as for any other sequence, namely $\left(\tfrac{1}{3}\right)\left(\tfrac{2}{3}\right)^4$, and that the 5 in the last line corresponds to the number of different sequences which give $X = 1$. You could have counted the number of sequences by using an argument involving combinations. There are 5 positions in each sequence and one of the positions must be filled with a success (s) and the remaining four must all be failures (f). The choice of which position to place the s in can be made in any one of $\binom{5}{1}$ ways.

Therefore $P(X = 1) = \binom{5}{1} \times \left(\tfrac{1}{3}\right) \times \left(\tfrac{2}{3}\right)^4.$

Similarly you could find that for $X = 2$ there are sequences such as $s_1 s_2 f_3 f_4 f_5$ and $f_1 s_2 f_3 s_4 f_5$. To see how many of these sequences there are, consider the following argument. There are 5 positions which have to be filled with 2 ss and 3 fs. After you choose the places in which to put the 2 ss, there is then no choice as to where the fs go.

There are 5 places to choose from for the 2 ss. From Section 5.3, you have seen that the number of choices is $\binom{5}{2}$. Each of these choices has probability $\left(\tfrac{1}{3}\right)^2 \times \left(\tfrac{2}{3}\right)^3$.

Using these results $P(X = 2) = \binom{5}{2} \times \left(\frac{1}{3}\right)^2 \times \left(\frac{2}{3}\right)^3$.

Continuing in this way, you can find the distribution of X, given in Table 7.2.

x	$P(X = x)$	
0	$\left(\frac{2}{3}\right)^5$	$= \frac{32}{243}$
1	$\binom{5}{1} \times \left(\frac{1}{3}\right) \times \left(\frac{2}{3}\right)^4$	$= \frac{80}{243}$
2	$\binom{5}{2} \times \left(\frac{1}{3}\right)^2 \times \left(\frac{2}{3}\right)^3$	$= \frac{80}{243}$
3	$\binom{5}{3} \times \left(\frac{1}{3}\right)^3 \times \left(\frac{2}{3}\right)^2$	$= \frac{40}{243}$
4	$\binom{5}{4} \times \left(\frac{1}{3}\right)^4 \times \left(\frac{2}{3}\right)$	$= \frac{10}{243}$
5	$\binom{5}{5} \times \left(\frac{1}{3}\right)^5$	$= \frac{1}{243}$

Table 7.2. Probability distribution for the number of times out of 5 that the spinner shows black.

Notice that $\sum_{x=0}^{5} P(X = x)$ is 1. This is a useful check for the probabilities in any distribution table.

Notice also that as $\left(\frac{1}{3}\right)^0 = 1$ and $\left(\frac{2}{3}\right)^0 = 1$ you could write $P(X = 0)$ as $\binom{5}{0} \times \left(\frac{1}{3}\right)^0 \times \left(\frac{2}{3}\right)^5$, and $P(X = 5)$ as $\binom{5}{5} \times \left(\frac{1}{3}\right)^5 \times \left(\frac{2}{3}\right)^0$. These results enable you to write $P(X = x)$ as a formula:

$$P(X = x) = \binom{5}{x} \times \left(\frac{1}{3}\right)^x \times \left(\frac{2}{3}\right)^{5-x}.$$

However the formula on its own is not sufficient, because you must also give the values for which the formula is defined. In this case x can take integer values from 0 to 5 inclusive. So a more concise definition of the distribution of X than Table 7.2 would be

$$P(X = x) = \binom{5}{x} \times \left(\frac{1}{3}\right)^x \times \left(\frac{2}{3}\right)^{5-x} \qquad \text{for } x = 0, 1, 2, \ldots, 5.$$

Although the case of the spinner is not important in itself, it is an example of an important and frequently occurring situation.

- A single trial has just two possible outcomes (often called success, s, and failure, f).
- There is a fixed number of trials, n.
- The outcome of each trial is independent of the outcome of all the other trials.
- The probability of success at each trial, p, is constant.

The random variable X, which represents the number of successes in n trials of this experiment, is said to have a **binomial distribution**.

A consequence of the last condition is that the probability of failure will also be a constant, equal to $1 - p$. This probability is usually denoted by q, which means that $q = 1 - p$.

In a binomial distribution, the random variable X has a probability distribution given by

$$P(X = x) = \binom{n}{x} p^x q^{n-x} \quad \text{for} \quad x = 0, 1, 2, \ldots, n.$$

You will see the reason for the name 'binomial' a little later. Provided you are given the values of n and p, you can evaluate all of the probabilities in the distribution table. The values of n and p are therefore the essential pieces of information about the probability distribution. In the example, n was 5 and p was $\frac{1}{3}$. You did not need to be told q, because its value is always $1 - p$, so in the example the value of q was $\frac{2}{3}$.

The values of n and p are called the **parameters** of the binomial distribution. You need to know the parameters of a probability distribution to calculate the probabilities numerically.

To denote that a random variable X has a binomial distribution with parameters n and p, you write $X \sim B(n, p)$. So for the probability distribution in Table 7.2 you write $X \sim B(5, \frac{1}{3})$.

Example 7.1.1

Given that $X \sim B(8, \frac{1}{4})$, find   (a) $P(X = 6)$,   (b) $P(X \le 2)$,   (c) $P(X > 0)$.

(a) Using the binomial probability formula with $n = 8$ and $p = \frac{1}{4}$ you get

$$P(X = 6) = \binom{8}{6} \times \left(\tfrac{1}{4}\right)^6 \times \left(\tfrac{3}{4}\right)^2 = 28 \times \left(\tfrac{1}{4}\right)^6 \times \left(\tfrac{3}{4}\right)^2 = 0.003\,85,$$

correct to 3 significant figures.

(b) $P(X \le 2) = P(X = 0) + P(X = 1) + P(X = 2)$

$$= \binom{8}{0} \left(\tfrac{1}{4}\right)^0 \left(\tfrac{3}{4}\right)^8 + \binom{8}{1} \left(\tfrac{1}{4}\right)^1 \left(\tfrac{3}{4}\right)^7 + \binom{8}{2} \left(\tfrac{1}{4}\right)^2 \left(\tfrac{3}{4}\right)^6$$

$$= 0.1001\ldots + 0.2669\ldots + 0.3114\ldots$$

$$= 0.6785\ldots = 0.679, \text{ correct to 3 significant figures.}$$

(c) The easiest way to find $P(X > 0)$ is to use the fact that $P(X > 0)$ is the complement of $P(X = 0)$.

So $P(X > 0) = 1 - P(X = 0)$

$$= 1 - \binom{8}{0} \left(\tfrac{1}{4}\right)^0 \left(\tfrac{3}{4}\right)^8 \quad \text{(from part (b))}$$

$$= 1 - 0.1001\ldots$$

$$= 0.8998\ldots = 0.900, \text{ correct to 3 significant figures.}$$

To check that the binomial formula does represent a probability distribution you must show that $\sum_{x=0}^{n} P(X = x) = 1$. Consider the example involving the spinner, but use p and q instead of $\frac{1}{3}$ and $\frac{2}{3}$ respectively. Table 7.3 shows the distribution.

If you sum the probabilities in the right column you get

$$\sum_{x=0}^{5} P(X = x) = q^5 + 5pq^4$$
$$+ 10p^2q^3 + 10p^3q^2 + 5p^4q + p^5.$$

The right side of this equation is the binomial expansion of $(q + p)^5$ (see C2 Chapter 3).

You could check for yourself by multiplying out $(q + p)(q + p)(q + p)(q + p)(q + p)$, so

$$\sum_{x=0}^{5} P(X = x) = (q + p)^5 = 1^5 = 1.$$

You can use a similar argument to show that

$$\sum_{x=0}^{n} P(X = x) = \sum_{x=0}^{n} \left[\binom{n}{x} \times p^x \times q^{n-x} \right] = (q + p)^n = 1^n = 1.$$

x	$P(X = x)$	
0	q^5	$= q^5$
1	$\binom{5}{1} \times p \times q^4$	$= 5pq^4$
2	$\binom{5}{2} \times p^2 \times q^3$	$= 10p^2q^3$
3	$\binom{5}{3} \times p^3 \times q^2$	$= 10p^3q^2$
4	$\binom{5}{4} \times p^4 \times q$	$= 5p^4q$
5	p^5	$= p^5$

Table 7.3. Probability distribution for the number of times out of 5 that the spinner shows black.

The individual probabilities in the binomial distribution are the terms of the binomial expansion of $(q + p)^n$: these are two similar uses of the word 'binomial'.

Before using the binomial distribution as a model for a situation you need to convince yourself that all the conditions are satisfied. The following example illustrates some of the problems that can occur.

Example 7.1.2
A school car park has 5 parking spaces. A student decides to do a survey to see whether this is enough. At the same time each day, she observes the number of spaces which are filled. Let X be the number of spaces filled at this time on a randomly chosen day. Is it reasonable to model the distribution of the random variable X with a binomial distribution?

She looks at each parking space to see whether it is occupied or not. This represents a single trial.

Are there exactly two outcomes for each trial (parking space), and are these mutually exclusive? In other words, is each parking space either occupied by a single car or not? The answer will usually be yes, but sometimes poorly parked vehicles will give the answer no.

Are there a fixed number of trials? The answer is yes. On each day there are 5 parking spaces available so the number of trials is 5 times the number of days on which observations were made.

Are the trials independent? This is not likely. Drivers may be less inclined to park in one of the centre spaces if it is surrounded by cars, because getting out of their own car may be more difficult.

Is the probability p of success (in this case a parking space being filled by a car) constant? Probably not, because people may be more likely to choose the space closest to the school entrance, for example.

You can see that, when you are proposing to model a practical situation with a binomial distribution, many of the assumptions may be questionable and some may not be valid at all. In this case, however, provided you are aware that the binomial model is far from perfect, you could still use it as a reasonable approximation. You might also have realised that you do not know the value of p in this example, so you would have to estimate it. To do this you would divide the total number of cars observed by the total number of available car parking spaces, which in this case is

$5 \times$ (the number of days for which the survey was carried out).

Example 7.1.3
State whether a binomial distribution could be used in each of the following problems. If the binomial distribution is an acceptable model, define the random variable clearly and state its parameters.

(a) A fair cubical dice is rolled 10 times. Find the probability of getting three fours, four fives and three sixes.

(b) A fair coin is spun until a head occurs. Find the probability that eight spins are necessary, including the one on which the head occurs.

(c) A jar contains 49 balls numbered 1 to 49. Six of the balls are selected at random. Find the probability that four of the six have an even score.

(a) In this case you are interested in three different outcomes: a four, a five and a six. A binomial distribution depends on having only two possible outcomes, success and failure, so it cannot be used here.

> You could use the binomial distribution if you just wanted the probability of getting three fours, say.

(b) The binomial distribution requires a fixed number of trials, n, and this is not the case here, since the number of trials is unknown. In fact, the number of trials is the random variable of interest here.

(c) Whether a binomial model is appropriate or not depends on whether the selection of the balls is done with replacement or without replacement. If the selection is without replacement, then the outcome of each trial will not be independent of all the other trials. If the selection is with replacement, then define the random variable X to be the number of balls with an even score out of six random selections. X will then have a binomial distribution with parameters 6 and $\frac{24}{49}$. You write this as $X \sim B(6, \frac{24}{49})$. You are assuming, of course, that the balls are thoroughly mixed before each selection and that every ball has an equal chance of being selected.

Example 7.1.4
A card is selected at random from a standard pack of 52 playing cards. The suit of the card is recorded and the card is replaced. This process is repeated to give a total of 16 selections, and on each occasion the card is replaced in the pack before another selection is made. Calculate the probability that

(a) exactly five hearts occur in the 16 selections,

(b) at most 8 hearts occur,

(c) at least three hearts occur.

Let X be the number of hearts in 16 random selections (with replacement) of a playing card from a pack. Then X satisfies all the conditions for a binomial distribution.

- Each trial consists of selecting a card from the pack, with replacement.

- Each trial has exactly two possible outcomes, and these are mutually exclusive; getting a heart is a success and not getting a heart is a failure.

> You may think that there are 52 possible outcomes for each trial, but you are only interested in whether the card is a heart or not a heart.

- The outcome of each trial is independent of any other trial. This is true since each card is replaced before the next one is selected. But you must ensure that each selection is random and that the cards are thoroughly shuffled before each selection.

- The probabilities of success and failure are constant. P(selecting a heart) = P(success) = $\frac{1}{4}$ and P(not selecting a heart) = P(failure) = $\frac{3}{4}$, so this condition is fulfilled.

X therefore has a binomial distribution with parameters $n = 16$ and $p = \frac{1}{4}$. That is,

$$X \sim B(16, \tfrac{1}{4}).$$

(a) Using the binomial formula,

$$P(X = 5) = \binom{16}{5} \times \left(\tfrac{1}{4}\right)^5 \times \left(\tfrac{3}{4}\right)^{11} = 0.180, \text{ correct to 3 significant figures.}$$

(b) You need to find $P(X \le 8)$. From first principles

$$P(X \le 8) = P(X = 0) + P(X = 1) + \cdots + P(X = 8)$$
$$= \binom{16}{0} \times \left(\tfrac{1}{4}\right)^0 \times \left(\tfrac{3}{4}\right)^{16} + \binom{16}{1} \times \left(\tfrac{1}{4}\right)^1 \times \left(\tfrac{3}{4}\right)^{15} + \cdots + \binom{16}{8} \times \left(\tfrac{1}{4}\right)^8 \times \left(\tfrac{3}{4}\right)^8.$$

This calculation would take a considerable time to carry out. Fortunately, there are cumulative probability tables, as on pages 208–213, which you could use for this kind of calculation. For certain values of n and p the cumulative probability $P(X \le x)$ is given for values of x from $0, 1, \ldots, n - 1$.

From the table on page 210, $n = 16$ and $p = 0.25$ give $P(X \le 8) = 0.9925$ correct to 4 decimal places.

(c) To find $P(X \geq 3)$, first use the fact that $P(X \geq 3) = 1 - P(X \leq 2)$, and then find $P(X \leq 2)$ from tables.

$$P(X \geq 3) = 1 - P(X \leq 2)$$
$$= 1 - 0.1971 = 0.8029.$$

You can use subtraction to find the probabilities of single values of X. For example, using the tables for part (a),

$$P(X = 5) = P(X \leq 5) - P(X \leq 4)$$
$$= 0.8103 - 0.6302 = 0.1801,$$

which agrees with the earlier result when corrected to 3 significant figures.

Example 7.1.5
Given that $Y \sim B(10, 0.3)$ find

(a) $P(Y < 8)$,   (b) $P(Y > 5)$,   (c) $P(3 < Y \leq 5)$,   (d) $P(2 \leq Y < 7)$.

(a) $P(Y < 8) = P(Y \leq 7) = 0.9984$ (from tables).

(b) $P(Y > 5) = 1 - P(Y \leq 5)$
$$= 1 - 0.9527 \text{ (from tables)}$$
$$= 0.0473.$$

(c) $P(3 < Y \leq 5) = P(Y \leq 5) - P(Y \leq 3)$
$$= 0.9894 - 0.6496 \text{ (from tables)}$$
$$= 0.3031.$$

(d) $P(2 \leq Y < 7) = P(Y \leq 6) - P(Y \leq 1)$
$$= 0.9894 - 0.1493 \text{ (from tables)}$$
$$= 0.8401.$$

Here is a summary of the binomial distribution.

> **Binomial distribution**
> - A single trial has exactly two possible outcomes (success and failure) and these are mutually exclusive.
> - A fixed number, n, of trials takes place.
> - The outcome of each trial is independent of the outcome of all the other trials.
> - The probability of success at each trial is constant.
>
> The random variable X, which represents the number of successes in the n trials of this experiment, has a probability distribution given by
>
> $$P(X = x) = \binom{n}{x} p^x q^{n-x} \qquad \text{for } x = 0, 1, 2, \ldots, n, \qquad (7.1)$$
>
> where p is the probability of success and $q = 1 - p$ is the probability of failure.
>
> When the random variable X satisfies these conditions, $X \sim B(n, p)$.

7.2 Practical activity

Penalties or shots

(a) Select a group of students and ask them each to take either 8 penalties at football or 8 shots at basketball. For each student record the number of successful penalties or shots.

(b) Does the binomial distribution provide a reasonable model for these results? Is it necessary to use the same goalkeeper for all of the football penalties?

(c) Does the skill level of each person matter if the binomial distribution is to be a reasonable model? Is the basketball example more likely to be fitted by a binomial model than the football example?

Exercise 7A

In this exercise give probabilities correct to 4 decimal places.

1 The random variable X has a binomial distribution with $n = 6$ and $p = 0.2$. Calculate

(a) $P(X = 3)$,   (b) $P(X = 4)$,   (c) $P(X = 6)$.

2 Given that $Y \sim B(7, \frac{2}{3})$, calculate

(a) $P(Y = 4)$,   (b) $P(Y = 6)$,   (c) $P(Y = 0)$.

3 Given that $Z \sim B(9, 0.45)$, calculate

(a) $P(Z = 3)$,   (b) $P(Z = 4$ or $5)$,   (c) $P(Z \geq 7)$.

4 Given that $D \sim B(12, 0.7)$, calculate

(a) $P(D < 4)$,   (b) the smallest value of d such that $P(D > d) < 0.90$.

5 Given that $H \sim B(9, \frac{1}{2})$, calculate the probability that H is

(a) exactly 5,   (b) 5 or 6,   (c) at least 8,   (d) more than 2.

6 Given that $S \sim B(7, \frac{1}{6})$, find the probability that S is

(a) exactly 3,   (b) at least 4.

7 In a certain school, 30% of the students are in the age group 16–19.

(a) Ten students are chosen at random. What is the probability that fewer than four of them are in the 16–19 age group?

(b) If the ten students were chosen by picking ten who were sitting together at lunch, explain why a binomial distribution might no longer have been suitable.

8 A factory makes large quantities of coloured sweets, and it is known that on average 20% of the sweets are coloured green. A packet contains 20 sweets. Assuming that the packet forms a random sample of the sweets made by the factory, calculate the probability that exactly seven of the sweets are green.

If you knew that, in fact, the sweets could have been green, red, orange or brown, would it have invalidated your calculation?

9 Eggs produced at a farm are packaged in boxes of six. Assume that, for any egg, the probability that it is broken when it reaches the retail outlet is 0.1, independent of all other eggs. A box is said to be bad if it contains at least two broken eggs. Calculate the probability that a randomly selected box is bad.

It is known that, in fact, breakages are more likely to occur after the eggs have been packed into boxes, and while they are being transported to the retail outlet. Explain why this fact is likely to invalidate the calculation.

10 On a particular tropical island, the probability that there is a hurricane in any given month can be taken to be 0.08. Use a binomial distribution to calculate the probability that there is a hurricane in more than two months of the year. State two assumptions needed for a binomial distribution to be a good model. Why may one of the assumptions not be valid?

11 The random variable X has a binomial distribution with $n = 5$ and $p = 0.35$. Use tables to find

(a) $P(X \leq 2)$,   (b) $P(X = 3)$,   (c) $P(X < 3)$,   (d) $P(X > 2)$.

12 The random variable Y has a binomial distribution B(10,0.4). Use tables to find

(a) $P(Y \leq 5)$,   (b) $P(Y = 2)$,   (c) $P(Y < 4)$,   (d) $P(Y \geq 6)$.

13 The random variable Z has a binomial distribution B(10, 0.7). Use tables to find

(a) $P(Z \leq 5)$,   (b) $P(Z \geq 4)$,   (c) $P(Z < 8)$.

14 It is given that, at a stated time of day, 35% of the adults in the country are wearing jeans. At that time, a sample of twelve adults is selected. Use a binomial distribution to calculate the probability that exactly five out of these twelve are wearing jeans. Explain carefully two assumptions that must be made for your calculation to be valid. (If you say 'sample is random' you must explain what this means in the context of the question.)

15 Explain why a binomial distribution would not be a good model in the following problem. (Do not attempt any calculation.)

Thirteen cards are chosen at random from an ordinary pack. Find the probability that there are four clubs, four diamonds, three hearts and two spades.

16 Explain why the binomial distribution B(6, 0.5) would not be a good model in each of the following situations. (Do not attempt any calculations.)

(a) It is known that 50% of the boys in a certain school are over 170 cm in height. They are arranged, for a school photograph, in order of ascending height. A group of six boys standing next to each other is selected at random. Find the probability that exactly three members of the sample are over 170 cm in height.

(b) It is known that, on average, the temperature in London reaches at least 20 °C on exactly half the days in the year. A day is picked at random from each of the months January, March, May, July, September and November. Find the probability that the temperature in London reaches 20 °C on exactly three of these six days.

17 A bag contains six red and four green counters. Four counters are selected at random, without replacement. The events A, B, C and D represent obtaining a red counter on the first, second, third and fourth selection, respectively.

Use a tree diagram to show that $P(A) = P(B) = P(C) = P(D) = 0.6$.

Explain why the total number of red counters could not be well modelled by the distribution $B(4, 0.6)$.

> The purpose of this and the preceding question is to illustrate that the properties 'the probability of a success is constant' and 'the outcomes are independent' are not the same, and you should try to distinguish carefully between them. Notice also that 'the outcomes are independent' is not the same thing as 'sampling with replacement'.

7.3 The geometric distribution

Consider the following three examples.

1 A dice is rolled until a six is scored. Let X be the number of rolls up to and including the roll on which the first six occurs.

2 A card is selected with replacement from a standard pack of cards until an ace is drawn. Let Y be the number of selections up to and including the one on which the first ace occurs.

3 A person has a 1 in 17 chance of winning a prize in a lottery. She keeps playing the lottery once each week. Let W be the number of weeks up to and including the week in which she first wins a prize.

The three random variables have certain similarities.

In the first example,

$$P(X = 1) = P(\text{a six occurs on the first throw}) = \tfrac{1}{6}.$$

If you let s represent the event that a six occurs on a trial and let f represent the event that a six does not occur, then $\{X = 2\}$ corresponds to the sequence $f_1 s_2$. Similarly the event $\{X = 3\}$ corresponds to the sequence $f_1 f_2 s_3$. Notice that there is only one possible sequence for each value of X. Contrast this with the binomial distribution.

You can now calculate the probability distribution for X:

$$P(X = 2) = P(f_1 s_2) = \left(\tfrac{5}{6}\right) \times \left(\tfrac{1}{6}\right) = \tfrac{5}{36},$$
$$P(X = 3) = P(f_1 f_2 s_3) = \left(\tfrac{5}{6}\right)^2 \times \left(\tfrac{1}{6}\right) = \tfrac{25}{216},$$
$$P(X = 4) = P(f_1 f_2 f_3 s_4) = \left(\tfrac{5}{6}\right)^3 \times \left(\tfrac{1}{6}\right) = \tfrac{125}{1296},$$

and so on.

You can generalise this as

$$P(X = x) = \left(\tfrac{5}{6}\right)^{x-1} \times \left(\tfrac{1}{6}\right) \quad \text{for } x = 1, 2, 3, \dots$$

In the second example the probability distribution formula for Y will be
$P(Y = y) = \left(\frac{12}{13}\right)^{y-1} \times \left(\frac{1}{13}\right)$ for values of $y = 1, 2, 3 \ldots$ since

$$P(Y = y) = P\left(\frac{y-1}{\underbrace{ff \ldots fs}}\right) = \overbrace{\frac{12}{13} \times \frac{12}{13} \times \cdots \times \frac{12}{13}}^{y-1 \text{ of these}} \times \frac{1}{13}.$$

In the third example, by a similar argument,

$$P(W = w) = \left(\frac{16}{17}\right)^{w-1} \times \left(\frac{1}{17}\right) \quad \text{for } w = 1, 2, 3, \ldots$$

There is no upper limit to the possible values of X, Y and W for these distributions. Contrast this with the binomial distribution.

Some of the ideas you met when studying the binomial distribution will be helpful for this distribution.

- A single trial consists of, for example, throwing a dice once.
- At each trial of the experiment there are exactly two possible outcomes (success and failure), and these are mutually exclusive.
- The trials are independent.
- The probability of success is constant at each trial.

Let X be the number of trials up to and including the first success. The random variable X satisfying these conditions is said to have a **geometric distribution**.

Let p be the probability of a success. The probability function for this geometric distribution is then

$$P(X = x) = q^{x-1} \times p \quad \text{for } x = 1, 2, 3, \ldots$$

where $q = 1 - p$.

You can write down the probabilities for a geometric distribution as in Table 7.4.

x	1	2	3	4	$\ldots$
$P(X = x)$	p	pq	pq^2	pq^3	$\ldots$

Table 7.4. Probability distribution for the geometric distribution.

The ratio between successive probabilities is constant, and always equal to q. A sequence in which successive terms are in a constant ratio is called a **geometric sequence**, or a **geometric progression**. (See C2 Chapter 6.) So the probabilities are in a geometric sequence.

The geometric distribution has only one parameter, p. You can use a piece of notation similar to that for the binomial distribution to denote this. You write $X \sim \text{Geo}(p)$.

The difference between the geometric and binomial distributions is that in the geometric distribution the number of trials is not fixed, and the random variable is the number of trials up to and including the first success.

Example 7.3.1

A darts player must start a game by hitting a certain section of the dart-board, The probability that any single dart hits this section is $\frac{2}{5}$. The player keeps throwing darts until he hits the required section. Calculate the probability that he needs

(a)   exactly 5 throws,

(b)   at most 2 throws,

(c)   at least 8 throws,

(d)   at most 10 throws.

(e)* How many throws does the player need to make to be at least 99.999% sure of hitting the required section?

(f)   What assumptions have you made in using the geometric distribution to model this situation?

> Let X be the number of throws needed to hit the required section of the dart-board. X has a geometric distribution, with parameter $\frac{2}{5}$.
>
> (a)   You need to find $P(X = 5)$. From the probability distribution formula
>
> $$P(X = 5) = \left(\frac{3}{5}\right)^4 \times \frac{2}{5} = 0.0518, \text{ correct to 3 significant figures.}$$
>
> (b)   You need to find $P(X \le 2)$. This can be found by adding probabilities.
>
> $$\begin{aligned} P(X \le 2) &= P(X = 1) + P(X = 2) \\ &= \frac{2}{5} + \frac{3}{5} \times \frac{2}{5} \\ &= 0.64 \end{aligned}$$
>
> (c)   Finding $P(X \ge 8)$ is best done by realising that $\{X \ge 8\}$ is equivalent to there having been 7 failures. Therefore
>
> $$P(X \ge 8) = \left(\frac{3}{5}\right)^7 = 0.0280, \text{ correct to 3 significant figures.}$$
>
> (d)   You can find $P(X \le 10)$ from the probability of the complementary event by using $P(X \le 10) = 1 - P(X \ge 11)$. Then, using a similar argument to that of part (c),
>
> $$\begin{aligned} P(X \le 10) &= 1 - P(X \ge 11) \\ &= 1 - \left(\frac{3}{5}\right)^{10} = 0.994, \text{ correct to 3 significant figures.} \end{aligned}$$
>
> (e)* To find m such that $P(X \le m) \ge 0.99999$, use the argument in part (d) to get
>
> $$P(X \le m) = 1 - P(X \ge m + 1) = 1 - \left(\frac{3}{5}\right)^m,$$
>
> so, to find m, you must solve the inequality $1 - \left(\frac{3}{5}\right)^m \ge 0.99999$, which is the same as $\left(\frac{3}{5}\right)^m \le 0.00001$, or $\left(\frac{5}{3}\right)^m \ge 100000$.
>
> Trying some values of m gives
>
> $$\left(\frac{5}{3}\right)^{22} \approx 75975 \quad \text{and} \quad \left(\frac{5}{3}\right)^{23} \approx 126625.$$
>
> So the required number of throws is 23.

(f)   The assumptions which have been made are that the probability of success, here $\frac{2}{5}$, is constant for every throw. This means that the darts player does not improve with practice, nor does he get worse as he gets tired. The results of individual throws are also assumed to be independent, so that each throw has no effect on any other throw.

The method used in parts (c) and (d) of Example 7.3.1 can be generalised as follows:

For the geometric distribution $X \sim \text{Geo}(p)$

$$P(X \geq x) = (1 - p)^{x-1},$$
$$P(X \leq x) = 1 - (1 - p)^{x}.$$

There is an alternative approach to solving problems such as Example 7.3.1 parts (c) and (d), which uses the formula for the sum of a geometric progression (see C2 Section 6.2). The sum to n terms of a geometric progression with first term a and common ratio r is given by

$$S_n = \frac{a(1 - r^n)}{1 - r}.$$

For part (c),

$$P(X \geq 8) = 1 - P(X \leq 7)$$
$$= 1 - S_7 \quad \text{where } r = \tfrac{3}{5}, a = \tfrac{2}{5} \text{ and } n = 7$$
$$= 1 - \frac{\tfrac{2}{5}\left(1 - \left(\tfrac{3}{5}\right)^7\right)}{1 - \tfrac{3}{5}} = 0.0280, \text{ correct to 3 significant figures,}$$

which agrees with the original answer to part (c).

Here is a summary of the conditions for the geometric distribution

The geometric distribution

- A single trial has exactly two possible outcomes (success and failure) and these are mutually exclusive.
- The outcome of each trial is independent of the outcome of all the other trials.
- The probability of success at each trial is constant.
- The trials are repeated until a success occurs.

The random variable X, which represents the number of trials up to and including the first success, then has a probability distribution given by the formula

$$P(X = x) = pq^{x-1} \quad \text{for } x = 1, 2, 3, \ldots \tag{7.2}$$

where p is the probability of success, and $q = 1 - p$ is the probability of failure.

When the random variable X satisfies these conditions $X \sim \text{Geo}(p)$.

7.4   Practical activity

Waste paper   Use the results of Practical activity 3 from Section 3.10 to determine whether the geometric model is appropriate for both sets of data. If so, does the parameter appear to be similar for each set of data? If the geometric distribution is not appropriate, state which of the modelling assumptions underlying a geometric distribution you think is not valid and why.

Exercise 7B

In this exercise give probabilities to 4 decimal places.

1 The random variable X represents the number of trials up to and including a success. The probability of a success on any given trial is $p = 0.3$, independently of any other trial. Find the probability that

(a) $X = 5$, (b) $X = 6$, (c) $X = 5$, 6 or 7.

2 The random variable Y represents the number of trials up to and including a success. The probability of a success on any given trial is $p = 0.4$, independently of any other trial. Find the probability that

(a) $Y = 3$, (b) $Y = 4$, (c) $Y = 2$, 3 or 4.

3 Trials are repeated until a success is obtained. The probability of a success on any given trial is 0.8, independently of any other trial. Find the probability that the total number of trials needed, including the successful one, is

(a) exactly 3, (b) less than or equal to 3, (c) more than 5.

4 The random variable G has a geometric distribution, and the probability of a success on the first trial is 0.025. Find the probability that the first success

(a) occurs on the 10th trial,

(b) occurs after the 10th trial,

(c) occurs on or before the 10th trial.

5 It is given that the random variable T, which can take values $1, 2, 3, \ldots$, has a geometric distribution and $P(T = 1) = 0.15$. Calculate

(a) $P(T > 7)$, (b) $P(T > 11)$, (c) $P(T \geq 12)$ (d) $P(T \leq 11)$.

6 A card is chosen at random from an ordinary pack, and replaced after its value has been noted. The process continues until a picture card (K, Q, J) is obtained. Z is the total number of cards drawn, including the picture card. Find the probability that

(a) $P(Z = 5)$, (b) $P(Z > 7)$, (c) $P(Z \leq 7)$.

7 In order to start a board game each player must throw at least one six with a pair of dice. Find the probability that for Gaye to start, she needs

(a) one throw, (b) five throws, (c) more than eight throws.

8 Wayne is counting cars going past the front gate of the school. He has been told that, on average, one car in 12 on the roads is green. Assuming that car colours are independent of each other, find the probability that

(a) the first green car he sees is the 8th that passes,

(b) the first green car is not among the first 15 cars,

(c) there is at least one green car among the first 10 cars.

9 A certain irrational number has a decimal expansion in which each digit is randomly chosen from the set $\{0, 1, 2, 3, 4, 5, 6, 7, 8, 9\}$. Find the probability that

(a) the first 9 occurs in the 8th place,

(b) there is no 9 in the first 10 places,

(c) there is no pair of 9s in the first 100 pairs of digits.

10 It is known that, on average, one person in three at a shopping centre is wearing trainers. A market researcher observes people entering the shopping centre. Use a geometric distribution, with $p = \frac{1}{3}$, to calculate the probability that

(a) the first person wearing trainers is the fourth person observed,

(b) the first person wearing trainers is not among the first five people observed,

(c) the first person wearing trainers is either the fourth or the fifth person observed.

Give a reason why a geometric distribution might not be suitable in this context.

11 It is known that 9% of the population belongs to blood group B. A hospital consultant visits patients in a hospital and determines their blood groups, stopping when he has found one member of blood group B.

(a) What is the probability that he needs to examine at least 11 patients?

(b)* How many patients must he examine to be 99.8% confident of finding at least one in blood group B?

12 A biologist is collecting data about fruit flies (*Drosophila*). She knows that one fruit fly in 10 has a striped body, and this property occurs at random in the population of fruit flies. She needs to collect one fruit fly with a striped body.

(a) Find the probability that she needs to collect at least 15 fruit flies.

(b)* Find the number of fruit flies she must collect to be 99.99% sure of obtaining one with a striped body.

13 An ordinary cubical dice is thrown repeatedly. A six is obtained on the 5th throw. Find the probability that the next six is

(a) obtained on the 12th throw

(b) not obtained until at least the 13th throw.

14* The random variable S can take values $1, 2, 3, \ldots$ and has a geometric distribution. It is given that $P(S = 2) = 0.2244$. Find the value of $P(S = 1)$, given that it is less than 0.5.

15* The random variable T can take values $1, 2, 3, \ldots$ and has a geometric distribution. It is given that $P(T = 1 \text{ or } 2) = 0.4375$. Find the value of $P(T = 1)$.

Miscellaneous exercise 7

1 The probability of a novice archer hitting a target with any shot is 0.3. Given that the archer shoots six arrows, find the probability that the target is hit at least twice.   (OCR)

2 A biased coin for which the probability of landing heads is 0.4, is spun 10 times. Let S be the number of heads that occur.

(a) State the distribution of S and give its parameters.

(b) Use tables to calculate $P(3 \leq S \leq 7)$.

(c) Use tables to calculate the most likely value of S.   (OCR)

3 (a) A computer program produces, at random, a single letter from the list A, B, C, D, E.

(i) Write down the proportion of the letters produced that you would expect to be Ds

(ii) Calculate the probability that the first nine letters produced contain no Ds.

(b) The program is then run repeatedly letters until a D is produced, and the number N of letters up to and including the first D is recorded.

(i) Write down the probability that $N = 1$.

(ii) Calculate the probability that N is exactly 5.

(iii) Find the probability that N is greater than 5.   (OCR)

4 Joseph and four friends each have an independent probability of 0.45 of winning a prize. Find the probability that

(a) exactly two of the five friends win a prize,

(b) Joseph and only one friend win a prize.   (OCR)

5 A bag contains two biased coins: coin A shows Heads with probability 0.6, and coin B shows Heads with probability 0.25. A coin is chosen at random from the bag, and tossed three times.

Find the probability that the three tosses of the coin show two Heads and one Tail in any order   (OCR, adapted)

6 When a driving test is taken, the probability of passing is $\frac{1}{3}$ at any attempt. If a candidate fails, tests continue until the candidate passes. The random variable X is the number of tests a candidate takes to achieve a pass. State a distribution which can be used as a model for X. Find the probabilities that $X = 1$, $X = 2$, $X = 3$, $X = 4$.

Find the probability that a candidate will need ten or fewer attempts to pass the test, giving your answer correct to 3 decimal places.

In a sample of 486 candidates, find how many you would expect

(a) to pass at the second attempt,

(b)* to need more than three attempts.   (OCR)

7 (a) A fair coin is tossed 4 times. Calculate the probabilities that the tosses result in 0, 1, 2, 3 and 4 heads.

  (b) A fair coin is tossed 8 times. Calculate the probability that the first 4 tosses and the last 4 tosses result in the same number of heads.

  (c)* Two teams each consist of 3 players. Each player in a team tosses a fair coin once and the team's score is the total number of heads thrown. Find the probability that the teams have the same score.   (OCR)

8 On average, from a free kick, Manuel scores one goal in every four attempts.

  (a) Name the distribution which models the number of attempts needed to score his first goal.

  (b) Find the probability that he scores his first goal on his fourth attempt.

  (c) Find the probability that he scores his first goal after at least three failures.

  (d) What assumption must be made to answer this question?   (OCR)

9* State the conditions under which the binomial distribution may be used for the calculation of probabilities.

  The probability that a girl chosen at random has a weekend birthday in 1993 is $\frac{2}{7}$. Calculate the probability that, among a group of ten girls chosen at random,

  (a) none has a weekend birthday in 1993,

  (b) exactly one has a weekend birthday in 1993.

  Among 100 groups of ten girls, how many groups would you expect to contain more than one girl with a weekend birthday in 1993?   (OCR)

10 A gambler buys one lottery ticket each week. Assuming that the probability of any one ticket winning a prize is 0.05, independently of all other tickets, find the probability that

  (a) the gambler first wins a prize with the ticket bought in the fifth week,

  (b) the gambler's first prize occurs before the fifth week,

  (c) the gambler's first prize occurs after the fifth week,

  (d) The gambler wins more than 1 prize in the first five weeks.   (OCR)

11 Show that, when two fair dice are thrown, the probability of obtaining a 'double' is $\frac{1}{6}$, where a 'double' is defined as the same score on both dice. Four players play a board game which requires them to take it in turns to throw two fair dice. Each player throws the two dice once in each round. When a double is thrown the player moves forward six squares. Otherwise the player moves forward one square. Find

  (a) the probability that the first double occurs on the third throw of the game,

  (b) the probability that exactly one of the four players obtains a double in the first round,

  (c) the probability that a double occurs exactly once in 4 of the first 5 rounds.   (OCR)

12 Six hens are observed over a period of 20 days and the number of eggs laid each day is summarised in the following table.

Number of eggs	3	4	5	6
Number of days	2	2	10	6

Show that the mean number of eggs per day is 5.

It may be assumed that a hen never lays more than one egg in any day. State one other assumption that needs to be made in order to consider a binomial model, with $n = 6$, for the total number of eggs laid in a day. State the probability that a randomly chosen hen lays an egg on a given day.

Calculate the expected frequencies of 3, 4, 5 and 6 eggs.   (OCR)

13 A Personal Identification Number (PIN) consists of 4 digits in order, each of which is one of the digits 0, 1, 2, ..., 9. Susie has difficulty remembering her PIN. She tries to remember it and writes down what she thinks it is. The probability that the first digit is correct is 0.8 and the probability that the second digit is correct is 0.86. The probability that the first two digits are correct is 0.72. Find

 (a) the probability that the second digit is correct given that the first digit is correct,

 (b) the probability that the first digit is correct and the second digit is incorrect,

 (c) the probability that the first digit is incorrect and the second digit is correct,

 (d) the probability that the second digit is incorrect given that the first digit is incorrect.

The probability that all four digits are correct is 0.7. On 12 separate occasions Susie writes down independently what she thinks is her PIN. Find the probability that the number of occasions on which all four digits are correct is less than 10.   (OCR)

14* From long observation it is known that the probability of a randomly chosen egg sold by a certain farmer being broken is 0.07. Eggs are packed in boxes of six. Use a binomial distribution to show that the probability that a box contains two or more broken eggs is 0.0608 correct to 4 significant figures.

A box of six eggs is classified as bad if it contains two or more broken eggs. Find the probability that in a consignment of 20 boxes exactly three are bad.

A quality control manager finds that in fact a binomial distribution is not a good model for the number of bad boxes in a consignment. Suggest a reason why breakages might not be independent of one another.

15 Sasha is playing an arcade game on a machine. The game involves using a mechanical crane to try to grab a prize within a 30 second time interval. If Sasha is successful she wins the prize, otherwise she loses. She pays 20p for each game and she keeps playing until she wins. From past experience Sasha estimates that she has a 60% chance of winning at each attempt.

(a) Calculate the probability that it costs her exactly £1.40 to win a prize. Give your answer correct to three significant figures.

The value of the prize is £2.50.

(b) Calculate the probability that Sasha will pay more to win the prize than its value. Give your answer correct to three significant figures.

(c) Given that Sasha has already failed to win her first nine games find the conditional probability that it will take more than 16 games in total for her to win the prize.

Next to the machine on which Sasha is playing is an identical machine. After she has lost her first 9 games she is joined by her friend John who starts to play on the neighbouring machine. You may assume that he also has a 60% chance of winning at each attempt.

(d) Find the probability that John takes more than 7 games to win the prize on the machine that he is playing.

(e) Describe the property of the geometric distribution which the answers to, parts (c) and (d) illustrate.

8 Expectation and variance of a random variable

This chapter shows you how to calculate the mean and variance of a random variable. When you have completed it you should

- know the meaning of the notation $E(X)$ and $Var(X)$
- be able to calculate the mean, $E(X)$, of a random variable X
- be able to calculate the variance, $Var(X)$, of a random variable X
- use the formulae $E(X) = np$ and $Var(X) = np(1 - p)$ for a binomial distribution
- use the formula $E(X) = \dfrac{1}{p}$ for a geometric distribution.

8.1 Expectation

In a game at a fund-raising event, you can pay to have a turn at spinning a roulette wheel. The wheel is numbered 1, 2, 3, and so on, up to 37. If the ball lands on 10, you win £10; if it lands on a number ending in 5, you win £5; otherwise, you win nothing. The amount, X, that you win is a random variable. If the roulette wheel is fair, X takes the values 10, 5 and 0, with probabilities

$$P(X = 10) = P(\text{ball lands on } 10) = \tfrac{1}{37},$$
$$P(X = 5) = P(\text{ball lands on } 5, 15, 25, 35) = \tfrac{4}{37},$$
$$P(X = 0) = 1 - P(X = 5) - P(X = 10) = 1 - \tfrac{4}{37} - \tfrac{1}{37} = \tfrac{32}{37},$$

and the probability distribution of X is

x	0	5	10
$P(X = x)$	$\frac{32}{37}$	$\frac{4}{37}$	$\frac{1}{37}$

How much should the person running the game charge for a turn? Obviously the idea is to make a profit, so a starting point would be to find the charge if the game is to break even. This involves finding the mean amount won per turn. Consider the situation after 3700 turns at the game. You can calculate the frequencies you would expect using

$$\text{frequency} \approx \text{total frequency} \times \text{probability}$$

(see Section 6.3). You might expect to win nothing about $3700 \times \tfrac{32}{37} = 3200$ times, £5 about $3700 \times \tfrac{4}{37} = 400$ times and £10 about $3700 \times \tfrac{1}{37} = 100$ times. The total amount won in £s in 3700 turns would be about $(0 \times 3200) + (5 \times 400) + (10 \times 100) = 3000$ so the mean amount would be £$\tfrac{3000}{3700} = £0.8108\ldots$.

If you look at this calculation carefully, you will see that the result obtained is independent of the number of turns. For example, if you had 7400 turns, then the amount won would double but the mean amount would remain the same. This suggests that the person running the stall needs to charge at least 81.08... p, which in practice means 82p.

The same result can be obtained more directly by multiplying each value by its probability and summing. Using p_i as a shortened form of $P(X = x_i)$, this gives

$$\sum x_i p_i = \left(0 \times \tfrac{32}{37}\right) + \left(5 \times \tfrac{4}{37}\right) + \left(10 \times \tfrac{1}{37}\right) = \tfrac{30}{37}.$$

The value which has been calculated is a theoretical mean. It is denoted by μ (which is read as 'mu'), the Greek letter m, standing for 'mean'. The new symbol is used in order to distinguish the mean of a probability distribution from $\bar{x}$, the mean of a data set. The mean, μ, of a probability distribution does not represent the amount won at a single turn or even the mean amount won over a finite number of turns. It is the value to which the mean amount won tends as the number of turns gets larger and larger, or, as mathematicians say, 'tends to infinity'. In practice, it is helpful to think of μ as the mean amount you would expect to win in a very long run of turns. For this reason, μ is often called the **expectation** or **expected value** or **mean** of X and is denoted by $E(X)$.

> The expectation of a random variable X is defined by
>
> $$E(X) = \mu = \sum x_i p_i. \tag{8.1}$$

Note that the expected value is not the same as the mode. The mode is the value with the highest probability.

Example 8.1.1
Find the expected value of each of the variables X, Y and W, which have the probability distributions given below. The variables X, Y and W were discussed in Section 6.1 in connection with the number of squares moved in a turn at three different board games.

(a)

x	1	2	3	4	5	6	Total
$P(X = x)$	$\frac{1}{6}$	$\frac{1}{6}$	$\frac{1}{6}$	$\frac{1}{6}$	$\frac{1}{6}$	$\frac{1}{6}$	1

(b)

y	1	2	3	4	5	7	8	9	10	11	12	Total
$P(Y = y)$	$\frac{1}{6}$	$\frac{1}{6}$	$\frac{1}{6}$	$\frac{1}{6}$	$\frac{1}{6}$	$\frac{1}{36}$	$\frac{1}{36}$	$\frac{1}{36}$	$\frac{1}{36}$	$\frac{1}{36}$	$\frac{1}{36}$	1

(c)

w	2	3	4	5	6	7	8	9	10	11	12	Total
$P(W = w)$	$\frac{1}{36}$	$\frac{2}{36}$	$\frac{3}{36}$	$\frac{4}{36}$	$\frac{5}{36}$	$\frac{6}{36}$	$\frac{5}{36}$	$\frac{4}{36}$	$\frac{3}{36}$	$\frac{2}{36}$	$\frac{1}{36}$	1

(a) $E(X) = \sum x_i p_i = \left(1 \times \tfrac{1}{6}\right) + \left(2 \times \tfrac{1}{6}\right) + \left(3 \times \tfrac{1}{6}\right) + \left(4 \times \tfrac{1}{6}\right) + \left(5 \times \tfrac{1}{6}\right) + \left(6 \times \tfrac{1}{6}\right) = 3\tfrac{1}{2}.$

You may have spotted that there is a quicker way to find the mean in this example. Since the distribution is symmetrical about $3\frac{1}{2}$, the mean must equal $3\frac{1}{2}$.

(b) This distribution is not symmetrical and so the mean has to be calculated.

$$\mathrm{E}(Y) = \sum y_i p_i = \left(1 \times \tfrac{1}{6}\right) + \left(2 \times \tfrac{1}{6}\right) + \left(3 \times \tfrac{1}{6}\right) + \left(4 \times \tfrac{1}{6}\right) + \left(5 \times \tfrac{1}{6}\right) + \left(7 \times \tfrac{1}{36}\right)$$
$$+ \left(8 \times \tfrac{1}{36}\right) + \left(9 \times \tfrac{1}{36}\right) + \left(10 \times \tfrac{1}{36}\right) + \left(11 \times \tfrac{1}{36}\right) + \left(12 \times \tfrac{1}{36}\right)$$
$$= (1 + 2 + 3 + 4 + 5) \times \tfrac{1}{6} + (7 + 8 + 9 + 10 + 11 + 12) \times \tfrac{1}{36}$$
$$= 15 \times \tfrac{1}{6} + 57 \times \tfrac{1}{36} = 4\tfrac{1}{12}.$$

(c) As in part (a), the probability distribution is symmetrical, in this case about 7, so $\mathrm{E}(W) = 7$.

This calculation shows that you move round the board fastest in Game C and slowest in Game A.

Example 8.1.2
A random variable R has the probability distribution shown below.

r	1	2	3	4
$P(R = r)$	0.1	a	0.3	b

Given that $\mathrm{E}(R) = 3$, find a and b.

Since $\sum P(R = r) = 1$,

$$0.1 + a + 0.3 + b = 1, \quad \text{so} \quad a + b = 0.6.$$

Also $\mathrm{E}(R) = 3$, so $\sum r P(R = r) = 3$,

$$1 \times 0.1 + 2 \times a + 3 \times 0.3 + 4 \times b = 3, \quad \text{so} \quad 2a + 4b = 2.$$

Solving these two equations simultaneously gives $a = 0.2$ and $b = 0.4$.

8.2 The variance of a random variable

Example 8.1.1 showed that the random variables X, Y and W have different means. If you compare the probability distributions (which are illustrated in Fig. 6.6), you will see that X, Y and W also have different degrees of spread. Just as the spread in a data set can be measured by the standard deviation or variance, so it is possible to define a corresponding measure of spread for a random variable. The symbol used for the standard deviation of a random variable is σ (a small Greek s, read as 'sigma') and its square, σ^2, the variance of a random variable, is denoted by $\mathrm{Var}(X)$.

The **variance** of a random variable X is defined by

$$\sigma^2 = \mathrm{Var}(X) = \sum (x_i - \mu)^2 p_i = \sum x_i^2 p_i - \mu^2. \qquad (8.2), (8.3)$$

The **standard deviation** of a random variable is σ, the square root of $\mathrm{Var}(X)$.

$\sum x_i^2 p_i$ is sometimes written as $E(X^2)$.

In practice it is usually simpler to calculate $Var(X)$ from the second version rather than the first version.

*Below is an explanation of how the formula for $Var(X)$ is derived. You may omit this if you wish, and go straight to Example 8.2.1.

Before deriving a formula for $Var(X)$, it is helpful to look at another method of arriving at the formula for $E(X)$. Suppose you had n turns at the roulette wheel game described in Section 8.1 and won nothing with frequency f_1, £5 with frequency f_2 and £10 with frequency f_3. The mean for these n turns is given by

$$\bar{x} = \frac{\sum x_i f_i}{n} = \frac{0 \times f_1}{n} + \frac{5 \times f_2}{n} + \frac{10 \times f_3}{n}.$$

The right side of the expression can be written slightly differently in the form

$$\bar{x} = 0 \times \frac{f_1}{n} + 5 \times \frac{f_2}{n} + 10 \times \frac{f_3}{n} = \sum \left(x_i \times \frac{f_i}{n} \right).$$

Now consider what happens as n becomes very large: the value of $\bar{x}$ tends to μ, and the ratio $\frac{f_i}{n}$, which is the relative frequency, tends to the corresponding theoretical probability, p_i. This gives

$$\mu = E(X) = \sum x_i p_i$$

which was the result obtained in Section 8.1.

Now consider the formula given in Equation 3.3 for the variance of a data set. Replacing $\sum f_i$ by n and rearranging gives

$$\text{variance} = \frac{\sum (x_i - \bar{x})^2 f_i}{n} = \sum (x_i - \bar{x})^2 \times \frac{f_i}{n}.$$

Again consider what happens when n becomes large. The ratio $\frac{f_i}{n}$ tends to p_i, and $\bar{x}$ tends to μ, giving

$$\sigma^2 = Var(X) = \sum (x_i - \mu)^2 p_i.$$

Alternatively, starting from Equation 3.4 for the variance of a data set, replacing $\sum f_i$ by n and rearranging gives

$$\text{variance} = \frac{\sum x_i^2 f_i}{n} - \bar{x}^2 = \sum x_i^2 \times \frac{f_i}{n} - \bar{x}^2.$$

When n becomes large, $\frac{f_i}{n}$ tends to p_i and $\bar{x}$ tends to μ, giving

$$\sigma^2 = Var(X) = \sum x_i^2 p_i - \mu^2.$$

Example 8.2.1
Calculate the standard deviation of the random variable X in Example 8.1.1, using Equation 8.3.

First calculate $\sum x_i^2 p_i$:

$$\sum x_i^2 p_i = \left(1^2 \times \tfrac{1}{6}\right) + \left(2^2 \times \tfrac{1}{6}\right) + \left(3^3 \times \tfrac{1}{6}\right) + \left(4^2 \times \tfrac{1}{6}\right) + \left(5^2 \times \tfrac{1}{6}\right) + \left(6^2 \times \tfrac{1}{6}\right)$$

$$= (1^2 + 2^2 + 3^2 + 4^2 + 5^2 + 6^2) \times \tfrac{1}{6} = 91 \times \tfrac{1}{6} = 15\tfrac{1}{6}.$$

From Example 8.1.1, $\mu = E(X) = 3\tfrac{1}{2}$.

Using Equation 8.3:

$$\sigma^2 = \mathrm{Var}(X) = \sum x_i^2 p_i - \mu^2 = 15\tfrac{1}{6} - \left(3\tfrac{1}{2}\right)^2 = \tfrac{35}{12}.$$

Then calculate the standard deviation:

$$\sigma = \sqrt{\tfrac{35}{12}} = 1.71 \text{ correct to 3 significant figures.}$$

The standard deviations for the random variables Y and W in Example 8.1.1 are $\sqrt{\tfrac{10395}{1296}} = 2.83$ and $\sqrt{\tfrac{35}{6}} = 2.42$ respectively, both given to 3 significant figures.

You could check these values. If you look again at Fig. 6.6 you will see how the size of the standard deviation is related to the degree of spread of the distribution. Although Y and W have very similar ranges, W has a smaller standard deviation because the probability distribution rises to a peak at the centre.

Example 8.2.2
In a certain field, each mushroom which is growing gives rise to a number X of mushrooms in the following year. None of the mushrooms present in one year survives until the next year. The random variable X has the probability distribution given below.

x	0	1	2
$P(X = x)$	0.2	0.6	0.2

If there were two mushrooms present in one year, find the probability distribution of Y, the number of mushrooms present in the following year. Hence find the mean and variance of Y.

The possible values of Y are given below.

	First value of X		
Second value of X	0	1	2
0	0	1	2
1	1	2	3
2	2	3	4

The corresponding probabilities are given below.

		First value of X		
		0	1	2
Second value of X	0	0.2×0.2	0.2×0.6	0.2×0.2
	1	0.6×0.2	0.6×0.6	0.6×0.2
	2	0.2×0.2	0.2×0.6	0.2×0.2

Combining these two sets of results gives the probability distribution of Y, from which $E(Y)$ and $Var(Y)$ can be found.

y	$P(Y = y)$	$yP(Y = y)$	$y^2 P(Y = y)$
0	0.04	0	0
1	$0.12 + 0.12 = 0.24$	0.24	0.24
2	$0.04 + 0.36 + 0.04 = 0.44$	0.88	1.76
3	$0.12 + 0.12 = 0.24$	0.72	2.16
4	0.04	0.16	0.64
	Totals: $\sum P(Y = y) = 1$	$\sum yP(Y = y) = 2$	$\sum y^2 P(Y = y) = 4.8$

From the last row of the table $\sum yP(Y = y) = 2$, and $\sum y^2 P(Y = y) = 4.8$.

Then $E(Y) = \sum yP(Y = y) = 2$, and

$$Var(Y) = \sum y^2 P(Y = y) - (E(Y))^2 = 4.8 - 2^2 = 0.8.$$

Exercise 8A

In this exercise all variables are discrete. Give numerical answers to 4 significant figures when appropriate.

1 Find the mean of the random variables X and Y which have the following probability distributions.

(a)

x	0	1	2	3	4
$P(X = x)$	$\frac{1}{8}$	$\frac{3}{8}$	$\frac{1}{8}$	$\frac{1}{4}$	$\frac{1}{8}$

(b)

y	-2	-1	0	1	2	3
$P(Y = y)$	0.15	0.25	0.3	0.05	0.2	0.05

2 The random variable T has the probability distribution given in the following table.

t	1	2	3	4	5	6	7
$P(T = t)$	0.1	0.2	0.1	0.2	0.1	0.2	0.1

Find $E(T)$ and $Var(T)$.

3 Find the exact expectation and variance of the random variable Y, which has the following probability distribution.

y	3	4	5	6	7
$P = (Y = y)$	$\frac{1}{18}$	$\frac{5}{18}$	$\frac{7}{18}$	$\frac{1}{18}$	$\frac{4}{18}$

4 The six faces of a fair cubical dice are numbered 1, 2, 2, 3, 3 and 3. When the dice is thrown once, the score is the number appearing on the top face. This is denoted by X.

(a) Find the mean and standard deviation of X.

(b) The dice is thrown twice and Y denotes the sum of the scores obtained. Find the probability distribution of Y. Hence find $E(Y)$ and $Var(Y)$.

5 A construction company can bid for one of two possible projects and the finance director has been asked to advise on which to choose. She estimates that project A will yield a profit of £150,000 with probability 0.5, a profit of £250,000 with probability 0.2 and a loss of £100,000 with probability 0.3. Project B will yield a profit of £100,000 with probability 0.6, a profit of £200,000 with probability 0.3 and a loss of £50,000 with probability 0.1. Determine which project the finance director should support, by calculating $E(A)$ and $E(B)$.

6 Some of the eggs in a supermarket are sold in boxes of six. The number, X, of broken eggs in a box has the probability distribution given in the following table.

x	0	1	2	3	4	5	6
$P(X = x)$	0.80	0.14	0.03	0.02	0.01	0	0

(a) Find the expectation and variance of X.

(b) Find the expectation and variance of the number of unbroken eggs in a box.

(c) Comment on the relationship between your answers to part (a) and part (b).

7 Find $E(H)$ and $Var(H)$ for the H defined in Question 4 of Exercise 6A.

8 The random variable X has the probability distribution given in the following table.

x	1	2	3	4	5
$P(X = x)$	a	0.3	0.2	0.1	0.2

Find the values of a, μ and σ for the distribution.

9 The random variable Y has the probability distribution given in the following table.

y	2	3	4	5	6	7
$P(Y = y)$	0.05	0.25	a	b	0.1	0.3

Given that $E(Y) = 4.9$, show that $a = b$, and find the standard deviation of Y.

10* A game is played by throwing a fair dice until either a six is obtained or four throws have been made. Let X denote the number of throws made. Find

(a) the probability distribution of X,   (b) the standard deviation of X.

The number of sixes obtained in the game is denoted by Y. Find $E(Y)$.

If the player throws a six in the course of the game then the player wins 100 points. If a six is not thrown then 150 points are lost. Find the expectation of the number of points received by a player after one game.

11* A committee of 6 men and 4 women appoints two of its members to represent it. Assuming that each member is equally likely to be appointed, obtain the probability distribution of the number of women appointed. Find the expected number of women appointed.

12* The dice of Question 4 is thrown and then an unbiased coin is thrown the number of times indicated by the score on the dice. Let H denote the number of heads obtained.

(a) Show that $P(H = 2) = \frac{13}{48}$.

(b) Tabulate the probability distribution of H.

(c) Show that $E(H) = \frac{1}{2}E(X)$, where X denotes the score on the dice.

(d) Calculate $\text{Var}(H)$.

8.3   The expectation and variance of a binomial distribution

Suppose that you wanted to find the mean and variance of the random variable X, where $X \sim B\left(3, \frac{1}{4}\right)$. One way would be to write out the probability distribution and calculate $E(X)$ and $\text{Var}(X)$ using Equations 8.1 and 8.3.

Example 8.3.1
Calculate $E(X)$ and $\text{Var}(X)$ for $X \sim B\left(3, \frac{1}{4}\right)$ from the probability distribution.

The probability distribution is found using the binomial probability formula

$$P(X = x) = \binom{n}{x} p^x (1 - p)^{n-x} \text{ (see Equation 7.1)}.$$

The distribution is shown in the table on the next page.

> Remember that p_i is the same as $P(X = x_i)$.

Using the totals from the table,

$$\mu = E(X) = \sum x_i p_i = \frac{48}{64} = \frac{3}{4}.$$
$$\sigma^2 = \text{Var}(X) = \sum x_i^2 p_i - \mu^2 = \frac{72}{64} - \left(\frac{3}{4}\right)^2 = \frac{36}{64} = \frac{9}{16}.$$

x	$P(X = x)$	$xP(X = x)$	$x^2 P(X = x)$
0	$\binom{3}{0}\left(\frac{1}{4}\right)^0\left(\frac{3}{4}\right)^3 = \frac{27}{64}$	0	0
1	$\binom{3}{1}\left(\frac{1}{4}\right)^1\left(\frac{3}{4}\right)^2 = \frac{27}{64}$	$\frac{27}{64}$	$\frac{27}{64}$
2	$\binom{3}{2}\left(\frac{1}{4}\right)^2\left(\frac{3}{4}\right)^1 = \frac{9}{64}$	$\frac{18}{64}$	$\frac{36}{64}$
3	$\binom{3}{3}\left(\frac{1}{4}\right)^3\left(\frac{3}{4}\right)^0 = \frac{1}{64}$	$\frac{3}{64}$	$\frac{9}{64}$
	Totals: $\sum p_i = 1$	$\sum x_i p_i = \frac{48}{64}$	$\sum x_i^2 p_i = \frac{72}{64}$

Probability distribution for Example 8.3.1.

There are, however, formulae for calculating the mean and variance of a binomial distribution directly from n and p. If you consider the general case $X \sim B(n, p)$, then the mean would be given by $\sum x_i p_i = \sum x\binom{n}{x}p^x(1 - p)^{n-x}$.

Each term in this sum depends on the parameters n and p and so it would be reasonable to assume that $E(X)$ also depends on n and p. Although this sum looks very complicated, it can be shown that it simplifies to np.

Intuitively you might expect this result, since in n trials

number of successes $\approx$ number of trials $\times$ probability of success at a single trial
$$= n \times p = np.$$

Now $\sum x_i^2 p_i$ also depends on n and p and so, therefore, does $\text{Var}(X)$. It can be shown that $\text{Var}(X) = np(1 - p) = npq$, where $q = 1 - p$.

For $X \sim B(n, p)$,
$$E(X) = np \tag{8.4}$$
$$\text{Var}(X) = np(1 - p) = npq, \text{ where } q = 1 - p. \tag{8.5}$$

Example 8.3.2
Calculate $E(X)$ and $\text{Var}(X)$ for $X \sim B(3, \frac{1}{4})$ using Equations 8.4 and 8.5.

Using Equations 8.4 and 8.5,
$$E(X) = \mu = np = 3 \times \tfrac{1}{4} = \tfrac{3}{4},$$
$$\text{Var}(X) = \sigma^2 = np(1 - p) = 3 \times \tfrac{1}{4} \times \tfrac{3}{4} = \tfrac{9}{16}.$$

You can see that the second method (Example 8.3.2) is much quicker than the first (Example 8.3.1). The formulae for calculating the mean and variance of a binomial distribution are particularly useful when n is large, as in the following example.

Example 8.3.3

Nails are sold in packets of 100. Occasionally a nail is faulty. The number of faulty nails in a randomly chosen packet is denoted by X. Assuming that faulty nails occur independently and at random, calculate the mean and standard deviation of X, given that the probability of any nail being faulty is 0.04.

Since faulty nails occur independently and at random and with a fixed probability, the distribution of X can be modelled by the binomial distribution with $n = 100$ and $p = 0.04$. Therefore

$$E(X) = \mu = np = 100 \times 0.04 = 4,$$
$$\text{Var}(X) = \sigma^2 = np(1 - p) = 100 \times 0.04 \times 0.96 = 3.84.$$

Therefore

$$\sigma = \sqrt{3.84} = 1.96, \text{ correct to 3 significant figures.}$$

To have calculated μ and σ using Equations 8.1 and 8.3 would have involved writing out a probability distribution with 101 terms!

The following examples give further illustrations of the use of Equations 8.4 and 8.5.

Example 8.3.4

(a) Given that $X \sim B(10, 0.3)$, find $E(X)$ and $\text{Var}(X)$.

(b) For $X \sim B(10, 0.3)$, calculate $P(\mu - \sigma < X < \mu + \sigma)$.

(a) Since $n = 10$ and $p = 0.3$,

$$E(X) = \mu = np = 10 \times 0.3 = 3,$$
$$\text{Var}(X) = \sigma^2 = np(1 - p) = 10 \times 0.3 \times 0.7 = 2.1.$$

(b)
$$
\begin{aligned}
P(\mu - \sigma < X < \mu + \sigma) &= P(\mu - \sqrt{2.1} < X < \mu + \sqrt{2.1}) \\
&= P(3 - 1.444\ldots < X < 3 + 1.44\ldots) \\
&= P(1.55\ldots < X < 4.44\ldots) \\
&= P(X = 2) + P(X = 3) + P(X = 4) \\
&= 0.8497 - 0.1493 \text{ (using cumulative probability tables)} \\
&= 0.7004.
\end{aligned}
$$

Thus $P(\mu - \sigma < X < \mu + \sigma) = 0.700$, correct to 3 significant figures.

Example 8.3.5

Given that Y is B(n, p), and $E(Y) = 24$ and $\text{Var}(Y) = 8$, find the values of n and p.

Using Equations 8.4 and 8.5,

$$E(Y) = np = 24 \quad \text{and} \quad \text{Var}(Y) = np(1 - p) = 8.$$

Substituting the value of np from the first equation into the second equation gives:

$$24(1 - p) = 8, \quad \text{so} \quad 1 - p = \tfrac{1}{3} \quad \text{and} \quad p = \tfrac{2}{3}.$$

Using $np = 24$,

$$n = \frac{24}{p} = \frac{24}{\tfrac{2}{3}} = 24 \times \frac{3}{2} = 36.$$

8.4 The expectation of a geometric distribution

The probability formula for the geometric distribution is $P(X = x) = (1 - p)^{x-1} p = q^{x-1} p$ (see Equation 7.2). It has only one parameter, p. For example, X, the number of throws of a fair dice until a 3 is thrown, has a geometric distribution with parameter $p = \tfrac{1}{6}$. On average you would expect to get a 3 once in every six throws and so you might expect that, on average, you would need six throws before you got a 3. This suggests that the mean of a geometric distribution might be given by $\dfrac{1}{p}$. You could check this by calculating $\sum x_i p_i$:

$$\sum x_i p_i = \left(1 \times \tfrac{1}{6}\right) + \left(2 \times \tfrac{5}{6} \times \tfrac{1}{6}\right) + \left(3 \times \tfrac{5}{6} \times \tfrac{5}{6} \times \tfrac{1}{6}\right) + \left(4 \times \tfrac{5}{6} \times \tfrac{5}{6} \times \tfrac{5}{6} \times \tfrac{1}{6}\right) + \cdots.$$

You can see that there is a difficulty in evaluating this sum because, unlike all the distributions met so far in this chapter, there is no upper limit on the value of X. If you work out the sum of the first four terms given above you will find that it equals $1.177\ldots$. You can use your calculator to see what happens as you add further terms. Alternatively, you could use a spreadsheet to investigate what happens to this sum as the number of terms gets very large. You will find that, as you take more terms, the sum gets closer and closer to 6. For example, the sum of the first 20 terms is $5.32\ldots$ and the sum of the first 40 terms is $5.96\ldots$. This gives support for the formula $\dfrac{1}{p}$ for the mean of a geometric distribution.

For $X \sim \text{Geo}(p)$, $\mu = E(X) = \dfrac{1}{p}$. \hfill (8.6)

A proof of this result is given in Section 8.5.

Example 8.4.1
A certain brand of tea has a picture card in each packet. The cards form a set of 50 different pictures. They are distributed at random in the packets. A child has collected 49 of the picture cards and so needs one more to complete the set. What is the mean number of packets she will need to open in order to obtain the last picture?

The probability that the next packet she opens will contain the picture she needs is $\tfrac{1}{50} = 0.02$. So X, the number of packets opened, up to and including the first one to contain the required picture card, has a geometric distribution with parameter $p = 0.02$.

So $\quad E(X) = \dfrac{1}{p} = \dfrac{1}{0.02} = 50.$

The child can expect to open 50 packets to obtain the last picture.

Example 8.4.2
The random variable Y has a geometric distribution. If $P(Y = 2) = 0.24$ and $P(Y = 3) = 0.144$, find the expected value of Y.

If the geometric distribution has parameter p, then

$$P(Y = 2) = qp = 0.24, \quad \text{and} \quad P(Y = 3) = q^2 p = 0.144.$$

Therefore $\dfrac{q^2 p}{qp} = q = \dfrac{0.144}{0.24} = 0.6.$

Thus $p = 0.4$ and $E(Y) = \frac{1}{0.4} = 2.5$.

8.5*   Proof that $E(X) = \dfrac{1}{p}$ for a geometric distribution

Consider the random variable $X \sim \text{Geo}(p)$. Let $q = 1 - p$. The probability formula is $P(X = x) = q^{x-1} p$, where $q = 1 - p$.

From Equation 8.1,

$$\mu = \sum x P(X = x) = 1p + 2qp + 3q^2 p + 4q^3 p + 5q^4 p + \cdots.$$

Assuming that you can multiply both sides of this equation by q gives:

$$q\mu \qquad\qquad = \qquad qp \ + 2q^2 p + 3q^3 p + 4q^4 p + 5q^5 p + \cdots.$$

> The terms on the right side have been moved along so that they are underneath like terms in the equation above this one.

Subtracting the second equation from the first gives

$$\mu - q\mu = p + qp + q^2 p + q^3 p + q^4 p + \cdots.$$

The sum on the right side of this equation is $\sum P(X = x)$, which is equal to 1 for a probability distribution (see Section 6.2). The left side can be factorised:

$$\mu(1 - q) = 1, \quad \text{giving} \quad \mu p = 1 \quad \text{and} \quad \mu = \dfrac{1}{p}.$$

Exercise 8B

1 Given that $X \sim B(20, 0.14)$, calculate

   (a) $E(X)$ and $\text{Var}(X)$,   (b) $P(X \le E(X))$.

2 A batch of capsules of a certain drug contains 2% of damaged capsules. A bottle contains 42 of these capsules. Calculate the mean and standard deviation of the number of damaged capsules in such a bottle, assuming that each capsule is randomly selected.

3 In a certain examination 35% of candidates pass from year to year. Calculate the expectation and variance of the number of passes in a group of 30 randomly chosen candidates who take the examination.

4 The random variable X has a binomial distribution with mean 3 and variance 2.25. Find $P(X = 3)$.

5 The random variables X and Y are such that $X \sim B(n, p)$ and $Y \sim B(m, p)$. Given that $E(X) = 3$, $Var(X) = 2.4$ and $E(Y) = 2$, find $Var(Y)$.

6 For the random variable Y, for which $Y \sim B(16, 0.8)$, calculate $P(Y > \mu + \sigma)$.

7 The random variable X has a geometric distribution with $P(X > 1) = 0.75$. Find $E(X)$.

8 A fair coin is tossed until a head is obtained.

(a) Find the expected value of the number of tosses required.

(b) What is the expected value of the number of tails tossed?

9 A box of Chocobix cereal costs £1.50. One box in 25, on average, contains a silver button. If a student buys a box of this cereal every week, find the expected total cost of the boxes bought, up to and including the first box with a silver button.

10 A bag contains 4 £1 coins and 12 similar foreign coins. Sophie selects one coin at random from the bag. She keeps the coin if it is a £1 coin, otherwise she returns it to the bag and selects again.

(a) Find the expected number of selections that Sophie makes, up to and including the first £1 coin.

(b) Given that Sophie picks a £1 coin on her first selection, find the expected number of extra selections that Sophie makes to obtain a second £1 coin.

11 A random number generator on a computer is used to produce integers from 1 to 5, inclusive. Ahmed writes a program which will produce a sequence of these integers which ends when 5 has been obtained. The number, n, of integers in the sequence is counted and stored. This procedure is repeated 1000 times and $\sum n$ obtained. On a particular run of this program the value of $\sum n$ was 5096. Estimate the probability of the computer generating 5.

Those with programming skills might like to try to write and run the program described above. The number of repetitions could be an input variable, as could the terminating integer of the sequence.

Miscellaneous exercise 8

1 The number of times a certain factory machine breaks down each working week has been recorded over a long period. From the data, the following probability distribution for the number, X, of weekly breakdowns was produced.

x	0	1	2	3	4	5	6
$P(X = x)$	0.04	0.24	0.28	0.16	0.16	0.08	0.04

(a) Find the mean and standard deviation of X.

(b) What would be the expected total number of breakdowns that will occur over the next 48 working weeks?

2 Some of the eggs sold in a store are packed in boxes of 10. For any egg, the probability that it is cracked is 0.05, independently of all other eggs. Calculate the expected number of cracked eggs in a box.

3 'Paperslide' ball-point pens are sold in boxes of 50. The probability of any pen being faulty is 0.05, independently of all other pens. In a quality control process all pens in each box of a large batch of these boxes are tested until a box is obtained in which no pen is faulty.

(a) Calculate the probability that a box contains no faulty pens.

(b) Calculate the expected number of boxes that will be tested in the process.

4 The random variable X is such that $X \sim B(5, p)$. Given that $P(X = 0) = 0.01024$, find the values of $E(X)$, $Var(X)$ and $P(X = E(X))$.

5 The independent random variables X and Y have the following probability distributions.

x	0	1	2	3
$P(X = x)$	0.3	0.2	0.4	0.1

y	3	4	5
$P(Y = y)$	0.5	0.2	0.3

Find $E(X)$, $Var(X)$, $E(Y)$ and $Var(Y)$.

The sum of one random observation of X and one random observation of Y is denoted by Z.

(a) Obtain the probability distribution of Z.

(b) Show that $E(Z) = E(X) + E(Y)$ and $Var(Z) = Var(X) + Var(Y)$.

6 In a certain city area, 4% of vehicles are taxis. A man is waiting for a taxi to appear so that he can hail it.

(a) Assuming that a geometric distribution is appropriate, calculate the expected number of vehicles the man sees, up to and including the first taxi.

(b) Explain why a geometric distribution may not be appropriate in this situation.

(OCR, adapted)

7 In the proofs of books of a certain publisher, it has been found that, on average, one page in 15 contains at least one misprint. An expert proof-reader checks a book of 486 full pages.

(a) Find the probability that the first misprint occurs on or before the 32nd page.

(b) Find the expectation and variance of the number of pages without a misprint in the final 300 pages of the book.

8 A machine grinds metal rods to a given specification and, when working normally, 5% of the rods are of unacceptable quality. Each rod is inspected as it leaves the machine during a run. Let X denote the number of rods inspected up to and including the first unacceptable rod. If $X \leq 3$ then the machine will be stopped and checked.

(a) Calculate the probability that the machine is stopped during a run.

(b) Calculate $P(X < E(X))$.

(c) In a set of 12 runs, calculate the expectation and variance of the number of times the machine is stopped. State any necessary assumption for the validity of your calculations.

9 An absent-minded mathematician is attempting to log on to a computer, which is done by typing the correct password. Unfortunately he can't remember his password. If he types the wrong password he tries again. The computer allows a maximum of four attempts altogether. For each attempt the probability of success is 0.4, independently of all other attempts.

(a) Calculate the probability that he logs on successfully.

(b) The total number of attempts he makes, successful or not, is denoted by X (so that the possible values of X are 1, 2, 3 or 4). Tabulate the probability distribution of X.

(c) Calculate the expectation and variance of X.

10* In some families the parents continue to have children until at least one child of each sex is born. It may be assumed that for such families, the probability of having a child of either sex is $\frac{1}{2}$ independently of any other child. Find, for these families,

(a) the probability of having 4 children,

(b) the expected number of children.   (OCR)

9 Correlation

This chapter looks at ways of describing and measuring the strength of a relationship between two variables. When you have completed it you should

- recognise a set of bivariate data and know how to illustrate it by a scatter diagram
- be able to calculate the value of the product moment correlation coefficient for a set of bivariate data
- understand the basis of Spearman's rank correlation coefficient and be able to calculate its value
- understand that the value of a correlation coefficient is unaffected by a linear transformation of the variables
- be able to relate the value of a correlation coefficient (in particular values close to -1, 0 and 1) to the appearance of a scatter diagram.

9.1 Scatter diagrams

In the first three chapters of this book you studied data sets where values of a single variable had been recorded for each member of a group. It is often interesting to make measurements of *two* variables for each member of the group. Such data are called **bivariate data**. An example is given in Table 9.1. Bivariate data are of particular interest if you think that the two variables may be related in some way.

Student	A	B	C	D	E	F	G	H	I	J
Pure mathematics	42	21	25	32	34	27	23	40	20	16
Statistics	41	16	36	29	35	24	22	47	30	20

Table 9.1. Marks of ten students in two examinations.

This table gives the marks (out of 50) obtained by a group of ten students in each of two different examinations, pure mathematics and statistics. As you might expect, each student obtains similar marks in both papers.

Fig. 9.2 is a **scatter diagram** of these data. Each point on the diagram represents a student and the coordinates of the point give the marks of that student in the two examinations. You can see clearly from the scatter diagram that students with high marks in one examination tend to have high marks in the other and students with low marks in one

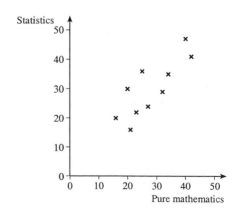

Fig. 9.2. Scatter diagram of the students' marks in Table 9.1.

examination have low marks in the other. The diagram illustrates **positive correlation** between the two variables.

Region	Unemployment (%)	Income (£)
North	8.9	291.7
York and Humberside	6.8	289.4
North West	7.7	318.2
West Midlands	6.0	325.0
East Midlands	5.1	342.3
East Anglia	3.7	357.1
South East	4.0	434.3
South West	4.4	348.6

Table 9.3. Weekly gross household income and unemployment levels in Great Britain, 1990. Data reproduced from *The Economist Book of Vital World Statistics*.

Table 9.3 gives weekly income and levels of unemployment for different regions of Great Britain and Fig. 9.4 is a scatter diagram of these data. Each point represents a different region. You can see from this diagram that high values of one variable are paired with low values of the other. This diagram illustrates **negative correlation** between the two variables.

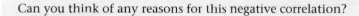

Can you think of any reasons for this negative correlation?

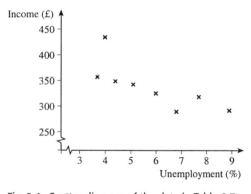

Fig. 9.4. Scatter diagram of the data in Table 9.3.

Table 9.5 gives the score on each of two dice when they were thrown together 15 times, and the corresponding scatter diagram is shown in Fig. 9.6. In this case you can see that the points on the diagram do not show any particular pattern. This means that there is no obvious correlation between the two variables.

Throw	1	2	3	4	5	6	7	8	9	10	11	12	13	14	15
Blue score	5	2	4	1	4	3	2	3	5	1	4	6	3	2	2
Red score	2	4	5	5	3	6	4	5	3	6	5	6	2	3	1

Table 9.5. Results when a pair of dice were thrown together 15 times.

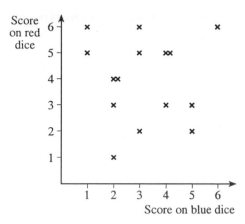

Fig. 9.6. Scatter diagram of the data in Table 9.5.

You would not expect any correlation in this situation, because the results of the throws on the two dice are independent events.

Exercise 9A

1 State in which of the following data sets x and y are bivariate data.

(a) Population: babies born in a given hospital in a given month

   x: height of baby at birth y: weight of baby at birth

(b) Population: babies born in a given hospital in a given month

   x: height of baby at birth (grouped) y: frequency of each group

(c) Population: days in June, July and August at a seaside resort

   x: volume of ice-cream sold y: number of calls on the life-guard

(d) Population: students at a given school

   x: end-of-year exam mark y: age to nearest month

(e) Population: sampled electrical components produced by a factory

   x: day of month of sampling y: number of defective items

(f) Population: Passenger journeys by railway

   x: month of year y: number of journeys made that month

2 For each of the following sets of bivariate data, say whether you would expect the correlation to be positive, zero or negative.

(a) maths mark and science mark in exams

(b) age (between 20 and 50), and income for an office worker

(c) age (between 20 and 50), and income for a professional sportsman or sportswoman

(d) cost of air ticket and length of flight

(e) number of houses per square mile, and average house price, in a city

(f) length of journey time to school, and height

(g) volume of gas consumed, and gas bill

3 Plot scatter diagrams for the following sets of data, and use your diagrams to decide whether there is any correlation between the two variables. Where there seems to be correlation, suggest a possible reason.

(a) Marks in English and Maths.

English	35	37	40	70	51	62	47	56	43	77	80	82
Maths	10	12	20	30	32	40	60	72	81	93	95	99

(b) Minimum daytime temperature in London, $t\,^\circ$C, and number, v, of overcoats sold per day in a store in Vancouver.

t	−3	−1	0	2	3	3	4	5	8	8	9
v	21	17	16	8	9	6	6	2	3	5	1

(c) Air resistance F N acting on a motorcyclist at various speeds v m.p.h.

v	10	20	30	40	50	60	70	80	90	100
F	31	59	92	121	148	216	294	384	486	600

(d) Maximum daytime temperature $t\,^\circ$C, and number n of road accidents.

t	1	3	4	7	10	15	17	22	29
n	21	6	4	3	7	2	6	5	17

4 For the 'Brain size' data on page 7, plot scatter diagrams for the following pairs of variables in order to decide whether there is any correlation between them. If there seems to be correlation, suggest a reason.

(a) the height and mass of female students

(b) the VIQ score and MRI value (rounded to the nearest thousand) for male students

9.2 Measurement of correlation

Scatter diagrams are a good means of seeing the correlation between two variables. Fig. 9.7 shows diagrams where it is easy to see differences in the strength of positive correlation.

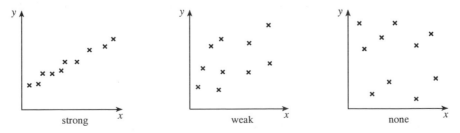

Fig. 9.7. Scatter diagrams illustrating different degrees of correlation.

However, in general it would more useful if you could calculate a value which measures the strength of correlation. Ideally, this value should be zero if there is no correlation, and it should increase as the strength of the correlation increases.

* You may omit the following explanation, and go straight to the box on
    page 154.

For one possible method, see Fig. 9.8, which reproduces Fig. 9.2 but has two new axes added: vertically through the mean pure mathematics mark $\bar{x} = 28$ and horizontally through the mean statistics mark $\bar{y} = 30$.

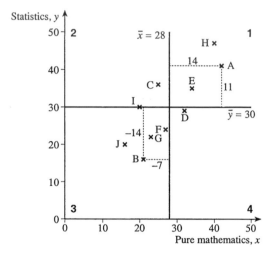

Fig. 9.8. Fig. 9.2 divided into four quadrants.

These new axes divide the diagram into four quadrants. Most of the points lie in the first (top right) and third (bottom left) quadrants. Now look at the deviations of the points from these new axes. For student A, in the first quadrant, $x - \bar{x} = 42 - 28 = 14$ and $y - \bar{y} = 41 - 30 = 11$. Both these numbers are positive and so their product, $14 \times 11 = 154$, is also positive. These values are shown in Table 9.9, which gives similar calculations for the other students. For student B, in the third quadrant, both deviations are negative but their product is still positive. For students C and D, in the second and fourth quadrants, one deviation is positive and the other negative, making the products negative. Clearly the sign of the product depends on the quadrant. Table 9.9 also gives the sum of the last column, which, in Σ-notation, is written as $\sum(x_i - \bar{x})(y_i - \bar{y})$. This sum is positive because the positive contribution of the points in quadrants 1 and 3 outweighs the negative contribution of the points in quadrants 2 and 4. This is why such correlation is called 'positive'.

If you applied the same method to Fig. 9.4, the contribution of the points in quadrants 2 and 4 would outweigh that of the points in quadrants 1 and 3. The resulting total would be negative, indicating negative correlation. For Fig. 9.6, where the points are roughly equally shared between the four quadrants, the total will be close to zero indicating a small degree of correlation.

Student	Pure, x_i	Statistics, y_i	$x_i - \bar{x}$	$y_i - \bar{y}$	$(x_i - \bar{x})(y_i - \bar{y})$
A	42	41	14	11	154
B	21	16	−7	−14	98
C	25	36	−3	6	−18
D	32	29	4	−1	−4
E	34	35	6	5	30
F	27	24	−1	−6	6
G	23	22	−5	−8	40
H	40	47	12	17	204
I	20	30	−8	0	0
J	16	20	−12	−10	120
					Total: 630

Table 9.9. Calculation of $\sum(x_i - \bar{x})(y_i - \bar{y})$ for the data in Table 9.1.

A disadvantage of $\sum(x_i - \bar{x})(y_i - \bar{y})$ as a measure of correlation is that it depends on the sample size, n. You can allow for this by dividing by n to give $\frac{1}{n}\sum(x_i - \bar{x})(y_i - \bar{y})$. This quantity is called the **covariance** of x and y. For the data in Table 9.9 the covariance is $\frac{630}{10} = 63$.

Unfortunately this new quantity is still not suitable as a measure of correlation because it depends on the scales used on the axes. For example, if the marks (out of 50) in Table 9.1 had been expressed as percentages, then all the values of x and y would be doubled. This would mean that the values of $(x_i - \bar{x})$ and $(y_i - \bar{y})$ in Table 9.9 would also be doubled. As a result the values in the last column of Table 9.9 would be four times as great and the covariance would now be $\frac{2520}{10} = 252$. However, the only effect on the scatter diagram in Fig. 9.8 would be that the scales would need to be renumbered, 10 becoming 20, 20 becoming 40 and so on. The appearance of the scatter diagram, and so the degree of correlation between x and y, would be unchanged.

This difficulty can be overcome by dividing the covariance by the product of the standard deviations of x and y. This quantity depends on scale in the same way as the covariance. You can see this by considering the effect of doubling the values of x and y. Each standard deviation will be doubled and the product of the standard deviations will be four times as great. Use your calculator to check this statement. You should find that the product of the standard deviations for the original values in Table 9.9 is $8.27\ldots \times 9.31\ldots = 77.05$ but if the values are doubled the product is $16.54\ldots \times 18.63\ldots = 308.21\ldots$. Thus the ratio of the covariance to the product of the standard deviations is unchanged: for the original values it equals $\frac{63}{77.05\ldots} = 0.817\ldots$ and for the doubled values it equals $\frac{252}{308.21\ldots} = 0.817\ldots$. This ratio is called the **product moment correlation coefficient**, r.

An expression for r written using Σ-notation can be found as follows. From Equation (3.1), the product of the standard deviations is

$$\sqrt{\frac{\sum(x_i - \bar{x})^2}{n}} \times \sqrt{\frac{\sum(y_i - \bar{y})^2}{n}} = \sqrt{\frac{\sum(x_i - \bar{x})^2 \times \sum(y_i - \bar{y})^2}{n^2}} = \frac{1}{n}\sqrt{\sum(x_i - \bar{x})^2 \times \sum(y_i - \bar{y})^2}.$$

Thus the ratio of the covariance of x and y to the product of the standard deviations is

$$\frac{\dfrac{1}{n}\sum(x_i - \bar{x})(y_i - \bar{y})}{\dfrac{1}{n}\sqrt{\sum(x_i - \bar{x})^2 \sum(y_i - \bar{y})^2}}$$

The ns cancel out giving

$$r = \frac{\sum(x_i - \bar{x})(y_i - \bar{y})}{\sqrt{\sum(x_i - \bar{x})^2}\sqrt{\sum(y_i - \bar{y})^2}} \tag{9.1}$$

The product moment correlation coefficient gives a measure of the strength of correlation which is independent of the choice of scale. It can be shown that r takes values between -1 and $+1$. These extreme values occur when the points on the scatter diagram lie exactly on a straight line: the value of $+1$ when the line has positive slope and the value -1 when the line has negative slope. As a consequence r gives a measure of how close the points on a scatter diagram are to a straight line, that is, r measures the strength of linear correlation. When there is little linear correlation r is close to 0.

> The **product moment correlation coefficient**, r, given by
>
> $$r = \frac{\sum(x_i - \bar{x})(y_i - \bar{y})}{\sqrt{\sum(x_i - \bar{x})^2 \sum(y_i - \bar{y})^2}}$$
>
> measures how close the points on a scatter diagram are to a straight line.
>
> The value of r is independent of scale.
>
> The largest value r can take is $+1$. This happens when the points on the scatter diagram lie exactly on a line with positive slope. The smallest value r can take is -1, when the points lie exactly on a line with negative slope. In other situations r will lie between these two values.
>
> The sign of r tells you whether the correlation is positive or negative and the size of r tells you how strong the correlation is.
>
> If there is very little linear correlation then r will be close to 0.

Exercise 9B gives you a chance to check these statements about r by calculation.

As you can see, finding r involves calculating three different sums. The symbols S_{xy}, S_{xx} and S_{yy} are often used to stand for these sums. You will find it easier if you calculate these sums first and then substitute them in the formula for r as follows:

$$S_{xx} = \sum(x_i - \bar{x})^2 \tag{9.2a}$$

$$S_{yy} = \sum(y_i - \bar{y})^2 \tag{9.2b}$$

$$S_{xy} = \sum(x_i - \bar{x})(y_i - \bar{y}) \tag{9.2c}$$

$$r = \frac{\sum(x_i - \bar{x})(y_i - \bar{y})}{\sqrt{\sum(x_i - \bar{x})^2 \sum(y_i - \bar{y})^2}} = \frac{S_{xy}}{\sqrt{S_{xx}S_{yy}}}. \tag{9.2d}$$

Example 9.2.1

Calculate the value of r for the data in Table 9.10, the marks of students in two examinations.

x_i	y_i	$x_i - \bar{x}$	$y_i - \bar{y}$	$(x_i - \bar{x})(y_i - \bar{y})$	$(x_i - \bar{x})^2$	$(y_i - \bar{y})^2$
42	41	14	11	154	196	121
21	16	−7	−14	98	49	196
25	36	−3	6	−18	9	36
32	29	4	−1	−4	16	1
34	35	6	5	30	36	25
27	24	−1	−6	6	1	36
23	22	−5	−8	40	25	64
40	47	12	17	204	144	289
20	30	−8	0	0	64	0
16	20	−12	−10	120	144	100
Totals: 280	300	0	0	630	684	868

Table 9.10. Calculating the correlation coefficient.

Note that it is always the case that $\sum(x_i - \bar{x}) = \sum(y_i - \bar{y}) = 0$.

$$\bar{x} = \tfrac{280}{10} = 28, \quad \bar{y} - \tfrac{300}{10} = 30, \quad S_{xy} - 630, \quad S_{xx} = 684, \quad S_{yy} = 868,$$

$$r = \frac{S_{xy}}{\sqrt{S_{xx}S_{yy}}} = \frac{630}{\sqrt{684 \times 868}} = 0.818, \text{ correct to 3 significant figures.}$$

The value of $r = 0.818$ tells you that there is quite strong positive linear correlation between the two variables, that is that the points lie fairly close to a straight line with positive slope. You can see that this is the case if you look back at the scatter diagram of these data (Fig. 9.2).

Exercise 9B

1 For each of the following data sets draw a scatter diagram and calculate r. Comment on the relationship between the value of r and the appearance of the scatter diagram.

(a)

x	1	2	3	4	5
y	1	3	5	7	9

(b)

x	2	3	4	5	6
y	4	3	2	1	0

(c)

x	1	3	2	1	3
y	1	1	2	3	3

(d)

x	2	3	4	5	6	7
y	3	4	3	6	5	7

If you have access to a computer you may find a spreadsheet program that includes a function for calculating r directly from the x- and y-values. Include a scatter diagram on your spreadsheet.

9.3   Making the calculation of *r* easier

In the example worked so far, x_i, y_i, $\bar{x}$ and $\bar{y}$ have been whole numbers, which has made the calculation of S_{xy}, S_{xx} and S_{yy} straightforward. In many examples x_i, y_i, $\bar{x}$ and $\bar{y}$ will not be whole numbers and it is helpful to find ways of making the calculation simple. In Section 3.6 you saw how the calculation of standard deviation could be made easier by using the fact that $\sum(x_i - \bar{x})^2 = \sum x_i^2 - \frac{1}{n}(\sum x_i)^2$. The left side of this identity is S_{xx}. There are corresponding identities for S_{yy} and S_{xy} and in most cases you will find it easier to calculate S_{xx}, S_{yy} and S_{xy} as follows.

$$S_{xx} = \sum x_i^2 - \frac{1}{n}\left(\sum x_i\right)^2 \tag{9.3a}$$

$$S_{yy} = \sum y_i^2 - \frac{1}{n}\left(\sum y_i\right)^2 \tag{9.3b}$$

$$S_{xy} = \sum x_i y_i - \frac{1}{n}\sum x_i \sum y_i \tag{9.3c}$$

Example 9.3.1

Table 9.11 gives the length and width (measured in mm) of 10 leaves taken from a rose bush. Calculate the value of *r* for these data.

Length, x_i	Width, y_i	x_i^2	y_i^2	$x_i y_i$
85	69	7 225	4 761	5 865
54	29	2 916	841	1 566
44	26	1 936	676	1 144
64	30	4 096	900	1 920
70	49	4 900	2 401	3 430
58	35	3 364	1 225	2 030
55	32	3 025	1 024	1 760
29	14	841	196	406
64	33	4 096	1 089	2 112
38	21	1 444	441	798
Totals: 561	338	33 843	13 554	21 031

Table 9.11. Lengths and widths of 10 rose leaves.

$$S_{xx} = \sum x_i^2 - \frac{(\sum x_i)^2}{n} = 33\,843 - \frac{561^2}{10} = 2370.9,$$

$$S_{yy} = \sum y_i^2 - \frac{(\sum y_i)^2}{n} = 13\,554 - \frac{338^2}{10} = 2129.6,$$

$$S_{xy} = \sum x_i y_i - \frac{\sum x_i \sum y_i}{n} = 21\,031 - \frac{561 \times 338}{10} = 2069.2,$$

$$r = \frac{S_{xy}}{\sqrt{S_{xx}S_{yy}}} = \frac{2069.2}{\sqrt{2370.9 \times 2129.6}}$$

$$= 0.921, \text{ correct to 3 significant figures.}$$

The value of r indicates strong linear correlation. You can also see this from the scatter diagram in Fig. 9.12, which shows that the points lie close to a straight line with positive slope.

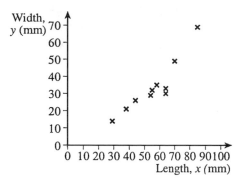

Fig. 9.12. Scatter diagram of data in Table 9.11.

Another way of easing the calculation of r is by re-scaling the variables with a linear transformation, a procedure known as **coding**. Two new variables, u and v, are calculated from x and y using the linear equations

$$u = \frac{x - A}{B}, \qquad v = \frac{y - C}{D}$$

where A, B, C and D are constants. The values of these constants are chosen so as to give values of u and v which are smaller than the original values and so easier to work with. The correlation coefficient for the variables u and v has exactly the same value as for x and y.

Subtracting a constant, A, from x does not alter $(x_i - \bar{x})$ because $\bar{x}$ also decreases by A. Dividing x by B has no effect on r because r is independent of scale (see Section 9.2).

A linear transformation (coding) of the variables does not affect the product moment correlation coefficient.

Example 9.3.2
The data in Table 9.13 give the heights and weights of 12 young men. Calculate the value of r after making a linear transformation to simplify the calculation.

The linear transformations to be made are $u = \dfrac{x - 1700}{10}$ and $v = y - 70$. Then

$$S_{uu} = \sum u_i^2 - \frac{\left(\sum u_i\right)^2}{n} = 993 - \frac{19^2}{12} = 962.91\ldots,$$

$$S_{vv} = \sum v_i^2 - \frac{\left(\sum v_i\right)^2}{n} = 561 - \frac{(-19)^2}{12} = 530.91\ldots,$$

$$S_{uv} = \sum u_i v_i - \frac{\sum u_i \sum v_i}{n} = 565 - \frac{19 \times (-19)}{12} = 595.08\ldots$$

$$r = \frac{S_{uv}}{\sqrt{S_{uu}S_{vv}}} = \frac{595.08\ldots}{\sqrt{962.91\ldots \times 530.91\ldots}}$$

$$= 0.832, \text{ correct to 3 significant figures.}$$

height, x_i (mm)	weight, y_i (kg)	u_i	v_i	u_i^2	v_i^2	$u_i v_i$
1670	72	−3	2	9	4	−6
1910	83	21	13	441	169	273
1800	67	10	−3	100	9	−30
1650	64	−5	−6	25	36	30
1800	75	10	5	100	25	50
1700	67	0	−3	0	9	0
1780	70	8	0	64	0	0
1730	69	3	−1	9	1	−3
1640	61	−6	−9	36	81	54
1560	57	−14	−13	196	169	182
1680	73	−2	3	4	9	−6
1670	63	−3	−7	9	49	21
		Totals: 19	−19	993	561	565

Table 9.13. Heights and weights of 12 young men.

This value of r indicates fairly strong positive correlation. You can see this in Fig. 9.14, which is the scatter diagram. The points go from the bottom left to the top right of the diagram, but there is no clear linear relationship.

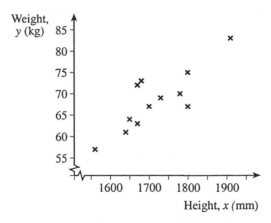

Fig. 9.14. Scatter diagram of data in Table 9.13.

You may like to check that you obtain the same value for r in this example if you calculate it from the original x and y values, particularly if you have a calculator which allows you to calculate r directly by keying in the values of x and y. Using a calculator in this way will make the calculation of r much quicker. Sometimes, however, you may be asked to calculate r from the sums $\sum x$, $\sum y$, $\sum x^2$, $\sum y^2$ and $\sum xy$ (rather than the individual x and y values) and so you need be familiar with the use of Equations 9.2 and 9.3.

Example 9.3.3
Calculate the product moment correlation coefficient between the variables l and p given that $n = 5$, $\sum p = 15$, $\sum l = 20$, $\sum p^2 = 55$, $\sum l^2 = 120$ and $\sum pl = 40$.

What does the value of the product moment correlation coefficient tell you about the appearance of a scatter diagram illustrating the data?

$$S_{pp} = \sum p^2 - \frac{(\sum p)^2}{n} = 55 - \frac{15^2}{5} = 10$$

$$S_{ll} = \sum l^2 - \frac{(\sum l)^2}{n} = 120 - \frac{20^2}{5} = 40$$

$$S_{pl} = \sum pl - \frac{\sum p \sum l}{n} = 40 - \frac{15 \times 20}{5} = -20$$

$$r = \frac{S_{pl}}{\sqrt{S_{pp}S_{ll}}} = \frac{-20}{\sqrt{10 \times 40}} = -1.$$

Since the value of the product moment correlation coefficient is -1, the points on a scatter diagram of the data must lie on a straight line of negative slope.

9.4 Practical activities

1 **Hand shape** The values in Example 9.3.1 suggest that rose leaves from the same bush have a very similar shape and differ only in their size. Is the same true for the hands of different people?

(a) Measure the length and width of the hands of at least 15 people. You will need to define carefully what you mean by the length and width of a hand before you start.

(b) Plot a scatter diagram of your results.

(c) Calculate the product moment correlation coefficient and compare it with the value obtained in Example 9.3.1.

2 **Travel to school**   (For this you will need a road map that shows your school or college and covers the area in which the students live.)

(a) For at least 15 people, measure how far from the school they live 'as the crow flies' and record how long it took them to travel to school today.

(b) Plot a scatter diagram of time against distance.

(c) Calculate the product moment correlation coefficient and comment on its value.

3 **Goals 'for' and 'against'**   (For this you will need details of football results.)

(a) Plot a scatter diagram of goals scored 'for' and 'against' for each club in one league.

(b) Is there a relationship between the two variables?

(c) Calculate the product moment correlation coefficient and comment on its value.

4 **Sporting physiques**   (For this you will need statistics relating to a sport which interests you.)

(a) Obtain the heights and weights of the members of a team for a sport of your choice.

(b) Plot a scatter diagram of weight against height.

(c) Compare your diagram with Fig. 9.14 and comment on any differences or similarities. Does the scatter diagram show the sort of pattern you would expect for your sport?

(d) Calculate a value for the product moment correlation coefficient.

9.5   Interpretation of a correlation coefficient

When you are looking for a relationship between two variables it is important that you draw a scatter diagram before you calculate a value of r. Fig. 9.15a and Fig. 9.15b show two examples where the value of r is not very helpful in interpreting a relationship. In both cases there is obviously a relationship between the two variables but it is not a linear relationship. For Fig. 9.15a the value of r is close to 1 because the points are nearly on a straight line. However, on the scatter diagram a gentle curve of some sort would fit the points better. For Fig. 9.15b the value of r is close to 0, but a quadratic function would give a good fit to the points.

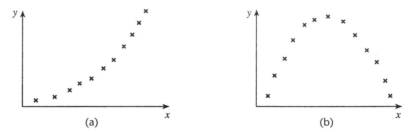

Fig. 9.15. Scatter diagrams showing non-linear correlation.

When there is a relationship between two variables, you need to take care in interpreting it. A correlation between two variables does not mean that one thing *causes* the other. In the first example in Section 9.1 there was a strong correlation between the two examination marks, but it is not true that a student's high mark in statistics would cause her high mark in pure mathematics (or vice versa). High marks in the two exams do tend to go together, but this is because both marks depend on a third variable: the student's mathematical ability.

In some cases, the correlation between two variables which depend on a third can suggest a ridiculous conclusion. For example, in the years 1955–65 there was a strong correlation between the number of TV licences and the number of road accidents in this country. Someone might deduce that watching TV made people worse at driving, but of course the correlation actually arose because both variables depend on the 'standard of living'. Such misleading correlations often arise when variables are measured over a period of time.

Exercise 9C

1   Calculate the value of the product moment correlation coefficient between the following sets of data:

(a) (to be done without a calculator)
     (7,0), (9,4), (10,8), (11,6), (13,12)

(b) (to be done with a calculator, but with all working set out as in Example 9.2.1)
     (5,20), (6,18), (8,17), (9,11), (12,9)

(c) (to be done with a calculator, but with all working set out as in Example 9.3.1)

x	4	6	7	11	14	18
y	3	7	11	12	5	4

(d) $n = 7$, $\sum x = 28$, $\sum y = 73$, $\sum x^2 = 140$, $\sum y^2 = 955$, $\sum xy = 364$

(e) $n = 5$, $\sum w = 31$, $\sum t = 90$, $\sum w^2 = 225$, $\sum t^2 = 1702$, $\sum wt = 508$

(f) (to be done using built-in calculator functions)

x	1	2	3	4	5	6
y	9.6	8.1	7.9	6.4	6.7	2.3

(g) (to be done using built-in calculator functions)

w	2.0	2.5	3.0	3.5	4.0	4.5	5.0
t	12.56	19.31	27.56	37.31	48.56	61.31	75.56

(h) (to be done using built-in calculator functions)

p	5	9	13	17	21	25
y	9.6	8.1	7.9	6.4	6.7	2.3

What is the relationship between p in this example and x in Question 1(f)?

(i) (to be done using built-in calculator functions)

x	4.0	6.25	9.0	12.25	16.0	20.25	25.0
t	12.56	19.31	27.56	37.31	48.56	61.31	75.56

What is the relationship between x in this example and w in Question 1(g)?

(j) $n = 7$, $\sum x = 28$, $\sum y = 73$, $\sum x^2 = 140$, $\sum y^2 = 955$, $\sum xy = 364$, together with the extra point $(8,11)$

(k) $n = 7$, $\sum x = 28$, $\sum y = 73$, $\sum x^2 = 140$, $\sum y^2 = 955$, $\sum xy = 364$, but with the point $(7,16)$ deleted. State what your answer tells you about the data in this question.

2 Explain what is wrong with each of these statements.

(a) If $r = 0.93$ then there is a linear relationship between the variables.

(b) If $r = 0.02$ then there is virtually no relationship between the data.

(c) If $r = 1$ then the two variables are proportional.

(d) If $r = 0.99$ then if you increase one of the x-values, the corresponding y-value will increase.

3 The following table gives the total monthly rainfall, w cm, and the total monthly sunshine, s hours, in each month of a given year at a certain resort.

	Jan.	Feb.	Mar.	Apr.	May	Jun.	Jul.	Aug.	Sep.	Oct.	Nov.	Dec.
w	12	14	16	13	8	5	4	12	3	6	11	12
s	80	70	100	120	170	210	230	220	200	160	90	80

$n = 12$, $\sum w = 116$, $\sum s = 1730$, $\sum w^2 = 1324$, $\sum s^2 = 290\,100$, $\sum ws = 14\,580$

Calculate the product moment correlation coefficient between w and s, and state what can be deduced about a scatter diagram illustrating the data.

4 The following table shows, in conventional units, the yield, y, of a chemical reaction at various temperatures t.

t	110	120	130	140	150	160	170
y	2.1	2.3	3.1	3.4	2.9	3.5	3.3

$n = 7$, $\sum t = 980$, $\sum y = 20.6$, $\sum t^2 = 140\,000$, $\sum y^2 = 62.42$, $\sum ty = 2942$

Calculate the product moment correlation coefficient between t and y, and explain what your answer tells you about a scatter diagram illustrating the data.

Another person who analysed this experiment coded the values of t using the formula $x = \dfrac{t - 100}{10}$. What can you say about the product moment correlation coefficient between x and y?

5 A large industry carries out a survey to investigate the relationship between the frequency f (orders per year) of placing orders for a certain expensive component and the total annual ordering and holding costs, $£A$, of those components. The results are in the table.

f	1	2	3	4	5	6	7	8	9	10
A	2080	1160	910	820	800	810	850	890	940	1000

$n = 10$, $\sum f = 55$, $\sum A = 10\,260$, $\sum f^2 = 385$, $\sum A^2 = 11\,866\,800$, $\sum fA = 50\,800$

Calculate the value of the product moment correlation coefficient and comment on any possible relationship between f and A.

Draw a scatter diagram to illustrate the data and comment further on whether there appears to be a strong relationship between f and A.

6 A company manufacturing CDs makes the following estimates of the proportion of defective CDs, d %, produced by the factory, and the cost of quality control, $£c$ thousand, required to achieve that proportion.

c	50	100	150	250	500	750	1000	2000
d	8.0	5.5	3.8	3.0	2.3	2.0	1.5	1.0

$n = 8$, $\sum c = 4800$, $\sum d = 27.1$, $\sum c^2 = 5\,910\,000$, $\sum d^2 = 130.23$, $\sum cd = 8420$

Calculate the product moment correlation coefficient between c and d. State what its value tells you about the likely relationship between c and d.

Plot a scatter diagram to illustrate the data, and comment on what further information the diagram gives.

7* By calculating the product moment correlation coefficients between

(a) x and y,   (b) x^2 and y,   (c) x^3 and y,

for the following data, determine which of the relationships

$$y = ax + b, \quad y = ax^2 + b, \quad y = ax^3 + b$$

best fits the data.

x	2	3	5	6	8	9
y	1.1	2.0	5.3	7.5	13.1	16.5

8 For the 'Cereals' data on pages 2 and 3, investigate whether there is a relationship between sodium content and rating. Take a sample by starting with the first cereal on the list and then every 10th cereal after that.

9.6 Rank correlation

A manufacturer is experimenting with flavours for a new cola-flavoured drink and wishes to test public reaction to them. Two tasters put eight different flavours, labelled A to H, in order of preference, starting with their favourite. The results are given in Table 9.16.

Taster 1	D	C	G	B	A	E	F	H
Taster 2	C	D	B	G	H	E	A	F

Table 9.16. Order of preference of eight flavours for two tasters.

Unsurprisingly, the two tasters do not agree exactly on their order of preference. However there are some flavours which they both rate highly, namely C and D, and others appear near the bottom of both lists, for example F. It would be useful to measure how well the tasters agree. As a first step, you can give each flavour a **rank** for each taster, according to where it appears in their list. The rankings of the flavours for the two tasters are given in Table 9.17.

Fig. 9.18 shows a scatter diagram of the ranks.

Flavour	Rank for taster 1, x_i	Rank for taster 2, y_i
A	5	7
B	4	3
C	2	1
D	1	2
E	6	6
F	7	8
G	3	4
H	8	5

Table 9.17. Rankings of eight flavours for two tasters.

This diagram suggests that there is some measure of agreement between the two tasters because the points on the scatter diagram show positive correlation. It would seem reasonable to measure the degree of agreement by calculating the product moment correlation coefficient for the two sets of ranks. However, in order to emphasise that x and y are ranks rather than continuous variables (such as height or weight), the coefficient is given a new symbol, r_s. The subscript s honours the British psychologist, Charles Spearman, who studied this coefficient which is called **Spearman's rank correlation coefficient**. Table 9.19 shows the calculation of r_s for the data in Table 9.17.

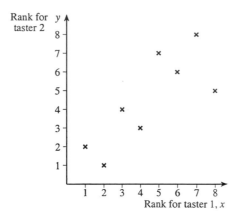

x_i	y_i	x_i^2	y_i^2	$x_i y_i$
5	7	25	49	35
4	3	16	9	12
2	1	4	1	2
1	2	1	4	2
6	6	36	36	36
7	8	49	64	56
3	4	9	16	12
8	5	64	25	40
Totals: 36	36	204	204	195

Fig. 9.18. Scatter diagram of the ranks in Table 9.17.

Table 9.19. Calculation of r_s using Equation 9.3.

$$S_{xx} = \sum x_i^2 - \frac{\left(\sum x_i\right)^2}{n} = 204 - \frac{36^2}{8} = 42,$$

$$S_{yy} = \sum y_i^2 - \frac{\left(\sum y_i\right)^2}{n} = 204 - \frac{36^2}{8} = 42,$$

$$S_{xy} = \sum x_i y_i - \frac{\sum x_i \sum y_i}{n} = 195 - \frac{36 \times 36}{8} = 33,$$

$$r_s = \frac{S_{xy}}{\sqrt{S_{xx}}\sqrt{S_{yy}}} = \frac{33}{\sqrt{42} \times \sqrt{42}} = 0.786, \text{ correct to 3 significant figures.}$$

You can interpret this value by recalling that r_s is the product moment correlation coefficient of the ranks. If the rank orders for the two tasters had been identical, then the points on a scatter diagram of the ranks would fall exactly on the line $y = x$ and r_s would equal 1. If one rank order was the exact reverse of the other then the points would fall on the line $y = -x$ and $r_s = -1$. If there was little agreement between the two rank orders, then the scatter diagram would show little correlation and r_s would be close to 0. The value of 0.79, correct to 2 significant figures, obtained in this example indicates a fair degree of agreement between the two tasters.

> **Spearman's rank correlation coefficient** takes values between
> $+1$ and -1.
>
> It has the value $+1$ when both rank orders are identical and the value -1 when one rank order is the exact reverse of the other.
>
> A value close to 0 indicates that there is little agreement between the two rank orders.

9.7 Another method of calculating Spearman's rank correlation coefficient

When r_s is calculated from the ranks of n items, x and y always take the values $1, 2, 3, \ldots , n$. It can be shown that in this case, there is an alternative formula for r_s.

> Spearman's rank correlation coefficient is
> $$r_s = 1 - \frac{6 \sum d_i^2}{n(n^2 - 1)}.$$ (9.4)
> where $d_i =$ difference between the ranks for the ith item $= x_i - y_i$.

Table 9.20 shows the calculation of r_s for the data in Table 9.17 using this formula.

Flavour	x_i	y_i	d_i	d_i^2
A	5	7	-2	4
B	4	3	1	1
C	2	1	1	1
D	1	2	-1	1
E	6	6	0	0
F	7	8	-1	1
G	3	4	-1	1
H	8	5	3	9
			Totals: 0	18

Table 9.20. Calculation of r_s for the ranks in Table 9.17 using Equation 9.4.

> Note that $\sum d_i$ is always equal to 0. This fact provides a useful check when you are calculating r_s.

$$r_s = 1 - \frac{6 \sum d_i^2}{n(n^2 - 1)} = 1 - \frac{6 \times 18}{8(8^2 - 1)} = 0.785, \text{ correct to 3 significant figures.}$$

The answer is the same as before, which gives support for the correctness of Equation 9.4. You can see that the arithmetic is more straightforward using this equation rather than the previous one, so r_s is usually calculated in this way. This version of the formula also shows clearly that when the rankings are the same, all the d_i will be zero, making $\sum d_i^2 = 0$ and $r_s = 1$.

> In this example the highest value of d is 3 for flavour H, so this is the flavour which the tasters agree least about.

When two people place a number of items in order of merit, they sometimes award marks rather than giving ranks or an ordered list. An example is shown in Table 9.21. The first two columns give the marks awarded to skaters from six different countries by two judges.

| Country | Mark | | Rank | | d_i | d_i^2 |
	Judge A	Judge B	Judge A	Judge B		
UK	5.8	5.6	3	3	0	0
France	5.5	5.4	5	5	0	0
Russia	6.0	5.8	1	1	0	0
Germany	5.9	5.7	2	2	0	0
USA	5.6	5.5	4	4	0	0
Canada	5.0	5.3	6	6	0	0
					Totals: 0	0

Table 9.21. Marks awarded to skaters from six different countries by two judges.

If you look at each skater in turn, you will see that the two judges do not award the same marks. However it would be interesting to see whether they place the competitors in the same order of merit. To see whether the judges agree on this, you must first find the ranks for each judge. These are given in the third and fourth columns. The remaining columns complete the calculations required to find r_s.

$$r_s = 1 - \frac{6 \sum d_i^2}{n(n^2 - 1)} = 1 - \frac{6 \times 0}{6(6^2 - 1)} = 1.$$

The result of $+1$ tells you that the judges agree exactly about the order of merit of the skaters (even though their marks for a particular skater are not the same). You could also come to this conclusion by looking at Fig. 9.22, which shows a scatter diagram of the marks, rather than the ranks. The points do not lie exactly on a straight line. However, each time x increases, y also increases, so the rankings are all the same and r_s equals 1.

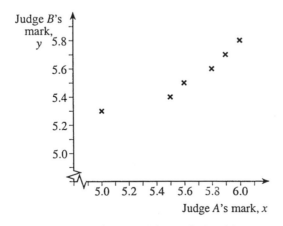

Fig. 9.22. Scatter diagram of the marks in Table 9.21.

In this example it would have been possible to calculate the product moment correlation coefficient for the marks. However this would have not been so appropriate because the data are 'subjective'. This means that the values of the marks reflect the judges' opinions. You can contrast this situation with that in Example 9.3.2 where the data are 'objective': the values given for the heights and weights are a matter of fact not opinion.

Example 9.7.1

A student calculated Spearman's rank correlation coefficient for each of three sets of bivariate data and obtained the values 0.027, −0.95, and −1.

State, with a reason in each case, which correlation coefficient corresponds to each of the diagrams A, B and C.

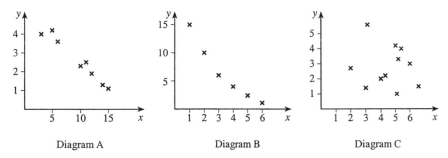

Diagram A   Diagram B   Diagram C

The value of 0.027 corresponds to diagram C because there is little correlation in this diagram and so the value of Spearman's rank correlation coefficient is close to 0.

The value of −1 corresponds to diagram B. This diagram shows negative correlation. Each increase in x is accompanied by a decrease in y so Spearman's rank correlation coefficient is −1.

The value of −0.95 corresponds to diagram A. This diagram shows high negative correlation but y does not always decrease as x increases. For this reason Spearman's rank correlation coefficient is close, but not equal, to −1.

9.8 Practical Activities

1 **Choosing a university**   Do male and female students have different priorities when selecting a university?

   (a) Make a list of about 10 factors which might influence your choice of university. Ask one male and one female student to rank these factors, starting with the most important.

   (b) Calculate Spearman's rank correlation coefficient for the two rankings and comment on its value.

2 **Popularity and position**   (For this you will need details of football statistics.)

   (a) Plot a scatter diagram of attendance against league position for the football teams in one league.

   (b) Is attendance higher for the more successful teams?

   (c) Calculate a value of Spearman's rank correlation coefficient between league position and attendance rank.

   (d) Repeat for other leagues. Does the value of the rank correlation coefficient differ from one league to another?

3 TV programmes

(a) Make a list of your 10 favourite TV programmes, ranking them in order of preference. Rewrite the list with the order mixed up and ask a friend to rank them in order of preference.

(b) Calculate Spearman's rank correlation coefficient between the two rankings and comment on its value.

4 Names   Do parents with long surnames tend to give their children short first names? Collect the names of about 15 students and calculate Spearman's rank correlation coefficient between length of first name and length of surname. What is your conclusion?

9.9*   A comparison of the two correlation coefficients

For some sets of data it would be reasonable to calculate both r and r_s, for example Table 9.1. For these data $r = 0.817\ldots$ (see Example 9.2.1). Table 9.23 shows the ranks. You can verify that the value of r_s is $0.745\ldots$.

Student	A	B	C	D	E	F	G	H	I	J
Rank for pure mathematics	1	8	6	4	3	5	7	2	9	10
Rank for statistics	2	10	3	6	4	7	8	1	5	9

Table 9.23. Ranks for the marks in Table 9.1.

The two values are not the same, because they are measuring different things. r is measuring how close the points on the scatter diagram are to a straight line, which is the strength of the linear relationship between x and y, whereas r_s is measuring the tendency for y to increase as x increases, not necessarily in a linear way.

For negative correlation, r_s measures the tendency for y to decrease as x increases.

Even though you can calculate both r and r_s for the data in Table 9.1, in practice you would normally calculate only one of them in order to assess the strength of the correlation. Where there is a choice the product moment correlation coefficient is usually preferred, since replacing values by ranks involves some loss of information. An exception would be if the scatter diagram indicated a non-linear relationship like, for example, Fig. 9.15a. Then it would be better to calculate a rank correlation coefficient. For this scatter diagram r would be close to, but not equal to, 1 whereas r_s would equal 1 exactly.

Exercise 9D

1 Calculate Spearman's rank correlation coefficient for the following ranked data.

Rank 1	1	2	3	4	5	6	7
Rank 2	3	4	2	1	7	6	5

2 Calculate Spearman's rank correlation coefficient for the following ranked data.

Rank 1	1	2	3	4	5	6	7
Rank 2	5	6	7	1	2	4	3

3 What is the relationship between the values of Rank 2 in Question 1 and the values of Rank 2 in Question 2? What is the effect on the value of Spearman's rank correlation coefficient if one set of rankings is replaced by its exact reverse?

4 Rank the following data (highest data value = ranking 1) and hence calculate Spearman's rank correlation coefficient between x and y.

Data x	107	125	138	152	160	199
Data y	87	92	66	73	60	59

What does your answer show about the data?

5 Rank the following data (lowest data value = ranking 1) and hence calculate Spearman's rank correlation coefficient between x and y.

Data x	3.7	4.9	2.6	8.7	1.6	5.4
Data y	−0.3	1.4	1.7	3.8	4.4	6.8

What does your answer show about the data?

6 At a wine-tasting, two judges ranked wines A to H as follows.

Wine	A	B	C	D	E	F	G	H
Judge 1	4	7	3	5	1	8	6	2
Judge 2	5	7	1	2	3	8	4	6

Calculate Spearman's rank correlation coefficient and state what its value tells you about the judges' rankings.

7 A student was shown photographs of eight people and asked to estimate their ages. The table below shows the actual age and the student's estimate.

Actual age in years	54	88	22	70	30	15	47	6
Estimated age in years	56	70	24	60	35	16	50	11

(a) Calculate the value of Spearman's rank correlation coefficient between the actual age and the estimated age.

(b) Does the high value of Spearman's rank correlation coefficient indicate that the student is good at estimating age? Give a reason for you answer.

8 Two newspapers published the following 'league tables' allocating scores to six different universities. The scores were as follows.

University	A	B	C	D	E	F
Newspaper 1	981	950	948	947	946	805
Newspaper 2	488	430	431	433	432	367

Calculate Spearman's rank correlation coefficient and comment on your answer. What important feature of these data is not made evident from the value of Spearman's rank correlation coefficient?

9 Three students, Ashish, Bella and Clive allocated scores to seven favourite films.

Film	A	B	C	D	E	F	G
Ashish	100	90	85	80	75	70	60
Bella	65	60	40	90	80	30	70
Clive	40	60	50	70	90	80	100

Calculate the values of Spearman's rank correlation coefficient for

(a) Ashish and Bella,   (b) Ashish and Clive.

On the basis of these results, Clive says that Ashish and Bella disagree with each other. Bella says that Ashish and Clive disagree with each other. Are they right?

10 Overhearing the discussion about the previous question, a statistics student tells Ashish, Bella and Clive that their scores for the films are too arbitrary and they should have used a clearly specified scale (such as 100 for their favourite film, then 90, 80, 70, 60, 50 and 40 for the film they liked least). Explain whether this would have made any difference to their answers.

Would it have made any difference if they had used the product moment correlation coefficient instead of Spearman's rank correlation coefficient?

11 Sketch separate scatter diagrams to illustrate data with the following properties.

(a) $r_s = 1$ but $r \neq 1$ (b) $r_s \neq 1$ but $r \approx 1$

Each diagram should include about eight data points.

Miscellaneous exercise 9

1 (a) The product moment correlation coefficient for the data illustrated is known to take one of the values -0.9, -0.5, 0, 0.5, 0.9.

State which value is correct.

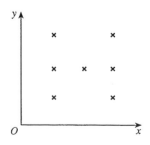

(b) Describe the nature of the correlation between the variables x and y shown here.   (OCR)

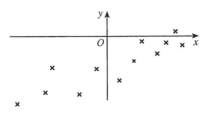

2 The diagrams illustrate two sets of bivariate data. State the value of the product moment correlation coefficient for

(a) data set A,   (b) data set B.   (OCR)

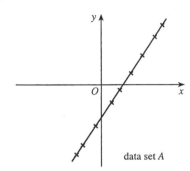
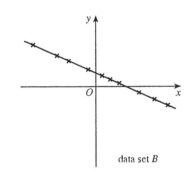

data set A data set B

3 The scatter diagrams illustrate four sets of bivariate data, P, Q, R and S.

(a) State the value of the product moment correlation coefficient for

(i) data set P,   (ii) data set R.

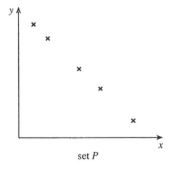
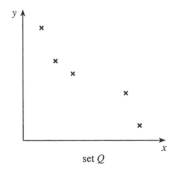

set P set Q

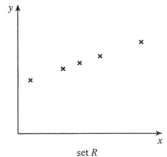
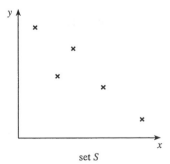

set R set S

(b) Two of the data sets have the same value of Spearman's rank correlation coefficient. State which two sets they are. (OCR)

4 At a film festival two judges rank six films (*A* to *F*) as follows.

Film	*A*	*B*	*C*	*D*	*E*	*F*
First judge	2	3	5	6	1	4
Second judge	6	5	1	3	4	2

Calculate Spearman's rank correlation coefficient for these rankings. (OCR)

5 Data published by London Research Centre and the Department of Transport give the proportion $x\%$ of unemployed adults, and the length y km of roads, in London boroughs in 1991. The data can be summarised as follows:

$n = 33$, $\sum x = 420.2$, $\sum y = 13\,247$, $\sum x^2 = 6079.82$, $\sum y^2 = 6\,157\,699$,

$\sum xy = 159\,149.1$.

Calculate the product moment correlation coefficient.

A councillor argues that 'This calculation shows that unemployment in our borough can be reduced by building more roads'. State, with a reason, whether or not you agree with the logic of this argument. (OCR)

[Data © Crown Copyright]

6 Three critics were asked to rank eight plays they had seen, in order of preference. The results are shown in the following table.

Play	*A*	*B*	*C*	*D*	*E*	*F*	*G*	*H*
Critic *P*	1	2	3	4	5	6	7	8
Critic *Q*	3	1	8	4	2	7	5	6
Critic *R*	7	5	6	3	8	1	2	4

(a) Calculate the value of Spearman's rank correlation coefficient between critics *P* and *Q*.

(b) The value of Spearman's rank correlation coefficient between critics *P* and *R* is approximately −0.548. Giving a reason for your answer, state whether *Q* or *R* agrees better with *P*.

(c) The rankings given by a fourth critic, *S*, have been lost, but it is known that the value of Spearman's rank correlation coefficient between critics *Q* and *S* was −1. Use this information to write down the rankings given by *S* to the eight plays.

7 The rules for a flower competition at a village fete are as follows.

'Three judges each give a score out of 100 to each entry. The two judges whose rankings are in closest agreement are identified, and their scores for each entry are added. The three prize-winners are those whose total score from these two judges are the highest. The scores of the third judge are ignored.'

The judges awarded marks as shown in the table below.

Contestant	A	B	C	D	E	F	G
Judge X	89	83	80	72	69	54	41
Judge Y	77	84	85	65	79	72	69
Judge Z	73	83	89	80	67	75	69

The value of Spearman's rank correlation coefficient between X and Y is 0.5, and between X and Z is 0.46, correct to 2 decimal places. Calculate the value of Spearman's rank correlation coefficient between judges Y and Z, and hence establish which were the three prize-winners and in what order. (OCR, adapted)

8 Two students, Arif and Beth, collected the following data relating the mean diversity d of plant species with the distance s metres up an irregular cliff face.

s	0	1.25	2.5	3.85	5.2	6.5	7.8	9.1
d	8.17	8.65	7.47	7.77	6.80	7.21	6.23	6.77

$n = 8$, $\sum s = 36.2$, $\sum d = 59.07$, $\sum s^2 = 235.575$, $\sum d^2 = 440.6151$, $\sum sd = 251.828$

(a) Arif finds the product moment correlation coefficient between s and d. Calculate the answer he should get.

(b) Beth finds Spearman's rank correlation coefficient between s and d. Calculate the answer she should get.

Subsequently the vertical heights, h metres, above sea level were measured (see diagram). The students now find their respective correlation coefficients between h and d. State, with a reason in each case, whether

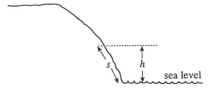

(c) Arif

(d) Beth

should obtain the same answer as before. (OCR)

9 Values of x and y for a set of bivariate data are given in the following table.

x	0.1	0.2	0.3	0.4	0.5	0.6	0.7	0.8	0.9
y	1.97	1.94	1.89	1.82	1.73	1.62	1.49	1.34	1.17

$n = 9$, $\sum x = 4.5$, $\sum y = 14.97$, $\sum x^2 = 2.85$, $\sum y^2 = 25.5309$, $\sum xy = 6.885$

(a) Calculate the product moment correlation coefficient for these data and state what its value tells you about the relationship between x and y.

The scatter diagram representing the data is shown.

(b) State the value of Spearman's rank correlation coefficient for these data, and state what further information its value gives about the relationship between x and y.

(c) State which of the following best indicates the relationship between x and y.

(i) The product moment correlation coefficient.

(ii) Spearman's rank correlation coefficient.

(iii) The scatter diagram.

Give a reason for your answer.

10 Regression

This chapter looks at the method for obtaining a linear equation relating two variables. When you have completed it you should

- understand the difference between an independent variable and a dependent variable
- understand what a controlled variable is
- understand the method of least squares
- be able to calculate the equation of a regression line
- understand the distinction between the regression line of y on x and the regression line of x on y
- know that both regression lines pass through $(\bar{x}, \bar{y})$
- select and use the appropriate line to estimate a value, and understand the uncertainties of such an estimation.

10.1 Linear relationships

Table 10.1 gives the electricity bill, £y, for a sample of 7 households (who get their electricity from the same company) and the number of units of electricity, x, which each of them used in one quarter.

Units of electricity, x	1009	567	248	1243	1098	976	1219
Bill, y (£)	58.85	36.75	20.80	70.55	63.30	57.20	69.35

Table 10.1. Amount of electricity used, and electricity bills, for a sample of 7 households.

This is a set of bivariate data, and you can illustrate it by a scatter diagram, as shown in Fig. 10.2. You can see that the points in this scatter diagram lie exactly on a straight line. You should be able to show that the equation of this line is

$$y = 8.4 + 0.05x.$$

It is not surprising that the points lie exactly on a straight line, because each household is charged according to the same rule: it pays a standing charge of £8.40 and then £0.05 for each unit of electricity consumed. Once you know how much electricity a household has used, you can calculate its bill exactly. Conversely, if you knew the value of a bill, you could calculate the amount of electricity used, x, by rearranging $y = 8.4 + 0.05x$ to give $x = -168 + 20y$.

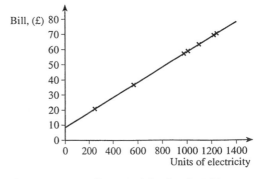

Fig. 10.2. Scatter diagram of the data in Table 10.1.

10.2   The method of least squares

In Chapter 9 you met examples where points on a scatter diagram representing bivariate data lay close to, but not exactly on, a straight line. Table 10.3 shows another example. This gives the height, y metres, and the circumference of the trunk, x metres, for a random sample of 6 pine trees. The height and circumference are random variables: if a tree is chosen at random you cannot say in advance what values its height and circumference will take.

Circumference, x (m)	0.75	0.55	0.72	0.61	0.66	0.58
Height, y (m)	8.7	6.8	7.9	7.0	7.1	6.1

Table 10.3. Height and circumference of a sample of 6 pine trees.

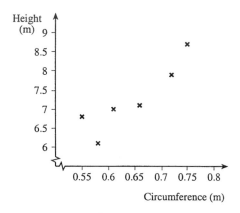

Fig. 10.4. Scatter diagram of the data in Table 10.3.

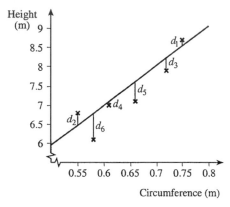

Fig. 10.5. Scatter diagram for trees with the line $y = 1 + 10x$ added.

Fig. 10.4 shows a scatter diagram of the data. These data were collected by the manager of a tree plantation from a sample of trees which had been cut down. He wanted to find a simple way of estimating the height of a tree which was still standing from the circumference of its trunk. In contrast to the previous example, there is not an exact answer to a question like 'What is the height of a tree with a trunk circumference of 0.64 m?', because trees with the same circumference can have different heights. The best that the manager can do is to obtain a simple equation which allows him to predict the average height of trees with a given circumference.

Finding such an equation involves drawing a straight line on the scatter diagram in Fig. 10.4. Many different possible lines could be drawn and you need some criterion to decide which line gives the 'best' fit to the points. The method used is called the **method of least squares**. It is based on an analysis of the errors made in using a straight line to fit the points. Fig. 10.5 shows the scatter diagram and a possible position for the line. This line has the equation $y = 1 + 10x$. The vertical deviations of the points from the line, such as d_1 and d_2, measure the errors which would be made in using this line to predict the heights of these trees. For example, for the first tree in Table 10.3, with circumference 0.75 m, the line predicts a height of $1 + 10 \times 0.75 = 8.5$ m. The actual height was 8.7 m. The deviation of this point from the line is $8.7 - 8.5 = 0.2$ m. Table 10.6 gives the deviations for each tree.

The best position for the line would be where the deviations are as small as possible. One way to achieve this is to minimise $\sum d_i^2$. This is the basis of the method of least squares. (The deviations are squared so each contributes positively to the sum: the deviations themselves tend to cancel out.) Table 10.6 also calculates $\sum d_i^2$ for the line $y = 1 + 10x$.

x_i	y_i	predicted y_i	d_i	d_i^2
0.75	8.7	8.5	0.2	0.04
0.55	6.8	6.5	0.3	0.09
0.72	7.9	8.2	−0.3	0.09
0.61	7.0	7.1	−0.1	0.01
0.66	7.1	7.6	−0.5	0.25
0.58	6.1	6.8	−0.7	0.49
			$\sum d_i^2 = 0.97$	

Table 10.6. Calculation of $\sum d_i^2$ for the line $y = 1 + 10x$.

For this line $\sum d_i^2 = 0.97$. Table 10.7 shows the computation of $\sum d_i^2$ for another possible line, $y = 0.1 + 11x$.

x_i	y_i	predicted y_i	d_i	d_i^2
0.75	8.7	8.35	0.35	0.1225
0.55	6.8	6.15	0.65	0.4225
0.72	7.9	8.02	−0.12	0.0144
0.61	7.0	6.81	0.19	0.0361
0.66	7.1	7.36	−0.26	0.0676
0.58	6.1	6.48	−0.38	0.1444
			$\sum d_i^2 = 0.8075$	

Table 10.7. Calculation of $\sum d_i^2$ for the line $y = 0.1 + 11x$.

For this line $\sum d_i^2$ is smaller than for the previous line, so this line gives a better fit.

Computer activity: construct a spreadsheet which allows you to investigate how $\sum d_i^2$ depends on the slope and intercept of the line relating y and x for the data in Table 10.3. Try to find the equation of the line for which $\sum d_i^2$ is a minimum.

Fortunately it is not necessary to try all the possible lines to see which one gives the smallest value of $\sum d_i^2$: there are formulae for the slope and intercept of the best line.

The equation of the line for which $\sum d_i^2$ is a minimum is $y = a + bx$ where

$$b = \frac{S_{xy}}{S_{xx}} \qquad (10.1) \qquad\qquad a = \bar{y} - b\bar{x} \qquad (10.2)$$

This line is called the **least-squares regression line of y on x,** and b is called **the regression coefficient of y on x** .

S_{xx} and S_{xy} are two of the sums you met in Chapter 9 (see Equations 9.3a and 9.3c). Note that Equation 10.2 can be rearranged to give $\bar{y} = a + b\bar{x}$. This shows that the point $(\bar{x}, \bar{y})$ lies on the regression line, since it satisfies the equation $y = a + bx$.

Question 3 in Exercise 10B explains the origin of the term 'regression'.

Example 10.2.1
(a) Calculate the regression line of y on x for the data in Table 10.3.
(b) Draw this line on a scatter diagram of the data.

(a)

x_i	y_i	x_i^2	$x_i y_i$
0.75	8.7	0.5625	6.525
0.55	6.8	0.3025	3.74
0.72	7.9	0.5184	5.688
0.61	7.0	0.3721	4.27
0.66	7.1	0.4356	4.686
0.58	6.1	0.3364	3.538
Totals: 3.87	43.6	2.5275	28.447

Using Equations 9.3a and 9.3c,

$$S_{xx} = \sum x_i^2 - \frac{\left(\sum x_i\right)^2}{n} = 2.5275 - \frac{3.87^2}{6} = 0.03135,$$

$$S_{xy} = \sum x_i y_i - \frac{\sum x_i \sum y_i}{n} = 28.447 - \frac{3.87 \times 43.6}{6} = 0.325.$$

Using Equation 10.1,

$$b = \frac{S_{xy}}{S_{xx}} = \frac{0.325}{0.03135} = 10.36\ldots$$

Using Equation 10.2,

$$a = \bar{y} - b\bar{x} = \frac{43.6}{6} - 10.36\ldots \times \frac{3.87}{6} = 0.5800\ldots$$

Round off b and a to 3 significant figures. The equation relating height, y, to circumference, x, is $y = 0.580 + 10.4x$.

The exact value of b was used in Equation 10.2 in order to avoid rounding-off errors.

If you did not construct a spreadsheet to solve this question, you can do a calculation similar to those in Tables 10.6 and 10.7 in order to find $\sum d_i^2$ for this line. Its value is 0.764. This is lower than the two previous values obtained. You would expect this since the least-squares method gives the line for which $\sum d_i^2$ has the least possible value.

(b) In order to draw this line on the scatter diagram you need to find the coordinates of two points which lie on it. You know that one point on the line is given by

$$(\bar{x}, \bar{y}) = \left(\frac{3.87}{6}, \frac{43.6}{6}\right) = (0.645, 7.27),$$

to 3 significant figures. You can find another point by substituting a value for x into the regression equation, for example $x = 0.7$, which gives

$$y = 0.58 + 10.4 \times 0.7 = 7.86.$$

You can now draw the regression line by joining the points $(0.645, 7.27)$ and $(0.7, 7.86)$. It is shown in Fig. 10.8.

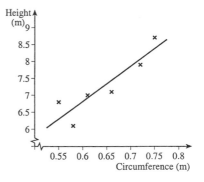

Fig. 10.8. Scatter diagram for the trees showing the regression line of y on x.

Many calculators will tell you the values of a and b directly if you key in all the values of x and y. However, you should be familiar with Equations 10.1 and 10.2 in case you are given information in the form of the sums $\sum x$, $\sum y$, $\sum x^2$ and $\sum xy$.

Example 10.2.2

Data were collected about the height, h m, and the length l m, jumped by 10 athletes. The results can be summarised as follows.

$n = 10$, $\sum h = 19$, $\sum l - 66$, $\sum h^2 = 36.44$, $\sum l^2 = 441.5$ and $\sum hl = 126.22$.

Find the equation of the regression line of h on l.

The regression line will have the form $h = a + bl$.

The number b, the regression coefficient of h on l, is given by $b = \dfrac{S_{hl}}{S_{ll}}$

Note that the line required is the regression line of h on l and only the variable l appears in the suffix of the denominator. Both variables appear in the suffix of the numerator.

Now

$$S_{hl} = \sum hl - \frac{\sum h \sum l}{n} = 126.22 - \frac{19 \times 66}{10} = 0.82$$

$$S_{ll} = \sum l^2 - \frac{(\sum l)^2}{n} = 441.5 - \frac{66^2}{10} = 5.9$$

So $b = \dfrac{S_{hl}}{S_{ll}} = \dfrac{0.82}{5.9} = 0.139$, correct to 3 significant figures.

The point $(\bar{l}, \bar{h})$ lies on the line so

$$\bar{h} = a + b\bar{l}.$$

The value of a can be found by rearranging this equation in the form

$$a = \bar{h} - b\bar{l} = \frac{19}{10} - \frac{0.82}{5.9} \times \frac{66}{10} = 0.983, \text{ correct to 3 significant figures.}$$

The regression line of h on l is $h = 0.983 + 0.139l$.

10.3   Making predictions with a regression line

The plantation manager can use the regression line of y on x (from Example 10.2.1) to predict the height of a tree from its circumference. For example, if he measures the circumference of a tree and finds that it is 0.74 m, he would calculate

$$y = 0.58 + 10.4x$$
$$= 0.58 + 10.4 \times 0.74 = 8.276,$$

and his estimate of the height of the tree is 8.3 m.

The tree may not actually have this height, because this value is an estimate for the *average* height of trees with this circumference. However, the closer the points are to a straight line on the scatter diagram, the closer the estimated value is likely to be to the actual value. In this example, the scatter of the points about the regression line means that there is little point in giving an estimate to more than 2 significant figures.

In this example an equation was found which describes how the height of a tree depends on its circumference. For this reason the height is called the **dependent** variable. The circumference is called the **independent** variable. This equation allows you to estimate an unknown value of the dependent variable from a known value of the independent variable.

When you have obtained a regression equation, it is tempting to think that it is true for all values of x, since it is possible to calculate a value of y for any value of x. For example, it is quite possible to calculate an estimate of the height of a tree with circumference 1.00 m. Substituting 1.00 for x in the equation $y = 0.58 + 10.4x$ gives

$$y = 0.58 + 10.4 \times 1.00 = 10.98.$$

The estimate of the height of the tree is 11.0 m.

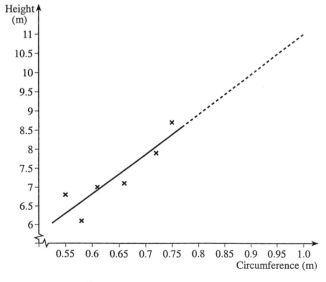

Fig. 10.9. Extrapolating a regression line.

If you look at Fig. 10.9 you will see that this prediction involves extending the regression line outside the range where it was fitted, into the region indicated by the dotted line. However, the rule relating circumference and height may no longer be true for such large trees. For example, as the trees get larger, the points on the scatter diagram might start to follow a curve rather than the dotted line which is shown. Extending a regression line outside the range where it was fitted is called 'extrapolation': it should be used with extreme caution.

10.4 Practical activities

1 **Pocket money and age**

   (a) For a sample of about 20 children, record their age, A, and their weekly pocket money, W.

   (b) Plot a scatter diagram of the results.

   (c) Calculate the regression line which would allow you to predict the average weekly pocket money for children of a given age and add it to your scatter diagram.

2 **Travel to school** If you collected data for this activity in the previous chapter (Section 9.4), and if you found a reasonable degree of correlation between the variables, calculate the regression line which would allow you to predict the average travel time from distance. Add it to your scatter diagram.

Exercise 10A

1 Calculate the equation of the regression line of y on x (or t on w) in the following cases. Use the methods indicated, and give each answer in the form $y = a + bx$ (or $t = a + bw$).

   (a) (to be done without a calculator)

   $$(x, y) = (7,0),\ (9,4),\ (10,8),\ (11,6),\ (13,12)$$

   (b) (to be done with a calculator, but with all working set out as in Example 10.2.1)

   $$(x, y) = (5,20),\ (6,18),\ (8,17),\ (9,11),\ (12,9)$$

   (c) (to be done with a calculator, but with all working set out as in Example 10.2.1)

x	4	6	7	11	14	18
y	3	7	11	12	5	4

   (d) $n = 7$, $\sum x = 28$, $\sum y = 73$, $\sum x^2 = 140$, $\sum y^2 = 955$, $\sum xy = 364$.

   (e) $n = 5$, $\sum w = 31$, $\sum t = 90$, $\sum w^2 = 225$, $\sum t^2 = 1702$, $\sum wt = 508$.

   (f) (Use built-in calculator functions.)

x	1	2	3	4	5	6
y	9.6	8.1	7.9	6.4	6.7	2.3

(g) (Use built-in calculator functions.)

w	2.0	2.5	3.0	3.5	4.0	4.5	5.0
t	12.56	19.31	27.56	37.31	48.56	61.31	75.56

2 Use your answer to Question 1 part (c) to estimate the value of y corresponding to $x = 10$.

3 Explain why an estimate obtained from the data in Question 1 part (c) for the value of y corresponding to $x = 25$ is unreliable. Explain also why it is difficult to assess the reliability of any estimates obtained from the data in Question 1 parts (d) and (e).

4 Use your answer to Question 1 part (f) to estimate the value of y corresponding to $x = 2.5$. Can you get this answer directly from the calculator?

5 An acoustician carried out tests on various concert halls, collecting data on the front–back distance, d metres, and the reverberation time, t seconds. The results were as follows.

d	20	35	41	42	50	56	60
t	1.2	1.4	2.7	2.6	2.9	3.1	4.5

$n = 7$, $\sum d = 304$, $\sum t = 18.4$, $\sum d^2 = 14\,306$, $\sum t^2 = 55.72$, $\sum dt = 881.5$

(a) Calculate the regression line of t on d in the form $t = a + bd$.

(b) Use your line to estimate the reverberation time of a hall with $d = 30$.

6 The table shows data relating the amount of investment per track mile, £x thousand, by various railway companies, together with the percentage of trains, y%, that run on time.

x	4.3	2.1	7.8	6.2	3.4	9.2	5.5
y	88.3	86	94.2	92.6	88.7	93.5	90.8

$n = 7$, $\sum x = 38.5$, $\sum y = 634.1$, $\sum x^2 = 248.63$, $\sum y^2 = 57\,495.87$, $\sum xy = 3530.35$

Calculate the equation of the regression line of y on x, in the form $y = a + bx$. Interpret the values of a and b in terms of amount of investment and percentage of punctual trains.

7 The table shows data collected from a trial of a weedkiller. Trial field areas, each of area 1 acre, were treated with different volumes of weedkiller. The volume of weedkiller applied is v litres, and x is the number of weeds found in the corresponding acre.

v	10	20	30	40	50	60	70	80	90
x	46	32	31	27	18	15	14	12	11

$n = 9$, $\sum v = 450$, $\sum x = 206$, $\sum v^2 = 28\,500$, $\sum x^2 = 5840$, $\sum vx = 7840$

Calculate the equation of the regression line of x on v in the form $x = a + bv$. Use your answer to estimate the number of weeds that would be found in an area of 1 acre treated with 35 litres of weedkiller.

Interpret the coefficient b in the context of volume of weedkiller and number of weeds. Explain why a does not necessarily give the expected number of weeds per acre when no weedkiller is used. How can you tell that a linear model will not be valid for very large values of v?

8 If you have access to a computer, design a spreadsheet which calculates the equation of the regression line of y on x for the data in Question 1 part (b). Include a scatter diagram on your spreadsheet, together with a plot of the regression line.

Investigate how the regression line changes when values of x and y are changed.

10.5 Two possible regression lines

Table 10.10 gives the mark, x (out of 25), obtained by students in an aptitude test at the start of a course and their marks, y%, in the final exam, for a class of 14 students.

x	22	22	9	19	24	9	20	24	14	23	18	8	13	14
y	60	73	26	70	63	29	74	77	50	65	66	17	40	30

Table 10.10. Marks of 14 students in an initial aptitude test and a final exam.

The data are illustrated in Fig. 10.11.

You can see that there is a strong positive linear correlation between the two variables. This can be confirmed by calculating the value of the product moment correlation coefficient, r. For these data,

$$\sum x_i = 239, \qquad \sum x_i^2 = 4521,$$
$$\sum y_i = 740, \qquad \sum y_i^2 = 44\,590,$$
$$\sum x_i y_i = 14\,050, \quad n = 14.$$

You can check that $S_{xx} = 440.92\dots$, $S_{yy} = 5475.7\dots$, $S_{xy} = 1417.1\dots$, giving $r = 0.912\dots$. This value of r is close to 1, indicating strong positive linear correlation.

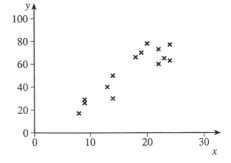

Fig. 10.11. Marks of 14 students in two tests.

A value of r which was close to zero would indicate that there was no relationship between the two variables. In this case there would be no point in calculating the equation of a regression line.

The tutor in charge of this course wants to find an equation which will allow her to predict how future students will perform in the final exam, on the basis of their mark in the aptitude test. Since y is being predicted from x, she needs to calculate the regression line of y on x. Using Equation 10.1 (with the values of S_{xx} and S_{xy} already calculated),

$$b = \frac{S_{xy}}{S_{xx}} = \frac{1417.1\dots}{440.92\dots} = 3.213\dots$$

Using Equation 10.2,

$$a = \bar{y} - b\bar{x} = \frac{740}{14} - \frac{1417.1\dots}{440.92\dots} \times \frac{239}{14} = -2.010\dots$$

Taking b and a to 3 significant figures, the regression line of y on x is $y = -20.1 + 3.21x$. Fig. 10.12 shows the scatter diagram with this line added to it.

You can use this line to estimate the mark that a student will obtain in the final test given their mark in the aptitude test, since x is being treated as the independent variable and y as the dependent variable. For example, students who obtain 15 in the initial test will, on average, obtain $y = -20.1 + 3.21 \times 15 = 46$ (to 2 significant figures) in the final test.

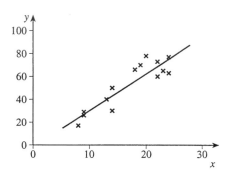

Fig. 10.12. Finding the regression line of y on x.

The tutor has another use for these data The pass mark in the final exam is 35%. She would like to estimate the average mark in the aptitude test for students obtaining 35% in the final test. She could use this as a qualifying mark for entry to the course. Since she is now predicting x from y she needs to calculate the regression line of x on y. This line treats y as the independent variable and x as the dependent variable: for a given value of y the line estimates the unknown value of x. This regression line minimises the sum of the squares of the deviations in the x-direction of the points from the line. These deviations are shown in Fig 10.13. The equations for finding the slope and intercept are the same as those for the regression line of y on x, but with x and y interchanged:

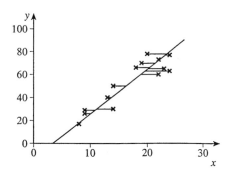

Fig. 10.13. Finding the regression line of x on y.

> The **least-squares regression line of x on y** is $x = a' + b'y$ where
> $$b' = \frac{S_{xy}}{S_{yy}} \quad \text{and} \quad a' = \bar{x} - b'\bar{y}.$$
> b' is the **regression coefficient of x on y**.

Note that b' is not the gradient of this line on a scatter diagram of y against x.

This regression line also passes through the point $(\bar{x}, \bar{y})$.

For the students' marks,

$$b' = \frac{S_{xy}}{S_{yy}} = \frac{1417.1\ldots}{5475.7\ldots} = 0.2588\ldots, \quad a' = \bar{x} - b'\bar{y} = \frac{239}{14} - 0.2588\ldots \times \frac{740}{14} = 3.391\ldots,$$

so the regression line of x on y is $x = 3.39 + 0.259y$.

From the pass mark of the final exam, 35%, the tutor calculates a qualifying mark of

$$x = 3.39 + 0.259 \times 35 = 12$$

(correct to 2 significant figures). Fig. 10.14 shows the scatter diagram with both regression lines. Since both lines go through the point $(\bar{x}, \bar{y})$, they intersect at this point. You may be surprised that the two regression lines are different, but you must remember that the two regression lines have different purposes:

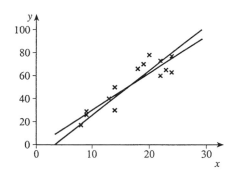

Fig. 10.14. The two regression lines.

For two random variables, x and y,

the regression line of y on x predicts the *average* value of y for a *given* value of x;

the regression line of x on y predicts the *average* value of x for a *given* value of y.

Only when the points on the scatter diagram lie exactly on a straight line, so that the relationship between x and y is exactly defined, will the two regression lines coincide.

For the data in Table 10.1 the two regression lines coincide.

10.6 Practical activity

Heights of parents and children   For about 15 students of the same sex as yourself, obtain a value for their height and also for the height of their parent of the same sex. Then, if you are male, calculate the regression line which would allow you to predict a male student's height from the height of his father; if you are female, calculate the regression line which would allow you to predict a female student's height from the height of her mother.

(a) Draw a scatter diagram of the results and add the regression line to the diagram. How reliable do you think the predictions will be? Use the line to predict your own height!

(b) Calculate the regression line which would allow you to estimate, as appropriate, either the average height of the mothers of girls of a given height or the average height of the fathers of boys of a given height. Add this line to your diagram. Explain why the two regression lines do not coincide.

Exercise 10B

1 Calculate the equations of the regression lines of x on y, and also of y on x, for each of the following sets of data. Give your answers in the form $y = a + bx$ and $x = a' + b'y$.

(a) $n = 12$, $\sum x = 540$, $\sum y = 948$, $\sum x^2 = 24\,732$, $\sum y^2 = 75\,084$, $\sum xy = 42\,780$

(b) (Set the working out as in Example 10.2.1.)

x	2	5	8	11	14
y	1	6	9	10	11

(c) (Use built-in calculator functions.)

x	1.2	1.8	2.7	3.0	3.9
y	5.6	7.3	9.3	11.7	12.5

(d) (Use built-in calculator functions.)

x	1.5	2.2	3.8	4.7	5.9	7.0
y	26	21	19	12	10	3

2 A mathematics exam consists of two papers, I and II. The marks of twelve candidates in the exam papers are given in the table.

Paper I, x	36	38	40	48	49	55	56	56	62	78	79	91
Paper II, y	24	39	36	35	42	47	43	51	60	85	79	86

$n = 12$, $\sum x = 688$, $\sum y = 627$, $\sum x^2 = 42\,792$, $\sum y^2 = 37\,503$, $\sum xy = 39\,790$

(a) A candidate who scored 43% in Paper II was absent for Paper II. It is desired to estimate a mark for this candidate on Paper II. Calculate the equation of an appropriate line of regression and use it to obtain the required estimate.

(b) A candidate who scored 70% in Paper II was absent for Paper I. It is desired to estimate a mark for this candidate on Paper I. Calculate the equation of an appropriate line of regression and use it to obtain the required estimate.

3 A statistician collected data on the heights, when fully grown, of 150 fathers and their sons. The results are summarised as follows, where x represents the father's height in inches, and y the son's height, also in inches.

$(n = 150$, $\sum x = 10\,500$, $\sum y = 10\,650$, $\sum x^2 = 738\,720$, $\sum y^2 = 758\,580$,

$\sum xy = 747\,900)$

(a) Calculate the equations of the regression lines of y on x, and of x on y.

(b) What is the fathers' mean height?

(c) Calculate the expected height of the son of a father whose height is

(i) 74 inches,   (ii) 66 inches.

(d) Calculate the value of the product moment correlation coefficient, and use it to assess the reliability of your estimates. Assume that the values $x = 74$ and $x = 66$ are within the range of the data.

(e) Find an estimate of the height of a father whose son is of height 65 inches.

(f)* The gradient of the regression line of y on x is positive, but less than 1. How does this explain the use of the term 'regression' (meaning 'movement back') in this context?

The term 'regression' was proposed by the British statistician Sir Francis Galton (1822–1911) when he analysed some similar experimental data. This has given rise to the general use of the term in other, often unrelated, contexts.

4 A student collected data about the latitude of various cities, $l°$, and the mean minimum daily temperature, $t°C$. Her results can be summarised as follows.

$$n = 40, \sum l = 1757.3, \sum t = 398.2, \sum l^2 = 92\,881.96, \sum t^2 = 10\,940.5,$$
$$\sum lt = 7402.639.$$

Calculate the product moment correlation coefficient.

By calculating the equations of suitable lines of regression, estimate

(a) the mean minimum daily temperature in London, latitude $51.3°$,

(b) the latitude of a city where the mean minimum daily temperature is $12.0\,°C$.

Comment on the reliability of your answers.

5 For the following data, calculate the product moment correlation coefficient and the equation of the regression line of y on x. Obtain the equation of the regression line of x on y with a minimum of calculation.

$$n = 6, \sum x = 21, \sum y = 81, \sum x^2 = 91, \sum y^2 = 1531, \sum xy = 371.$$

6 Is it true that:

(a) the equation of the regression line of x on y is a rearrangement of the equation of the regression line of y on x?

(b) it makes little difference which line is used for estimates if $r \approx \pm1$?

(c) it makes little difference which line is used for estimates if the value used for the estimate is close to the mean?

(d) if $r = 0.75$ then the gradient of the regression line of y on x must be less than 1?

7 If you have access to a computer, design a spreadsheet which displays a scatter diagram, together with plots of both regression lines.

Investigate how the regression lines change when values of x and y are changed. What happens to the two regression lines when the correlation is

(a) strong,   (b) weak?

10.7   Controlled variables

Table 10.15 shows the results of a simple scientific experiment which was carried out using the apparatus illustrated in Fig. 10.16. You may have done an experiment like this yourself. When masses are added to the scale pan, the spring stretches. The table shows values for x, the load on the scale pan (measured in newtons) and y, the length of the spring (measured in mm).

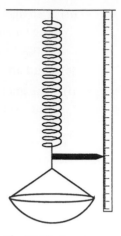

Load, x (N)	0.1	0.2	0.3	0.4	0.5	0.6
Length, y (mm)	102	107	123	130	144	149

Table 10.15. Results for measuring the length of a spring for different loads.

Fig. 10.16. A spring balance.

The scatter diagram in Fig. 10.17 illustrates this set of bivariate data.

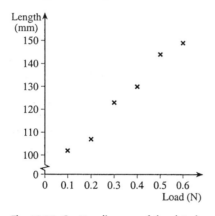

Fig. 10.17. Scatter diagram of the data in Table 10.15.

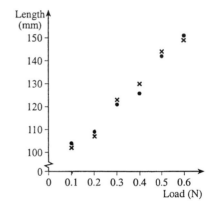

Fig. 10.18. Data from Table 10.15 and results of a repeat experiment.

In this experiment the load is not a random variable, because its values are chosen by the person doing the experiment. It is called a **controlled** variable. The length is called the **dependent** variable, because its value depends on the value of the load. Unlike the load, the measured length is a random variable. You can see this by looking at Fig. 10.18, which shows the original data and also the results of a repeat experiment. This diagram shows that the two values of y for each value of x differ slightly. This experimental variation means that you cannot know in advance exactly what the measured value of y will be for a given value of x.

The points on the scatter diagram are close to a straight line, which suggests that a linear model could be used to describe the relationship between x and y. It is assumed that the points do not lie exactly on a straight line because of experimental variation in y. To get a relationship between x and y, you draw a straight line on the scatter diagram. The best line to draw is the regression line of y on x.

Example 10.7.1

(a) Find the regression line of y on x for the data in Table 10.15, in the form $y = a + bx$.

(b) Give an interpretation of the coefficients a and b.

(c) Explain why the equation of the regression line should not be used to predict the length of the spring when a load of 10 newtons is hung from it.

(a)

x_i	y_i	x_i^2	$x_i y_i$
0.1	102	0.01	10.2
0.2	107	0.04	21.4
0.3	123	0.09	36.9
0.4	130	0.16	52.0
0.5	144	0.25	72.0
0.6	149	0.36	89.4
Totals: 2.1	755	0.91	281.9

Using Equations 9.3a and 9.3c,

$$S_{xx} = \sum x_i^2 - \frac{\left(\sum x_i\right)^2}{n} = 0.91 - \frac{2.1^2}{6} = 0.175.$$

$$S_{xy} = \sum x_i y_i - \frac{\sum x_i \sum y_i}{n} = 281.9 - \frac{2.1 \times 755}{6} = 17.65.$$

Using Equation 10.1,

$$b = \frac{S_{xy}}{S_{xx}} = \frac{17.65}{0.175} = 100.8\ldots$$

Using Equation 10.2,

$$a = \bar{y} - b\bar{x} = \frac{755}{6} - \frac{17.65}{0.175} \times \frac{2.1}{6} = 90.53\ldots$$

Round off b and a to 3 significant figures. The equation relating length, y, to load, x, is $y = 90.5 + 101x$.

(b) The coefficient $b = 101$ is the gradient. It gives an estimate of the increase in length (in mm) for each extra newton of load added. The coefficient $a = 90.5$ is the intercept of the regression line on the y-axis. It gives an estimate of the length of the unloaded spring in mm.

(c) The line should not be used to predict the length of the spring for a load of 10 newtons because this value is a long way outside the range of loads for which the line was fitted. In fact, such a load would probably break the spring.

Suppose you applied an unknown load to the spring and measured the length of the spring to be 127 mm. How should you estimate the value of the load? In the situation where x is controlled, the regression line of x on y has no meaning, because there is no random variation in x. Only the regression line of y on x has meaning, and this line is used to estimate the unknown load. Substituting $y = 127$ into the regression equation $y = 90.5 + 101x$ gives

$$127 = 90.5 + 101x$$
$$x = 0.361\ldots$$

The unknown load is estimated to be 0.36 N.

> If the variable x is controlled (that is, its values are not random) then only the regression line of y on x has meaning. This line is used to estimate y from x and also to estimate x from y.

10.8   Practical activity

Measuring an unknown load   (For this you will require a set of standard masses, a metre rule, a clamp stand and a spring.) Carry out the experiment described in Section 10.7 for yourself. Plot a scatter diagram of length against load. Calculate the regression line of length on load and add it to the scatter diagram. Apply an unknown load to the spring, measure the length of the spring and hence estimate a value for the load.

Exercise 10C

1 In the following data, x is the controlled variable. Calculate the equation of an appropriate line of regression, and use it to estimate

(a) the expected value of y when $x = 38$,

(b) the value of x corresponding to an expected y-value of 30.

x	20	25	30	35	40
y	17	23	26	38	42

2 In the following data, y is the controlled variable. Calculate the equation of an appropriate line of regression, and use it to estimate

(a) the value of x when $y = 3.6$,   (b) the value of y when $x = 90$.

x	83	84	96	94	99
y	4.2	3.9	3.3	3.0	2.7

3 The time taken, t seconds, for a loaded trolley of total mass m kg to reach a given speed from rest is shown in the following table.

m	3.2	3.7	4.2	4.7	5.2	5.7	6.2	6.7
t	2.5	3.0	3.4	4.0	4.5	4.9	5.3	5.8

$n = 8$, $\sum m = 39.6$, $\sum t = 33.4$, $\sum m^2 = 206.52$, $\sum t^2 = 148.8$, $\sum mt = 175.23$

Use linear regression to estimate

(a) the time t when $m = 5.0$,

(b) the mass m which would take 5.5 seconds to reach the given speed.

4 Experiments with a resistor show that its resistance R ohms varies with temperature $t\,^\circ C$ as in the following table.

t	20	22	24	26	28	30	32
R	101.4	101.3	100.5	100.2	99.5	99.4	99.0

$n = 7$, $\sum t = 182$, $\sum R = 701.3$, $\sum t^2 = 4844$, $\sum R^2 = 70\,265.55$, $\sum tR = 18\,209.8$

It is desired to set an operating temperature at which the resistance is as close to 100 ohms as possible. What temperature should be chosen?

5 In which of the following situations is it likely that the x-variable is controlled?

(a) x temperature $\qquad\qquad\qquad\qquad$ y rate of a chemical reaction

(b) x height of baby at birth $\qquad\qquad$ y weight of baby at birth

(c) x student's coursework mark $\qquad$ y student's exam mark

(d) x number of cigarettes smoked per day $\qquad$ y life expectancy in years

(e) x speed of a car $\qquad\qquad\qquad$ y petrol consumption of that car

(f) x quantity of drug taken $\qquad\quad$ y blood pressure

(g) x angle of slope $\qquad\qquad\qquad$ y time taken for marble to roll down

Miscellaneous exercise 10

1 A set of bivariate data can be summarised as follows:

$\qquad n = 6$, $\sum x = 21$, $\sum y = 43$, $\sum x^2 = 91$, $\sum y^2 = 335$, $\sum xy = 171$.

(a) Calculate the equation of the regression line of y on x. Give your answer in the form $y = a + bx$, where a and b should be stated correct to 3 significant figures.

(b) It is required to estimate the value of y for a given value of x. State circumstances under which the regression line of x on y should be used, rather than the regression line of y on x. $\hfill$ (OCR)

2 A firm investigates the effectiveness of a television advertising campaign. The number of sales, s thousands, in one day following television advertisements lasting a total of t minutes are given in the following table.

t	1.0	2.0	3.0	4.0	5.0
s	1.50	2.40	2.60	3.10	3.90

(a) It is required to estimate the value of s, correct to 2 significant figures, when $t = 3.4$. Calculate the equation of the appropriate regression line, and use it to find the required estimate.

(b) The product moment correlation coefficient between s and t is 0.98, correct to 2 significant figures. Without plotting the data points, state what this tells you about a scatter diagram illustrating the data. (OCR)

3 The table gives paired values of the variables g and h.

g	17	23	25	30	32	41
h	5	10	15	20	25	30

$n = 6$, $\sum g = 168$, $\sum h = 105$, $\sum g^2 = 5048$, $\sum h^2 = 2275$, $\sum gh = 3320$

(a) Obtain the equation of the line of regression of g on h. Give your answer in the form $g = p + qh$, stating the values of p and q.

(b) It is required to estimate the value of h when $g = 35$. State when the regression line of g on h, rather than that of h on g, is the correct one to use. Use the regression line of g on h to find the required estimate. (OCR)

4 A student found the following data for the female life expectancy, x years, and the Gross Domestic Product (GDP) per head, $\$y$, in six countries in South Asia in 1988.

Country	x	y
Afghanistan	42	143
Bangladesh	50	179
Bhutan	47	197
India	58	335
Pakistan	57	384
Sri Lanka	73	423

$n = 6$, $\sum x = 327$, $\sum y = 1661$, $\sum x^2 = 18\,415$, $\sum y^2 = 529\,909$, $\sum xy = 96\,412$

(a) It is required to estimate the value of x for Nepal, where the value of y was 160. Find the equation of a suitable line of regression. Simplify your answer as far as possible, giving the constants correct to 3 significant figures. Use your equation to obtain the required estimate.

(b) Use your equation to estimate the value of x for North Korea, where the value of y was 858. Comment on your answer. (OCR)

[Data © *The Economist Book of Vital World Statistics*, 1990]

5 An experiment to determine the effect of an organic liquid fertiliser on crop yield was carried out. A field was divided into 25 plots of equal area. Five different levels of concentration of fertiliser were used, each level being applied to five of the plots. The same quantity of liquid was applied to each plot. The results are shown in the following table, in

which x denotes the concentration of fertiliser in kilograms per litre and y denotes the crop yield in kilograms.

x	0.0	0.0	0.0	0.0	0.0	0.5	0.5	0.5	0.5	0.5
y	6.2	7.6	6.8	6.7	7.2	9.0	8.4	6.4	7.6	8.1

x	1.0	1.0	1.0	1.0	1.0	1.5	1.5	1.5	1.5	1.5
y	10.7	10.1	8.6	7.8	9.4	9.5	9.1	10.4	10.8	8.6

x	2.0	2.0	2.0	2.0	2.0
y	10.0	8.2	10.6	12.6	11.5

The data for all the plots is summarised by

$$n = 25, \ \sum x = 25, \ \sum y = 221.9, \ \sum x^2 = 37.5, \ \sum y^2 = 2037.15 \ \sum xy = 244.75.$$

(a) Calculate the product moment correlation coefficient between x and y.

(b) The equation of the line of regression of y on x can be written as $y = 7.048 + 1.828x$. Give interpretations of the meaning of the two coefficients, in terms of crop yield and concentration of fertiliser.

(c) Use the appropriate regression line to calculate an estimate of the concentration of fertiliser which would have produced a crop yield of 10.0 kg from one of the plots. Explain your choice of line.

6   An old film is treated with a chemical in order to improve the contrast. Preliminary tests on nine samples drawn from a segment of the film produce the following results.

Sample	A	B	C	D	E	F	G	H	I
x	1.0	1.5	2.0	2.5	3.0	3.5	4.0	4.5	5.0
y	49	60	66	62	72	64	89	90	96

The quantity x is a measure of the amount of chemical applied, and y is the contrast index, which takes values between 0 (no contrast) and 100 (maximum contrast).

(a) Plot a scatter diagram to illustrate the data.

(b) It is subsequently discovered that one of the samples of film was damaged and produced an incorrect result. State which sample you think this was.

In all subsequent calculations this incorrect sample is ignored. The remaining data can be summarised as follows:

$$n = 8, \ \sum x = 23.5, \ \sum y = 584, \ \sum x^2 = 83.75, \ \sum y^2 = 44\,622, \ \sum xy = 1883.$$

(c) Calculate the product moment correlation coefficient.

(d) State, with a reason, whether it is sensible to conclude from your answer to part (c) that x and y are linearly related.

(e) The line of regression of y on x has equation $y = a + bx$. Calculate the values of a and b, each correct to 3 significant figures.

(f) Use your regression line to estimate what the contrast index corresponding to the damaged piece of film would have been if the piece had been undamaged.

(g) State, with a reason, whether it would be sensible to use your regression equation to estimate the contrast index when the quantity of chemical applied to the film is zero.   (OCR)

7 When I travel to work each morning, my arrival time depends on when I depart. Over a period of ten consecutive days I made a note of my departure and arrival times. In the following table, x is the departure time, in minutes after 7 a.m., and y is the arrival time, in minutes after 8 a.m.

x	20	27	33	40	45	50	53	58	65	70
y	4	8	22	30	44	56	70	80	85	88

$n = 10$, $\sum x = 461$, $\sum y = 487$, $\sum x^2 = 23\,641$, $\sum y^2 = 32\,805$, $\sum xy = 27\,037$

(a) Plot a scatter diagram to illustrate the data.

(b) Calculate the product moment correlation coefficient, and explain what information your answer gives you about the relationship between x and y.

(c) Find the equation of the regression line of y on x in the form $y = a + bx$, giving a and b correct to 3 significant figures.

(d) I wish to estimate the time at which I should depart in order to arrive at 8.50 a.m. Give a reason why it will make little difference whether the regression line of y on x or the regression line of x on y is used.

Use the equation obtained in part (c) to calculate the required estimate.

(e) Give a reason why it would probably not be sensible to use either line to estimate the value of y when $x = 120$.

8 The speed of a car, v metres per second, at time t seconds after it starts to accelerate is shown in the table below, for $0 \le t \le 10$.

t	0	1	2	3	4	5	6	7	8	9	10
v	0	3.0	6.8	10.2	12.9	16.4	20.0	21.4	23.0	24.6	26.1

$n = 11$, $\sum t = 55$, $\sum v = 164.4$, $\sum t^2 = 385$, $\sum v^2 = 3267.98$, $\sum tv = 1117$

The relationship between t and v is initially modelled by using all the data above, and calculating a single regression line.

(a) Plot a scatter diagram of the data, with t on the horizontal axis and v on the vertical axis.

(b) Using all the data given, calculate the equation of the regression line of v on t. Give numerical coefficients in your answer correct to 3 significant figures.

(c) Calculate the product moment correlation coefficient for the given data.

(d)* Comment on the validity of modelling the data by a single straight line and on the answer obtained in (c).

In an alternative model, one straight line is fitted to the points for which $0 \leq t \leq 6$ and a different straight line to the points for which $6 \leq t \leq 10$.

(e)* Draw the two straight lines for the alternative model by eye on your scatter diagram. Find, from your graph, the equation of the line for $0 \leq t \leq 6$. (You need not calculate a regression line as in (b).)

(f)* Taking the alternative model as the more accurate one, calculate the percentage error in using the regression line in (b) to estimate the value of v when $t = 3.5$.   (OCR)

9* A statistician discovers the following part of an old research paper.

> giving us mean values $\bar{x} = 21$ and $\bar{y} =$
> The regression line of y on x may be written as $y = -\frac{1}{7}x +$
> and the regression line of x on y may be written as $y = -7x + 163$
> Treating y as the independent variable, we calculate that when y
> is known to be 128, an estimate for the value of x would be

(a) Show that $\bar{y} = 16$.

(b) Calculate the value of the missing term in the regression line of y on x.

(c) Use the appropriate regression line to calculate the missing estimate for the value of x.

(d) Using a formula she knows, the statistician works out that the product moment correlation coefficient r satisfies $r^2 = \frac{1}{49}$. Give a reason why the correct value of r is $-\frac{1}{7}$ and not $\frac{1}{7}$.

(e) Use the value of the product moment correlation coefficient to comment on the reliability of the estimate.

10* An office manager conducted an experiment to determine the number of letters per hour, l, answered by his office staff at various room temperatures $t\,°F$. (The values of t were controlled by means of a thermostat.) The data obtained are given in the table.

t	70	71	72	73	74	75	76	77	78	79	80
l	130	138	134	136	132	134	130	126	121	115	109

$n = 11,\ \sum t = 825,\ \sum t^2 = 61\,985,\ \sum l = 1405,\ \sum l^2 = 180\,299,\ \sum tl = 105\,117$

(a) Plot a scatter diagram of the data with t on the horizontal axis and l on the vertical axis.

(b) Calculate the product moment correlation coefficient between l and t, and state whether, on the basis of your answer and the appearance of the scatter diagram, a straight line would be a good model for the data.

(c) It is given that the product moment correlation coefficient for the data for values of t from 70 to 75 inclusive is 0.076, and for values of t from 75 to 80 inclusive is -0.995, both correct to 3 decimal places. Interpret these values by referring to your scatter diagram.

(d) Advise the manager as to whether there is a strong case for introducing air-conditioning into the office (which would prevent the temperature exceeding a specified maximum value).

(e) It is required to estimate the room temperature at which 125 letters per hour could be answered. State, with a reason, whether you would use the regression line of t on l, or the regression line of l on t for this purpose. Using data for t between 75 and 80 inclusive, calculate the equation of your chosen line of regression, simplifying your answer as far as possible. Use your answer to obtain the required estimate.

(f) Comment on the reliability of your estimate, in the light of the value of the product moment correlation coefficient. Explain whether an estimate of the temperature at which 100 letters per hour would be answered would be less, more or equally reliable.

(g) The manager's assistant says that different results would be obtained for the values of the product moment correlation coefficients if the temperatures had been measured in degrees Celsius rather than in degrees Fahrenheit. Explain why the assistant is in principle wrong, and give a reason why, in practice, slightly different results might well have been obtained.

Revision exercise

1 The table shows the length distribution of pebbles from the bed of a river.

Length, x (millimetres)	$0 \le x < 5$	$5 \le x < 10$	$10 \le x < 20$	$20 \le x < 50$	$50 \le x < 100$
Frequency	10	8	12	25	30

(a) You are given that the frequency density for the class $0 \le x < 5$ is 2. Write down the frequency densities for the other classes.

(b) Represent the data in a histogram.

(c) Calculate an estimate of the mean length of the pebbles in the sample, and of the standard deviation of the length of the pebbles in the sample.

2 The heights, h cm, and masses, w kg, of eight people are recorded in the table.

Person	A	B	C	D	E	F	G	H
h	170	120	180	135	165	175	150	155
w	56	32	72	44	62	68	54	52

You are given that $\sum h = 1250$, $\sum w = 440$, $\sum h^2 = 198\,300$, $\sum w^2 = 25\,368$, $\sum hw = 70\,550$.

(a) Use these values to calculate S_{hw}, S_{hh} and S_{ww}.

(b) Calculate the product moment correlation coefficient for these data, and state what this value tells you about the relationship between mass and height.

It is desired to estimate the mass of a person whose height is 160 cm.

(c) Calculate the appropriate least squares regression line, and use it to estimate the mass of a person whose height is 160 cm.

3 Eleanor has decided to play in a weekly lottery game. She is prepared to continue playing indefinitely. The lottery organisers claim that a participant in the lottery has a 1 in 57 chance of winning a prize. Let X be a random variable representing the number of games she plays up to and including her first win.

(a) Explain why a geometric distribution may be an appropriate model for the distribution of X.

(b) Calculate $P(X \le 12)$ and $P(13 \le X < 70)$.

(c)* Determine the minimum number of games Eleanor will need to play to be at least 95% certain of having won at least one prize by that time.

(d) State the value of $E(X)$.

4 An experiment consists of shuffling an ordinary pack of 52 cards. Once shuffled, the top card is examined. The card can be a 'picture card' (ace, king, queen or jack), an 'even card' or an 'odd card'. None of these categories overlap. If it is a 'picture card' (there are 16 in a pack), a score of 5 is awarded. Otherwise, if it is an 'even card' (there are 20), a score of 2 is awarded. A score of zero is given for an 'odd card'. This is summarised in the table.

Card	odd	picture	even
Score	0	5	2

(a) Write down the probability of a score of 5.

(b) Write down the probability distribution of the score, and calculate its mean and variance.

The experiment is repeated, with the top card being replaced before each shuffle. The repetitions continue until the examined card is a picture card. The number of shuffles is recorded.

(c) Identify an appropriate probability distribution to model the number of shuffles required and write down the mean number of shuffles.

(d) Find the probability of having to conduct the experiment more times than this expected number.

5 The six faces of an ordinary dice are numbered 1 to 6 in the usual fashion, where the total on opposite faces adds up to 7.

(a) State, with justification, the assumption that leads to the probability of a given number appearing on the uppermost face being $\frac{1}{6}$ when the dice is rolled.

(b) Let x be the random variable representing the outcome when the ordinary dice is rolled. Calculate the variance of X.

6 In training, a high jumper, on average, clears a particular height once in every four attempts. The data obtained in training are to be used to model the jumper's performance in a competition.

(a) In the competition the bar is at this height. Write down an estimate of the probability that the jumper fails at the first attempt.

In this competition each competitor is allowed three attempts at each height. If a competitor fails on the first attempt at the height he is allowed a second attempt. If he fails a second time he is allowed a third attempt. After a third failure at the same height he is eliminated from the competition. Any competitor who clears a height at either his first, second or third attempt proceeds to the next height.

(b) Stating clearly any assumptions you make, calculate the probability that the jumper

(i) succeeds at his second attempt at this height,

(ii) proceeds to the next height.

7 A certain type of examination consists of a number of questions all of equal difficulty. In a two-hour test the number of questions answered by a random sample of 1099 pupils is shown in the table.

No. of questions	0–4	5–9	10–14	15–19	20–24	25–29	30–34
No. of pupils	12	98	308	411	217	50	3

(a) Construct a cumulative frequency table and, on graph paper, draw a cumulative frequency curve.

(b) Use your graph to estimate the median and the interquartile range of these data.

(c) It should be possible for 3% of candidates to answer all the questions. Find how many questions the candidates should be asked to answer in the two hours.

8 The probability that a football club has all their first team players fit is 70%. When the club has a fully fit team it wins 90% of its home games. When the first team is not fully fit it wins 40% of its home games.

Calculate the probability that it will win its next home game.

9 A pupil conducting a coin tossing experiment was surprised when she dropped 20 coins on to the floor and obtained only 5 heads.

(a) Calculate, using an appropriate binomial distribution, the probability that 20 fair coins dropped onto the floor at random will show exactly 5 heads.

(b) Use appropriate tables to demonstrate clearly that the probability of obtaining either 5 heads or less, or 15 or more, when 20 coins are dropped at random, is less than 5%.

(c) State the expected number of heads when 20 fair coins are dropped onto the floor.

(d) Comment on the result obtained in part (b).

10 The lengths, in cm, of 19 fern fronds are shown ordered below.

2.3, 2.6, 2.7, 2.8, 3.0, 3.1, 3.2, 3.5, 3.6, 3.8, 4.3, 4.4, 4.9, 4.9, 5.6, 5.9, 6.4, 6.8, 7.2

(a) Present these data in a simple stem-and-leaf display.

(b) Use your display to identify the median length and the interquartile range.

(c) Construct a box-and-whisker plot of these data.

11 A student surveyed the ages, x years, and the prices, £y, of ten second-hand cars, of a particular type, in a local newspaper and obtained the data shown in the table.

Age of car, x (years)	6	2	9	5	13	4	7	8	3	10
Price, £y	2790	5990	850	3100	650	3350	3790	1350	4590	990

(a) Calculate, for these data, the value of Spearman's rank correlation coefficient.

(b) State clearly what the value found in part (a) tells you about the relationship between the variables age and price for this type of car.

12 (a) How many arrangements can be made of the letters of the word *STATISTICS*?

One of these arrangements is chosen at random.

(b) What is the probability that all the Ss are together?

Four letters are chosen at random from the letters of the word *STATISTICS*. Calculate the probability that the selection contains

(c) exactly two vowels,

(d) at least two vowels.

Practice examination 1

Time 1 hour 30 minutes

Answer all the questions.

1 Two magazines assessed the value for money offered by 8 hotels, based on quality of accommodation, standard of service, etc. Each magazine gave a mark out of 25 to each hotel, with higher marks indicating better value. The results are shown in the table.

Hotel	A	B	C	D	E	F	G	H
Mark from magazine 1	13	20	22	18	19	11	10	15
Mark from magazine 2	17	19	23	16	20	10	11	18

Calculate Spearman's rank correlation coefficient for the data, and comment briefly on the assessments made by the two magazines. [6]

2 The box-and-whisker plots in the diagram illustrate the scores in an aptitude test taken by people applying for a job. The scores are expressed on a scale of 0–50, and the results for men and women are shown separately.

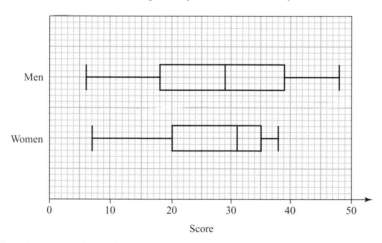

(i) For the men taking the aptitude test, state the value of
    (a) the median score, [1]
    (b) the range of the scores, [1]
    (c) the inter-quartile range of the scores. [1]

(ii) Compare briefly the scores obtained by men and women, stating one similarity and one difference. [2]

(iii) The scores might alternatively have been illustrated by means of a pair of cumulative frequency graphs. State one advantage of cumulative frequency graphs compared with box-and-whisker plots, and one disadvantage. [2]

3 Three married couples, Mr & Mrs Lee, Mr & Mrs Martin, and Mr & Mrs Shah, stand in a line for a photograph to be taken. Find the number of different ways in which these six people can be arranged

   (i) if there are no restrictions on the order in which they stand,   [1]

   (ii) if each man stands next to his wife,   [3]

   (iii) if no man stands next to another man.   [4]

4   (i) State conditions which need to be satisfied for a random variable to be modelled by a geometric distribution, and give one real-life example of a situation where a geometric distribution would be an appropriate model.   [3]

A discrete random variable X has a geometric distribution with mean 3.

   (ii) Calculate

      (a) $P(X = 5)$,   [2]
      (b) $P(X > 5)$.   [2]

   (iii) A random sample of three observations on this distribution is taken. Find the probability that all three observations are greater than 5.   [2]

5 A survey of traffic on a busy road showed that, on average, 75% of the cars using the road carried only the driver, while 25% carried one or more passengers in addition to the driver. Twelve cars using the road are chosen at random. Using tables of binomial probabilities, or otherwise, find the probability that the number of these cars carrying only the driver will be

   (i) exactly 9,   [2]

   (ii) at least 9.   [2]

The survey also showed that, on average, 18% of cars using the road carried exactly 1 passenger in addition to the driver. For a random sample of 20 cars using the road, calculate

   (iii) the expected number of cars carrying exactly 1 passenger,   [1]

   (iv) the probability that the number of cars carrying exactly 1 passenger is less than the expected number.   [4]

6 A bag contains 3 red balls and 2 green balls. Balls are drawn from the bag at random, one by one and without replacement, until a green ball is drawn. The number of draws required is denoted by the random variable X.

   (i) Draw a tree diagram to illustrate the situation, labelling all the outcomes and probabilities clearly.   [3]

   (ii) Hence copy and complete the following table to show the probability distribution of X.   [2]

x	1	2	3	4
$P(X = x)$		$\frac{3}{10}$		

   (iii) Show that $E(X) = 2$ and find $Var(X)$.   [5]

7 The value, in billions of dollars, of 100 companies registered in a certain country is summarised in the table below.

Value of company, $x billion	$1 \leq x < 2$	$2 \leq x < 3$	$3 \leq x < 5$	$5 \leq x < 10$	$10 \leq x < 20$
Number of companies	29	23	15	21	12

(i) Illustrate the data by means of a histogram, drawn accurately on graph paper. [4]

(ii) Calculate an estimate of the mean value of these companies, and explain briefly why your answer is only an estimate of the true mean value. [4]

(iii) The median value of x for these companies is known to be 2.92. State what feature of the data accounts for the mean being considerably greater than the median. [1]

(iv) Explain briefly why the mean might not be considered a very good measure of the 'average' value of the companies. [1]

8

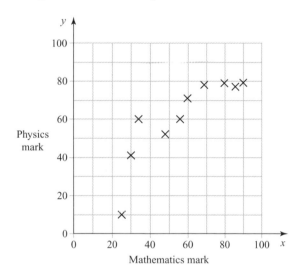

Ten students took end-of-term test papers in Mathematics and Physics. Their marks, x for Mathematics and y for Physics, are illustrated in the diagram, and summary totals are also given.

$$\sum x = 578, \sum y = 607,$$
$$\sum x^2 = 38\,378, \sum y^2 = 41\,221,$$
$$\sum xy = 39\,070.$$

(i) Calculate the product moment correlation coefficient between x and y. [2]

(ii) Explain briefly how the value of this correlation coefficient relates to the diagram. [2]

(iii) Calculate the equation of the regression line of y on x, giving your answer in the form $y = a + bx$. [3]

Two other students, *A* and *B*, were each absent from one test paper. Student *A* scored 85 in Mathematics, and student *B* scored 65 in Physics.

(iv) State for which student it would be appropriate to use the regression line calculated in part (iii) to estimate a mark for the paper which the student did not take, and calculate the estimated mark.   [4]

 (v) Comment briefly on the reliability of the estimated mark found in part (iv).   [2]

Practice examination 2

Time 1 hour 30 minutes

Answer all the questions.

1 The random variable X takes the values 0, 1, 2, 3 only, and its probability distribution is shown in the following table.

x	0	1	2	3
$P(X = x)$	a	b	0.2	0.05

    (i) Show that $a + b = 0.75$.   [1]

    (ii) Given that $E(X) = 1$, find the value of b and deduce the value of a.   [3]

    (iii) Does X have a binomial distribution? Give reasons for your answer.   [2]

2 Two passengers on a cruise were asked to give numerical ratings, out of 100, to ten aspects of the cruise. Their ratings are given in the table.

Aspect	A	B	C	D	E	F	G	H	I	J
Passenger P	100	50	90	40	10	20	80	30	60	70
Passenger Q	70	60	50	98	97	100	90	80	95	75

    (i) Calculate Spearman's rank correlation coefficient.   [5]

    (ii) Explain briefly what your answer tells you about the passengers' ratings.   [1]

3 In a class of 20 pupils, 7 are left-handed and 13 are right-handed. Five pupils are selected at random from the class; the order in which they are chosen is not important.

    (i) Find the number of possible selections in which 2 of the 5 are left-handed and 3 are right-handed.   [3]

    (ii) Find the probability that the sample of 5 will include 2 or fewer who are left-handed.   [4]

4 An amateur weather forecaster has a theory about the chances of flooding affecting the region where he lives. He believes that if there are floods in one year the probability of floods again the next year is 0.7, while if there are no floods one year the probability of no floods the next year is 0.6. Last year, there were no floods in his region.

    (i) Draw a tree diagram showing probabilities for floods and no floods for this year and the next two years, according to the weather forecaster's theory.   [3]

    (ii) Hence find the probability that

        (a) there is flooding in all of these three years,   [2]

        (b) there is flooding in exactly one of these three years.   [3]

5 A game is played in which a contestant spins three fair coins. A prize is won if all three coins show a head.

   (i) Calculate the probability that in a particular game a prize is won.   [1]

   Anna plays the game repeatedly. Let X be the number of games up to and including the game in which she first wins a prize.

   (ii) (a) Give two reasons why a geometric distribution might provide a reasonable model for this situation.   [2]

   (b) State the expectation of the geometric distribution that models X.   [2]

   (iii) Using this geometric distribution, calculate the following probabilities:

   (a) $P(X = 2)$;   [2]

   (b) $P(X < 30)$.   [3]

6 An investigation concerning air pollution and the acidity of a lake was carried out. The acidity of the water was measured on 9 occasions and at the same time a score representing the level of air pollution was recorded. The data are given in the table below.

Air pollution (x)	42	53	30	62	27	11	72	30	85
Acidity (y)	4.7	4.1	4.8	4.1	5.2	6.0	3.5	5.0	3.2

$$\left[\sum x = 412, \quad \sum y = 40.6, \quad \sum x^2 = 23\,476, \quad \sum y^2 = 189.28, \quad \sum xy = 1693.3.\right]$$

   (i) Illustrate the data by means of a suitable diagram.   [3]

   (ii) Calculate the product moment correlation coefficient for the data, and state briefly how the value obtained relates to your diagram in part (i).   [4]

   (iii) It is desired to predict the level of acidity in the lake for a given level of air pollution. Calculate the equation of a regression line that is appropriate for this purpose.   [3]

   (iv) Use this equation to calculate an estimate of the acidity in the lake on a day when the level of air pollution has a score of 50.   [1]

7 Batches of 400 shells in the First World War were classified as 'accepted' or 'rejected' by testing a small number of shells from the batch. Tested shells are either 'good' or 'bad'. The probability that a randomly selected shell is good is p.

   (i) In one testing method, 8 shells from a batch (of 400) are selected at random and tested. The batch is accepted if at least 3 of these 8 shells are good. Taking $p = 0.2$, use cumulative binomial tables to find the probability that the batch is accepted.   [2]

   (ii) In a second testing method, each batch of 400 is subdivided into four sub-batches of 100 shells each. Two shells from each sub-batch are tested, and the sub-batch is accepted if at least one of the two shells is good. Use a binomial distribution, with $p = 0.2$,

   (a) to show that the probability that one particular sub-batch is accepted is 0.36,   [2]

   (b) to find the probability that, out of four sub-batches, at least three are accepted.   [3]

(iii) In a third testing method, 4 shells are selected and the batch (of 400) is accepted if all 4 of the shells are good. The probability that the batch is accepted is 0.01. Assuming a binomial distribution, find the value of p. [2]

(iv) State one condition which must be satisfied by the shells if a binomial model is to be valid, and give a reason why it may not be satisfied in this context. [2]

8 Each car owner in a sample of 100 car owners was asked the age of his or her present car. The results are shown in the table below.

Age of car, t years	$0 \leq t < 2$	$2 \leq t < 4$	$4 \leq t < 6$	$6 \leq t < 10$	$10 \leq t < 15$	$t \geq 15$
Number of cars	25	32	20	12	7	4

(i) Making a suitable assumption about the ages of the oldest cars, draw a cumulative frequency graph on graph paper to illustrate the data. [4]

(ii) Hence find estimates for

(a) the proportion of cars in the sample that are more than 5 years old, [2]

(b) the age which is exceeded by the oldest 15% of cars. [2]

(iii) Use the figures in the table to calculate an estimate of the mean age of the cars. [3]

(iv) Explain briefly why the assumption made in part (i) has no effect on the answers obtained in part (ii) but does have an effect on the calculation in part (iii). [2]

Cumulative binomial probabilities

n = 5

p	0.05	0.10	0.15	1/6	0.20	0.25	0.30	1/3	0.35	0.40	0.45	0.50	0.55	0.60	0.65	2/3	0.70	0.75	0.80	5/6	0.85	0.90	0.95
x = 0	0.7738	0.5905	0.4437	0.4019	0.3277	0.2373	0.1681	0.1317	0.1160	0.0778	0.0503	0.0313	0.0185	0.0102	0.0053	0.0041	0.0024	0.0010	0.0003	0.0001	0.0001	0.0000	0.0000
1	0.9774	0.9185	0.8352	0.8038	0.7373	0.6328	0.5282	0.4609	0.4284	0.3370	0.2562	0.1875	0.1312	0.0870	0.0540	0.0453	0.0308	0.0156	0.0067	0.0033	0.0022	0.0005	0.0000
2	0.9988	0.9914	0.9734	0.9645	0.9421	0.8965	0.8369	0.7901	0.7648	0.6826	0.5931	0.5000	0.4069	0.3174	0.2352	0.2099	0.1631	0.1035	0.0579	0.0355	0.0266	0.0086	0.0012
3	1.0000	0.9995	0.9978	0.9967	0.9933	0.9844	0.9692	0.9547	0.9460	0.9130	0.8688	0.8125	0.7438	0.6630	0.5716	0.5391	0.4718	0.3672	0.2627	0.1962	0.1648	0.0815	0.0226
4	1.0000	1.0000	0.9999	0.9999	0.9997	0.9990	0.9976	0.9959	0.9947	0.9898	0.9815	0.9688	0.9497	0.9222	0.8840	0.8683	0.8319	0.7627	0.6723	0.5981	0.5563	0.4095	0.2262
5	1.0000	1.0000	1.0000	1.0000	1.0000	1.0000	1.0000	1.0000	1.0000	1.0000	1.0000	1.0000	1.0000	1.0000	1.0000	1.0000	1.0000	1.0000	1.0000	1.0000	1.0000	1.0000	1.0000

n = 6

p	0.05	0.10	0.15	1/6	0.20	0.25	0.30	1/3	0.35	0.40	0.45	0.50	0.55	0.60	0.65	2/3	0.70	0.75	0.80	5/6	0.85	0.90	0.95
x = 0	0.7351	0.5314	0.3771	0.3349	0.2621	0.1780	0.1176	0.0878	0.0754	0.0467	0.0277	0.0156	0.0083	0.0041	0.0018	0.0014	0.0007	0.0002	0.0001	0.0000	0.0000	0.0000	0.0000
1	0.9672	0.8857	0.7765	0.7368	0.6554	0.5339	0.4202	0.3512	0.3191	0.2333	0.1636	0.1094	0.0692	0.0410	0.0223	0.0178	0.0109	0.0046	0.0016	0.0007	0.0004	0.0001	0.0000
2	0.9978	0.9842	0.9527	0.9377	0.9011	0.8306	0.7443	0.6804	0.6471	0.5443	0.4415	0.3438	0.2553	0.1792	0.1174	0.1001	0.0705	0.0376	0.0170	0.0087	0.0059	0.0013	0.0001
3	0.9999	0.9987	0.9941	0.9913	0.9830	0.9624	0.9295	0.8999	0.8826	0.8208	0.7447	0.6563	0.5585	0.4557	0.3529	0.3196	0.2557	0.1694	0.0989	0.0623	0.0473	0.0159	0.0022
4	1.0000	0.9999	0.9996	0.9993	0.9984	0.9954	0.9891	0.9822	0.9777	0.9590	0.9308	0.8906	0.8364	0.7667	0.6809	0.6488	0.5798	0.4661	0.3446	0.2632	0.2235	0.1143	0.0328
5	1.0000	1.0000	1.0000	1.0000	0.9999	0.9998	0.9993	0.9986	0.9982	0.9959	0.9917	0.9844	0.9723	0.9533	0.9246	0.9122	0.8824	0.8220	0.7379	0.6651	0.6229	0.4686	0.2649
6	1.0000	1.0000	1.0000	1.0000	1.0000	1.0000	1.0000	1.0000	1.0000	1.0000	1.0000	1.0000	1.0000	1.0000	1.0000	1.0000	1.0000	1.0000	1.0000	1.0000	1.0000	1.0000	1.0000

n = 7

p	0.05	0.10	0.15	1/6	0.20	0.25	0.30	1/3	0.35	0.40	0.45	0.50	0.55	0.60	0.65	2/3	0.70	0.75	0.80	5/6	0.85	0.90	0.95
x = 0	0.6983	0.4783	0.3206	0.2791	0.2097	0.1335	0.0824	0.0585	0.0490	0.0280	0.0152	0.0078	0.0037	0.0016	0.0006	0.0005	0.0002	0.0001	0.0000	0.0000	0.0000	0.0000	0.0000
1	0.9556	0.8503	0.7166	0.6698	0.5767	0.4449	0.3294	0.2634	0.2338	0.1586	0.1024	0.0625	0.0357	0.0188	0.0090	0.0069	0.0038	0.0013	0.0004	0.0001	0.0001	0.0000	0.0000
2	0.9962	0.9743	0.9262	0.9042	0.8520	0.7564	0.6471	0.5706	0.5323	0.4199	0.3164	0.2266	0.1529	0.0963	0.0556	0.0453	0.0288	0.0129	0.0047	0.0020	0.0012	0.0002	0.0000
3	0.9998	0.9973	0.9879	0.9824	0.9667	0.9294	0.8740	0.8267	0.8002	0.7102	0.6083	0.5000	0.3917	0.2898	0.1998	0.1733	0.1260	0.0706	0.0333	0.0176	0.0121	0.0027	0.0002
4	1.0000	0.9998	0.9988	0.9980	0.9953	0.9871	0.9712	0.9547	0.9444	0.9037	0.8471	0.7734	0.6836	0.5801	0.4677	0.4294	0.3529	0.2436	0.1480	0.0958	0.0738	0.0257	0.0038
5	1.0000	1.0000	0.9999	0.9999	0.9996	0.9987	0.9962	0.9931	0.9910	0.9812	0.9643	0.9375	0.8976	0.8414	0.7662	0.7366	0.6706	0.5551	0.4233	0.3302	0.2834	0.1497	0.0444
6	1.0000	1.0000	1.0000	1.0000	1.0000	0.9999	0.9998	0.9995	0.9994	0.9984	0.9963	0.9922	0.9848	0.9720	0.9510	0.9415	0.9176	0.8665	0.7903	0.7209	0.6794	0.5217	0.3017
7	1.0000	1.0000	1.0000	1.0000	1.0000	1.0000	1.0000	1.0000	1.0000	1.0000	1.0000	1.0000	1.0000	1.0000	1.0000	1.0000	1.0000	1.0000	1.0000	1.0000	1.0000	1.0000	1.0000

n = 8

p	0.05	0.10	0.15	1/6	0.20	0.25	0.30	1/3	0.35	0.40	0.45	0.50	0.55	0.60	0.65	2/3	0.70	0.75	0.80	5/6	0.85	0.90	0.95
x = 0	0.6634	0.4305	0.2725	0.2326	0.1678	0.1001	0.0576	0.0390	0.0319	0.0168	0.0084	0.0039	0.0017	0.0007	0.0002	0.0002	0.0001	0.0000	0.0000	0.0000	0.0000	0.0000	0.0000
1	0.9428	0.8131	0.6572	0.6047	0.5033	0.3671	0.2553	0.1951	0.1691	0.1064	0.0632	0.0352	0.0181	0.0085	0.0036	0.0026	0.0013	0.0004	0.0001	0.0000	0.0000	0.0000	0.0000
2	0.9942	0.9619	0.8948	0.8652	0.7969	0.6785	0.5518	0.4682	0.4278	0.3154	0.2201	0.1445	0.0885	0.0498	0.0253	0.0197	0.0113	0.0042	0.0012	0.0004	0.0002	0.0000	0.0000
3	0.9996	0.9950	0.9786	0.9693	0.9437	0.8862	0.8059	0.7414	0.7064	0.5941	0.4770	0.3633	0.2604	0.1737	0.1061	0.0879	0.0580	0.0273	0.0104	0.0046	0.0029	0.0004	0.0000
4	1.0000	0.9996	0.9971	0.9954	0.9896	0.9727	0.9420	0.9121	0.8939	0.8263	0.7396	0.6367	0.5230	0.4059	0.2936	0.2586	0.1941	0.1138	0.0563	0.0307	0.0214	0.0050	0.0004
5	1.0000	1.0000	0.9998	0.9996	0.9988	0.9958	0.9887	0.9803	0.9747	0.9502	0.9115	0.8555	0.7799	0.6846	0.5722	0.5318	0.4482	0.3215	0.2031	0.1348	0.1052	0.0381	0.0058
6	1.0000	1.0000	1.0000	1.0000	0.9999	0.9996	0.9987	0.9974	0.9964	0.9915	0.9819	0.9648	0.9368	0.8936	0.8309	0.8049	0.7447	0.6329	0.4967	0.3953	0.3428	0.1869	0.0572
7	1.0000	1.0000	1.0000	1.0000	1.0000	1.0000	0.9999	0.9998	0.9998	0.9993	0.9983	0.9961	0.9916	0.9832	0.9681	0.9610	0.9424	0.8999	0.8322	0.7674	0.7275	0.5695	0.3366
8	1.0000	1.0000	1.0000	1.0000	1.0000	1.0000	1.0000	1.0000	1.0000	1.0000	1.0000	1.0000	1.0000	1.0000	1.0000	1.0000	1.0000	1.0000	1.0000	1.0000	1.0000	1.0000	1.0000

n = 9

p	0.05	0.10	0.15	1/6	0.20	0.25	0.30	1/3	0.35	0.40	0.45	0.50	0.55	0.60	0.65	2/3	0.70	0.75	0.80	5/6	0.85	0.90	0.95
x = 0	0.6302	0.3874	0.2316	0.1938	0.1342	0.0751	0.0404	0.0260	0.0207	0.0101	0.0046	0.0020	0.0008	0.0003	0.0001	0.0001	0.0000	0.0000	0.0000	0.0000	0.0000	0.0000	0.0000
1	0.9288	0.7748	0.5995	0.5427	0.4362	0.3003	0.1960	0.1431	0.1211	0.0705	0.0385	0.0195	0.0091	0.0038	0.0014	0.0010	0.0004	0.0001	0.0000	0.0000	0.0000	0.0000	0.0000
2	0.9916	0.9470	0.8591	0.8217	0.7382	0.6007	0.4628	0.3772	0.3373	0.2318	0.1495	0.0898	0.0498	0.0250	0.0112	0.0083	0.0043	0.0013	0.0003	0.0001	0.0000	0.0000	0.0000
3	0.9994	0.9917	0.9661	0.9520	0.9144	0.8343	0.7297	0.6503	0.6089	0.4826	0.3614	0.2539	0.1658	0.0994	0.0536	0.0424	0.0253	0.0100	0.0031	0.0011	0.0006	0.0001	0.0000
4	1.0000	0.9991	0.9944	0.9910	0.9804	0.9511	0.9012	0.8552	0.8283	0.7334	0.6214	0.5000	0.3786	0.2666	0.1717	0.1448	0.0988	0.0489	0.0196	0.0090	0.0056	0.0009	0.0000
5	1.0000	0.9999	0.9994	0.9989	0.9969	0.9900	0.9747	0.9576	0.9464	0.9006	0.8342	0.7461	0.6386	0.5174	0.3911	0.3497	0.2703	0.1657	0.0856	0.0480	0.0339	0.0083	0.0006
6	1.0000	1.0000	1.0000	0.9999	0.9997	0.9987	0.9957	0.9917	0.9888	0.9750	0.9502	0.9102	0.8505	0.7682	0.6627	0.6228	0.5372	0.3993	0.2618	0.1783	0.1409	0.0530	0.0084
7	1.0000	1.0000	1.0000	1.0000	1.0000	0.9999	0.9996	0.9990	0.9986	0.9962	0.9909	0.9805	0.9615	0.9295	0.8789	0.8569	0.8040	0.6997	0.5638	0.4573	0.4005	0.2252	0.0712
8	1.0000	1.0000	1.0000	1.0000	1.0000	1.0000	1.0000	0.9999	0.9999	0.9997	0.9992	0.9980	0.9954	0.9899	0.9793	0.9740	0.9596	0.9249	0.8658	0.8062	0.7684	0.6126	0.3698
9	1.0000	1.0000	1.0000	1.0000	1.0000	1.0000	1.0000	1.0000	1.0000	1.0000	1.0000	1.0000	1.0000	1.0000	1.0000	1.0000	1.0000	1.0000	1.0000	1.0000	1.0000	1.0000	1.0000

n = 10

p	0.05	0.10	0.15	1/6	0.20	0.25	0.30	1/3	0.35	0.40	0.45	0.50	0.55	0.60	0.65	2/3	0.70	0.75	0.80	5/6	0.85	0.90	0.95
x = 0	0.5987	0.3487	0.1969	0.1615	0.1074	0.0563	0.0282	0.0173	0.0135	0.0060	0.0025	0.0010	0.0003	0.0001	0.0000	0.0000	0.0000	0.0000	0.0000	0.0000	0.0000	0.0000	0.0000
1	0.9139	0.7361	0.5443	0.4845	0.3758	0.2440	0.1493	0.1040	0.0860	0.0464	0.0233	0.0107	0.0045	0.0017	0.0005	0.0004	0.0001	0.0000	0.0000	0.0000	0.0000	0.0000	0.0000
2	0.9885	0.9298	0.8202	0.7752	0.6778	0.5256	0.3828	0.2991	0.2616	0.1673	0.0996	0.0547	0.0274	0.0123	0.0048	0.0034	0.0016	0.0004	0.0001	0.0000	0.0000	0.0000	0.0000
3	0.9990	0.9872	0.9500	0.9303	0.8791	0.7759	0.6496	0.5593	0.5138	0.3823	0.2660	0.1719	0.1020	0.0548	0.0260	0.0197	0.0106	0.0035	0.0009	0.0003	0.0001	0.0000	0.0000
4	0.9999	0.9984	0.9901	0.9845	0.9672	0.9219	0.8497	0.7869	0.7515	0.6331	0.5044	0.3770	0.2616	0.1662	0.0949	0.0766	0.0473	0.0197	0.0064	0.0024	0.0014	0.0001	0.0000
5	1.0000	0.9999	0.9986	0.9976	0.9936	0.9803	0.9527	0.9234	0.9051	0.8338	0.7384	0.6230	0.4956	0.3669	0.2485	0.2131	0.1503	0.0781	0.0328	0.0155	0.0099	0.0016	0.0001
6	1.0000	1.0000	0.9999	0.9997	0.9991	0.9965	0.9894	0.9803	0.9740	0.9452	0.8980	0.8281	0.7340	0.6177	0.4862	0.4407	0.3504	0.2241	0.1209	0.0697	0.0500	0.0128	0.0010
7	1.0000	1.0000	1.0000	1.0000	0.9999	0.9996	0.9984	0.9966	0.9952	0.9877	0.9726	0.9453	0.9004	0.8327	0.7384	0.7009	0.6172	0.4744	0.3222	0.2248	0.1798	0.0702	0.0115
8	1.0000	1.0000	1.0000	1.0000	1.0000	1.0000	0.9999	0.9996	0.9995	0.9983	0.9955	0.9893	0.9767	0.9536	0.9140	0.8960	0.8507	0.7560	0.6242	0.5155	0.4557	0.2639	0.0861
9	1.0000	1.0000	1.0000	1.0000	1.0000	1.0000	1.0000	1.0000	1.0000	0.9999	0.9997	0.9990	0.9975	0.9940	0.9865	0.9827	0.9718	0.9437	0.8926	0.8385	0.8031	0.6513	0.4013
10	1.0000	1.0000	1.0000	1.0000	1.0000	1.0000	1.0000	1.0000	1.0000	1.0000	1.0000	1.0000	1.0000	1.0000	1.0000	1.0000	1.0000	1.0000	1.0000	1.0000	1.0000	1.0000	1.0000

n = 12

p	0.05	0.10	0.15	1/6	0.20	0.25	0.30	1/3	0.35	0.40	0.45	0.50	0.55	0.60	0.65	2/3	0.70	0.75	0.80	5/6	0.85	0.90	0.95
x = 0	0.5404	0.2824	0.1422	0.1122	0.0687	0.0317	0.0138	0.0077	0.0057	0.0022	0.0008	0.0002	0.0001	0.0000	0.0000	0.0000	0.0000	0.0000	0.0000	0.0000	0.0000	0.0000	0.0000
1	0.8816	0.6590	0.4435	0.3813	0.2749	0.1584	0.0850	0.0540	0.0424	0.0196	0.0083	0.0032	0.0011	0.0003	0.0001	0.0000	0.0000	0.0000	0.0000	0.0000	0.0000	0.0000	0.0000
2	0.9804	0.8891	0.7358	0.6774	0.5583	0.3907	0.2528	0.1811	0.1513	0.0834	0.0421	0.0193	0.0079	0.0028	0.0008	0.0005	0.0002	0.0000	0.0000	0.0000	0.0000	0.0000	0.0000
3	0.9978	0.9744	0.9078	0.8748	0.7946	0.6488	0.4925	0.3931	0.3467	0.2253	0.1345	0.0730	0.0356	0.0153	0.0056	0.0039	0.0017	0.0004	0.0001	0.0000	0.0000	0.0000	0.0000
4	0.9998	0.9957	0.9761	0.9636	0.9274	0.8424	0.7237	0.6315	0.5833	0.4382	0.3044	0.1938	0.1117	0.0573	0.0255	0.0188	0.0095	0.0028	0.0006	0.0002	0.0001	0.0000	0.0000
5	1.0000	0.9995	0.9954	0.9921	0.9806	0.9456	0.8822	0.8223	0.7873	0.6652	0.5269	0.3872	0.2607	0.1582	0.0846	0.0664	0.0386	0.0143	0.0039	0.0013	0.0007	0.0001	0.0000
6	1.0000	0.9999	0.9993	0.9987	0.9961	0.9857	0.9614	0.9336	0.9154	0.8418	0.7393	0.6128	0.4731	0.3348	0.2127	0.1777	0.1178	0.0544	0.0194	0.0079	0.0046	0.0005	0.0000
7	1.0000	1.0000	0.9999	0.9998	0.9994	0.9972	0.9905	0.9812	0.9745	0.9427	0.8883	0.8062	0.6956	0.5618	0.4167	0.3685	0.2763	0.1576	0.0726	0.0364	0.0239	0.0043	0.0002
8	1.0000	1.0000	1.0000	1.0000	0.9999	0.9996	0.9983	0.9961	0.9944	0.9847	0.9644	0.9270	0.8655	0.7747	0.6533	0.6069	0.5075	0.3512	0.2054	0.1252	0.0922	0.0256	0.0022
9	1.0000	1.0000	1.0000	1.0000	1.0000	1.0000	0.9998	0.9995	0.9992	0.9972	0.9921	0.9807	0.9579	0.9166	0.8487	0.8189	0.7472	0.6093	0.4417	0.3226	0.2642	0.1109	0.0196
10	1.0000	1.0000	1.0000	1.0000	1.0000	1.0000	1.0000	1.0000	0.9999	0.9997	0.9989	0.9968	0.9917	0.9804	0.9576	0.9460	0.9150	0.8416	0.7251	0.6187	0.5565	0.3410	0.1184
11	1.0000	1.0000	1.0000	1.0000	1.0000	1.0000	1.0000	1.0000	1.0000	1.0000	0.9999	0.9998	0.9992	0.9978	0.9943	0.9923	0.9862	0.9683	0.9313	0.8878	0.8578	0.7176	0.4596

Cumulative binomial probabilities

$n = 14$

p	0.05	0.10	0.15	1/6	0.20	0.25	0.30	1/3	0.35	0.40	0.45	0.50	0.55	0.60	0.65	2/3	0.70	0.75	0.80	5/6	0.85	0.90	0.95
$x = 0$	0.4877	0.2288	0.1028	0.0779	0.0440	0.0178	0.0068	0.0034	0.0024	0.0008	0.0002	0.0001	0.0000	0.0000	0.0000	0.0000	0.0000	0.0000	0.0000	0.0000	0.0000	0.0000	0.0000
1	0.8470	0.5846	0.3567	0.2960	0.1979	0.1010	0.0475	0.0274	0.0205	0.0081	0.0029	0.0009	0.0003	0.0001	0.0000	0.0000	0.0000	0.0000	0.0000	0.0000	0.0000	0.0000	0.0000
2	0.9699	0.8416	0.6479	0.5795	0.4481	0.2811	0.1608	0.1053	0.0839	0.0398	0.0170	0.0065	0.0022	0.0006	0.0001	0.0001	0.0000	0.0000	0.0000	0.0000	0.0000	0.0000	0.0000
3	0.9958	0.9559	0.8535	0.8063	0.6982	0.5213	0.3552	0.2612	0.2205	0.1243	0.0632	0.0287	0.0114	0.0039	0.0011	0.0007	0.0002	0.0000	0.0000	0.0000	0.0000	0.0000	0.0000
4	0.9996	0.9908	0.9533	0.9310	0.8702	0.7415	0.5842	0.4755	0.4227	0.2793	0.1672	0.0898	0.0426	0.0175	0.0060	0.0040	0.0017	0.0003	0.0000	0.0000	0.0000	0.0000	0.0000
5	1.0000	0.9985	0.9885	0.9809	0.9561	0.8883	0.7805	0.6898	0.6405	0.4859	0.3373	0.2120	0.1189	0.0583	0.0243	0.0174	0.0083	0.0022	0.0004	0.0001	0.0000	0.0000	0.0000
6	1.0000	0.9998	0.9978	0.9959	0.9884	0.9617	0.9067	0.8505	0.8164	0.6925	0.5461	0.3953	0.2586	0.1501	0.0753	0.0576	0.0315	0.0103	0.0024	0.0007	0.0003	0.0000	0.0000
7	1.0000	1.0000	0.9997	0.9993	0.9976	0.9897	0.9685	0.9424	0.9247	0.8499	0.7414	0.6047	0.4539	0.3075	0.1836	0.1495	0.0933	0.0383	0.0116	0.0041	0.0022	0.0002	0.0000
8	1.0000	1.0000	1.0000	0.9999	0.9996	0.9978	0.9917	0.9826	0.9757	0.9417	0.8811	0.7880	0.6627	0.5141	0.3595	0.3102	0.2195	0.1117	0.0439	0.0191	0.0115	0.0015	0.0000
9	1.0000	1.0000	1.0000	1.0000	1.0000	0.9997	0.9983	0.9960	0.9940	0.9825	0.9574	0.9102	0.8328	0.7207	0.5773	0.5245	0.4158	0.2585	0.1298	0.0690	0.0467	0.0092	0.0004
10	1.0000	1.0000	1.0000	1.0000	1.0000	1.0000	0.9998	0.9993	0.9989	0.9961	0.9886	0.9713	0.9368	0.8757	0.7795	0.7388	0.6448	0.4787	0.3018	0.1937	0.1465	0.0441	0.0042
11	1.0000	1.0000	1.0000	1.0000	1.0000	1.0000	1.0000	0.9999	0.9999	0.9994	0.9978	0.9935	0.9830	0.9602	0.9161	0.8947	0.8392	0.7189	0.5519	0.4205	0.3521	0.1584	0.0301
12	1.0000	1.0000	1.0000	1.0000	1.0000	1.0000	1.0000	1.0000	1.0000	0.9999	0.9997	0.9991	0.9971	0.9919	0.9795	0.9726	0.9525	0.8990	0.8021	0.7040	0.6433	0.4154	0.1530
13	1.0000	1.0000	1.0000	1.0000	1.0000	1.0000	1.0000	1.0000	1.0000	1.0000	1.0000	0.9999	0.9998	0.9992	0.9976	0.9966	0.9932	0.9822	0.9560	0.9221	0.8972	0.7712	0.5123
14	1.0000	1.0000	1.0000	1.0000	1.0000	1.0000	1.0000	1.0000	1.0000	1.0000	1.0000	1.0000	1.0000	1.0000	1.0000	1.0000	1.0000	1.0000	1.0000	1.0000	1.0000	1.0000	1.0000

$n = 16$

p	0.05	0.10	0.15	1/6	0.20	0.25	0.30	1/3	0.35	0.40	0.45	0.50	0.55	0.60	0.65	2/3	0.70	0.75	0.80	5/6	0.85	0.90	0.95
$x = 0$	0.4401	0.1853	0.0743	0.0541	0.0281	0.0100	0.0033	0.0015	0.0010	0.0003	0.0001	0.0000	0.0000	0.0000	0.0000	0.0000	0.0000	0.0000	0.0000	0.0000	0.0000	0.0000	0.0000
1	0.8108	0.5147	0.2839	0.2272	0.1407	0.0635	0.0261	0.0137	0.0098	0.0033	0.0010	0.0003	0.0001	0.0000	0.0000	0.0000	0.0000	0.0000	0.0000	0.0000	0.0000	0.0000	0.0000
2	0.9571	0.7892	0.5614	0.4868	0.3518	0.1971	0.0994	0.0594	0.0451	0.0183	0.0066	0.0021	0.0006	0.0001	0.0000	0.0000	0.0000	0.0000	0.0000	0.0000	0.0000	0.0000	0.0000
3	0.9930	0.9316	0.7899	0.7291	0.5981	0.4050	0.2459	0.1659	0.1339	0.0651	0.0281	0.0106	0.0035	0.0009	0.0002	0.0001	0.0000	0.0000	0.0000	0.0000	0.0000	0.0000	0.0000
4	0.9991	0.9830	0.9209	0.8866	0.7982	0.6302	0.4499	0.3391	0.2892	0.1666	0.0853	0.0384	0.0149	0.0049	0.0013	0.0008	0.0003	0.0000	0.0000	0.0000	0.0000	0.0000	0.0000
5	0.9999	0.9967	0.9765	0.9622	0.9183	0.8103	0.6598	0.5469	0.4900	0.3288	0.1976	0.1051	0.0486	0.0191	0.0062	0.0040	0.0016	0.0003	0.0000	0.0000	0.0000	0.0000	0.0000
6	1.0000	0.9995	0.9944	0.9899	0.9733	0.9204	0.8247	0.7374	0.6881	0.5272	0.3660	0.2272	0.1241	0.0583	0.0229	0.0159	0.0071	0.0016	0.0002	0.0000	0.0000	0.0000	0.0000
7	1.0000	0.9999	0.9989	0.9979	0.9930	0.9729	0.9256	0.8735	0.8406	0.7161	0.5629	0.4018	0.2559	0.1423	0.0671	0.0500	0.0257	0.0075	0.0015	0.0004	0.0002	0.0000	0.0000
8	1.0000	1.0000	0.9998	0.9996	0.9985	0.9925	0.9743	0.9500	0.9329	0.8577	0.7441	0.5982	0.4371	0.2839	0.1594	0.1265	0.0744	0.0271	0.0070	0.0021	0.0011	0.0001	0.0000
9	1.0000	1.0000	1.0000	1.0000	0.9998	0.9984	0.9929	0.9841	0.9771	0.9417	0.8759	0.7728	0.6340	0.4728	0.3119	0.2626	0.1753	0.0796	0.0267	0.0101	0.0056	0.0005	0.0000
10	1.0000	1.0000	1.0000	1.0000	1.0000	0.9997	0.9984	0.9960	0.9938	0.9809	0.9514	0.8949	0.8024	0.6712	0.5100	0.4531	0.3402	0.1897	0.0817	0.0378	0.0235	0.0033	0.0001
11	1.0000	1.0000	1.0000	1.0000	1.0000	1.0000	0.9997	0.9992	0.9987	0.9951	0.9851	0.9616	0.9147	0.8334	0.7108	0.6609	0.5501	0.3698	0.2018	0.1134	0.0791	0.0170	0.0009
12	1.0000	1.0000	1.0000	1.0000	1.0000	1.0000	1.0000	0.9999	0.9998	0.9991	0.9965	0.9894	0.9719	0.9349	0.8661	0.8341	0.7541	0.5950	0.4019	0.2709	0.2101	0.0684	0.0070
13	1.0000	1.0000	1.0000	1.0000	1.0000	1.0000	1.0000	1.0000	1.0000	0.9999	0.9994	0.9979	0.9934	0.9817	0.9549	0.9406	0.9006	0.8029	0.6482	0.5132	0.4386	0.2108	0.0429
14	1.0000	1.0000	1.0000	1.0000	1.0000	1.0000	1.0000	1.0000	1.0000	1.0000	0.9999	0.9997	0.9990	0.9967	0.9902	0.9863	0.9739	0.9365	0.8593	0.7728	0.7161	0.4853	0.1892
15	1.0000	1.0000	1.0000	1.0000	1.0000	1.0000	1.0000	1.0000	1.0000	1.0000	1.0000	1.0000	0.9999	0.9997	0.9990	0.9985	0.9967	0.9900	0.9719	0.9459	0.9257	0.8147	0.5599

$n = 18$

p	0.05	0.10	0.15	1/6	0.20	0.25	0.30	1/3	0.35	0.40	0.45	0.50	0.55	0.60	0.65	2/3	0.70	0.75	0.80	5/6	0.85	0.90	0.95
$x=0$	0.3972	0.1501	0.0536	0.0376	0.0180	0.0056	0.0016	0.0007	0.0004	0.0001	0.0000	0.0000	0.0000	0.0000	0.0000	0.0000	0.0000	0.0000	0.0000	0.0000	0.0000	0.0000	0.0000
1	0.7735	0.4503	0.2241	0.1728	0.0991	0.0395	0.0142	0.0068	0.0046	0.0013	0.0003	0.0000	0.0000	0.0000	0.0000	0.0000	0.0000	0.0000	0.0000	0.0000	0.0000	0.0000	0.0000
2	0.9419	0.7338	0.4797	0.4027	0.2713	0.1353	0.0600	0.0326	0.0236	0.0082	0.0025	0.0007	0.0001	0.0000	0.0000	0.0000	0.0000	0.0000	0.0000	0.0000	0.0000	0.0000	0.0000
3	0.9891	0.9018	0.7202	0.6479	0.5010	0.3057	0.1646	0.1017	0.0783	0.0328	0.0120	0.0038	0.0010	0.0002	0.0000	0.0000	0.0000	0.0000	0.0000	0.0000	0.0000	0.0000	0.0000
4	0.9985	0.9718	0.8794	0.8318	0.7164	0.5187	0.3327	0.2311	0.1886	0.0942	0.0411	0.0154	0.0049	0.0013	0.0003	0.0001	0.0000	0.0000	0.0000	0.0000	0.0000	0.0000	0.0000
5	0.9998	0.9936	0.9581	0.9347	0.8671	0.7175	0.5344	0.4122	0.3550	0.2088	0.1077	0.0481	0.0183	0.0058	0.0014	0.0009	0.0003	0.0000	0.0000	0.0000	0.0000	0.0000	0.0000
6	1.0000	0.9988	0.9882	0.9794	0.9487	0.8610	0.7217	0.6085	0.5491	0.3743	0.2258	0.1189	0.0537	0.0203	0.0062	0.0039	0.0014	0.0002	0.0000	0.0000	0.0000	0.0000	0.0000
7	1.0000	0.9998	0.9973	0.9947	0.9837	0.9431	0.8593	0.7767	0.7283	0.5634	0.3915	0.2403	0.1280	0.0576	0.0212	0.0144	0.0061	0.0012	0.0002	0.0000	0.0000	0.0000	0.0000
8	1.0000	1.0000	0.9995	0.9989	0.9957	0.9807	0.9404	0.8924	0.8609	0.7368	0.5778	0.4073	0.2527	0.1347	0.0597	0.0433	0.0210	0.0054	0.0009	0.0002	0.0001	0.0000	0.0000
9	1.0000	1.0000	0.9999	0.9998	0.9991	0.9946	0.9790	0.9567	0.9403	0.8653	0.7473	0.5927	0.4222	0.2632	0.1391	0.1076	0.0596	0.0193	0.0043	0.0011	0.0005	0.0000	0.0000
10	1.0000	1.0000	1.0000	1.0000	0.9998	0.9988	0.9939	0.9856	0.9788	0.9424	0.8720	0.7597	0.6085	0.4366	0.2717	0.2233	0.1407	0.0569	0.0163	0.0053	0.0027	0.0002	0.0000
11	1.0000	1.0000	1.0000	1.0000	1.0000	0.9998	0.9986	0.9961	0.9938	0.9797	0.9463	0.8811	0.7742	0.6257	0.4509	0.3915	0.2783	0.1390	0.0513	0.0206	0.0118	0.0012	0.0000
12	1.0000	1.0000	1.0000	1.0000	1.0000	1.0000	0.9997	0.9991	0.9986	0.9942	0.9817	0.9519	0.8923	0.7912	0.6450	0.5878	0.4656	0.2825	0.1329	0.0653	0.0419	0.0064	0.0002
13	1.0000	1.0000	1.0000	1.0000	1.0000	1.0000	1.0000	0.9999	0.9997	0.9987	0.9951	0.9846	0.9589	0.9058	0.8114	0.7689	0.6673	0.4813	0.2836	0.1682	0.1206	0.0282	0.0015
14	1.0000	1.0000	1.0000	1.0000	1.0000	1.0000	1.0000	1.0000	1.0000	0.9998	0.9990	0.9962	0.9880	0.9672	0.9217	0.8983	0.8354	0.6943	0.4990	0.3521	0.2798	0.0982	0.0109
15	1.0000	1.0000	1.0000	1.0000	1.0000	1.0000	1.0000	1.0000	1.0000	1.0000	0.9999	0.9993	0.9975	0.9918	0.9764	0.9674	0.9400	0.8647	0.7287	0.5973	0.5203	0.2662	0.0581
16	1.0000	1.0000	1.0000	1.0000	1.0000	1.0000	1.0000	1.0000	1.0000	1.0000	1.0000	1.0000	0.9999	0.9997	0.9987	0.9954	0.9932	0.9858	0.9605	0.9009	0.8272	0.5497	0.2265
17	1.0000	1.0000	1.0000	1.0000	1.0000	1.0000	1.0000	1.0000	1.0000	1.0000	1.0000	1.0000	1.0000	0.9999	0.9996	0.9993	0.9984	0.9944	0.9820	0.9624	0.9464	0.8499	0.6028
18	1.0000	1.0000	1.0000	1.0000	1.0000	1.0000	1.0000	1.0000	1.0000	1.0000	1.0000	1.0000	1.0000	1.0000	1.0000	1.0000	1.0000	1.0000	1.0000	1.0000	1.0000	1.0000	1.0000

$n = 20$

p	0.05	0.10	0.15	1/6	0.20	0.25	0.30	1/3	0.35	0.40	0.45	0.50	0.55	0.60	0.65	2/3	0.70	0.75	0.80	5/6	0.85	0.90	0.95
$x=0$	0.3585	0.1216	0.0388	0.0261	0.0115	0.0032	0.0008	0.0003	0.0002	0.0000	0.0000	0.0000	0.0000	0.0000	0.0000	0.0000	0.0000	0.0000	0.0000	0.0000	0.0000	0.0000	0.0000
1	0.7358	0.3917	0.1756	0.1304	0.0692	0.0243	0.0076	0.0033	0.0021	0.0005	0.0001	0.0000	0.0000	0.0000	0.0000	0.0000	0.0000	0.0000	0.0000	0.0000	0.0000	0.0000	0.0000
2	0.9245	0.6769	0.4049	0.3287	0.2061	0.0913	0.0355	0.0176	0.0121	0.0036	0.0009	0.0002	0.0000	0.0000	0.0000	0.0000	0.0000	0.0000	0.0000	0.0000	0.0000	0.0000	0.0000
3	0.9841	0.8670	0.6477	0.5665	0.4114	0.2252	0.1071	0.0604	0.0444	0.0160	0.0049	0.0013	0.0003	0.0000	0.0000	0.0000	0.0000	0.0000	0.0000	0.0000	0.0000	0.0000	0.0000
4	0.9974	0.9568	0.8298	0.7687	0.6296	0.4148	0.2375	0.1515	0.1182	0.0510	0.0189	0.0059	0.0015	0.0003	0.0000	0.0000	0.0000	0.0000	0.0000	0.0000	0.0000	0.0000	0.0000
5	0.9997	0.9887	0.9327	0.8982	0.8042	0.6172	0.4164	0.2972	0.2454	0.1256	0.0553	0.0207	0.0064	0.0016	0.0003	0.0002	0.0000	0.0000	0.0000	0.0000	0.0000	0.0000	0.0000
6	1.0000	0.9976	0.9781	0.9629	0.9133	0.7858	0.6080	0.4793	0.4166	0.2500	0.1299	0.0577	0.0214	0.0065	0.0015	0.0009	0.0003	0.0000	0.0000	0.0000	0.0000	0.0000	0.0000
7	1.0000	0.9996	0.9941	0.9887	0.9679	0.8982	0.7723	0.6615	0.6010	0.4159	0.2520	0.1316	0.0580	0.0210	0.0060	0.0037	0.0013	0.0002	0.0000	0.0000	0.0000	0.0000	0.0000
8	1.0000	0.9999	0.9987	0.9972	0.9900	0.9591	0.8867	0.8095	0.7624	0.5956	0.4143	0.2517	0.1308	0.0565	0.0196	0.0130	0.0051	0.0009	0.0001	0.0000	0.0000	0.0000	0.0000
9	1.0000	1.0000	0.9998	0.9994	0.9974	0.9861	0.9520	0.9081	0.8782	0.7553	0.5914	0.4119	0.2493	0.1275	0.0532	0.0376	0.0171	0.0039	0.0006	0.0001	0.0000	0.0000	0.0000
10	1.0000	1.0000	0.9999	0.9999	0.9994	0.9961	0.9829	0.9624	0.9468	0.8725	0.7507	0.5881	0.4086	0.2447	0.1218	0.0919	0.0480	0.0139	0.0026	0.0006	0.0002	0.0000	0.0000
11	1.0000	1.0000	1.0000	1.0000	0.9999	0.9991	0.9949	0.9870	0.9804	0.9435	0.8692	0.7483	0.5857	0.4044	0.2376	0.1905	0.1133	0.0409	0.0100	0.0028	0.0013	0.0001	0.0000
12	1.0000	1.0000	1.0000	1.0000	1.0000	0.9998	0.9987	0.9963	0.9940	0.9790	0.9420	0.8684	0.7480	0.5841	0.3990	0.3385	0.2277	0.1018	0.0321	0.0113	0.0059	0.0004	0.0000
13	1.0000	1.0000	1.0000	1.0000	1.0000	1.0000	0.9997	0.9991	0.9985	0.9935	0.9786	0.9423	0.8701	0.7500	0.5834	0.5207	0.3920	0.2142	0.0867	0.0371	0.0219	0.0024	0.0000
14	1.0000	1.0000	1.0000	1.0000	1.0000	1.0000	1.0000	0.9998	0.9997	0.9984	0.9936	0.9793	0.9447	0.8744	0.7546	0.7028	0.5836	0.3828	0.1958	0.1018	0.0673	0.0113	0.0003
15	1.0000	1.0000	1.0000	1.0000	1.0000	1.0000	1.0000	1.0000	1.0000	0.9997	0.9985	0.9941	0.9811	0.9490	0.8818	0.8485	0.7625	0.5852	0.3704	0.2313	0.1702	0.0432	0.0026
16	1.0000	1.0000	1.0000	1.0000	1.0000	1.0000	1.0000	1.0000	1.0000	1.0000	0.9997	0.9987	0.9951	0.9840	0.9556	0.9396	0.8929	0.7748	0.5886	0.4335	0.3523	0.1330	0.0159

Cumulative binomial probabilities

$n = 25$

p	0.05	0.10	0.15	1/6	0.20	0.25	0.30	1/3	0.35	0.40	0.45	0.50	0.55	0.60	0.65	2/3	0.70	0.75	0.80	5/6	0.85	0.90	0.95
$x = 0$	0.2774	0.0718	0.0172	0.0105	0.0038	0.0008	0.0001	0.0000	0.0000	0.0000	0.0000	0.0000	0.0000	0.0000	0.0000	0.0000	0.0000	0.0000	0.0000	0.0000	0.0000	0.0000	0.0000
1	0.6424	0.2712	0.0931	0.0629	0.0274	0.0070	0.0016	0.0005	0.0003	0.0001	0.0000	0.0000	0.0000	0.0000	0.0000	0.0000	0.0000	0.0000	0.0000	0.0000	0.0000	0.0000	0.0000
2	0.8729	0.5371	0.2537	0.1887	0.0982	0.0321	0.0090	0.0035	0.0021	0.0004	0.0001	0.0000	0.0000	0.0000	0.0000	0.0000	0.0000	0.0000	0.0000	0.0000	0.0000	0.0000	0.0000
3	0.9659	0.7636	0.4711	0.3816	0.2340	0.0962	0.0332	0.0149	0.0097	0.0024	0.0005	0.0001	0.0000	0.0000	0.0000	0.0000	0.0000	0.0000	0.0000	0.0000	0.0000	0.0000	0.0000
4	0.9928	0.9020	0.6821	0.5937	0.4207	0.2137	0.0905	0.0462	0.0320	0.0095	0.0023	0.0005	0.0001	0.0000	0.0000	0.0000	0.0000	0.0000	0.0000	0.0000	0.0000	0.0000	0.0000
5	0.9988	0.9666	0.8385	0.7720	0.6167	0.3783	0.1935	0.1120	0.0826	0.0294	0.0086	0.0020	0.0004	0.0001	0.0000	0.0000	0.0000	0.0000	0.0000	0.0000	0.0000	0.0000	0.0000
6	0.9998	0.9905	0.9305	0.8908	0.7800	0.5611	0.3407	0.2215	0.1734	0.0736	0.0258	0.0073	0.0016	0.0003	0.0000	0.0000	0.0000	0.0000	0.0000	0.0000	0.0000	0.0000	0.0000
7	1.0000	0.9977	0.9745	0.9553	0.8909	0.7265	0.5118	0.3703	0.3061	0.1536	0.0639	0.0216	0.0058	0.0012	0.0002	0.0001	0.0000	0.0000	0.0000	0.0000	0.0000	0.0000	0.0000
8	1.0000	0.9995	0.9920	0.9843	0.9532	0.8506	0.6769	0.5376	0.4668	0.2735	0.1340	0.0539	0.0174	0.0043	0.0008	0.0004	0.0001	0.0000	0.0000	0.0000	0.0000	0.0000	0.0000
9	1.0000	0.9999	0.9979	0.9953	0.9827	0.9287	0.8106	0.6956	0.6303	0.4246	0.2424	0.1148	0.0440	0.0132	0.0029	0.0016	0.0005	0.0000	0.0000	0.0000	0.0000	0.0000	0.0000
10	1.0000	1.0000	0.9995	0.9988	0.9944	0.9703	0.9022	0.8220	0.7712	0.5858	0.3843	0.2122	0.0960	0.0344	0.0093	0.0056	0.0018	0.0002	0.0000	0.0000	0.0000	0.0000	0.0000
11	1.0000	1.0000	0.9999	0.9997	0.9985	0.9893	0.9558	0.9082	0.8746	0.7323	0.5426	0.3450	0.1827	0.0778	0.0255	0.0164	0.0060	0.0009	0.0001	0.0000	0.0000	0.0000	0.0000
12	1.0000	1.0000	1.0000	0.9999	0.9996	0.9966	0.9825	0.9585	0.9396	0.8462	0.6937	0.5000	0.3063	0.1538	0.0604	0.0415	0.0175	0.0034	0.0004	0.0001	0.0000	0.0000	0.0000
13	1.0000	1.0000	1.0000	1.0000	0.9999	0.9991	0.9940	0.9836	0.9745	0.9222	0.8173	0.6550	0.4574	0.2677	0.1254	0.0918	0.0442	0.0107	0.0015	0.0003	0.0001	0.0000	0.0000
14	1.0000	1.0000	1.0000	1.0000	1.0000	0.9998	0.9982	0.9944	0.9907	0.9656	0.9040	0.7878	0.6157	0.4142	0.2288	0.1780	0.0978	0.0297	0.0056	0.0012	0.0005	0.0000	0.0000
15	1.0000	1.0000	1.0000	1.0000	1.0000	1.0000	0.9995	0.9984	0.9971	0.9868	0.9560	0.8852	0.7576	0.5754	0.3697	0.3044	0.1894	0.0713	0.0173	0.0047	0.0021	0.0001	0.0000
16	1.0000	1.0000	1.0000	1.0000	1.0000	1.0000	0.9999	0.9996	0.9992	0.9957	0.9826	0.9461	0.8660	0.7265	0.5332	0.4624	0.3231	0.1494	0.0468	0.0157	0.0080	0.0005	0.0000
17	1.0000	1.0000	1.0000	1.0000	1.0000	1.0000	1.0000	0.9999	0.9998	0.9988	0.9942	0.9784	0.9361	0.8464	0.6939	0.6297	0.4882	0.2735	0.1091	0.0447	0.0255	0.0023	0.0000
18	1.0000	1.0000	1.0000	1.0000	1.0000	1.0000	1.0000	1.0000	1.0000	0.9997	0.9984	0.9927	0.9742	0.9264	0.8266	0.7785	0.6593	0.4389	0.2200	0.1092	0.0695	0.0095	0.0002
19	1.0000	1.0000	1.0000	1.0000	1.0000	1.0000	1.0000	1.0000	1.0000	0.9999	0.9996	0.9980	0.9914	0.9706	0.9174	0.8880	0.8065	0.6217	0.3833	0.2280	0.1615	0.0334	0.0012
20	1.0000	1.0000	1.0000	1.0000	1.0000	1.0000	1.0000	1.0000	1.0000	1.0000	0.9999	0.9995	0.9977	0.9905	0.9680	0.9538	0.9095	0.7863	0.5793	0.4063	0.3179	0.0980	0.0072
21	1.0000	1.0000	1.0000	1.0000	1.0000	1.0000	1.0000	1.0000	1.0000	1.0000	1.0000	0.9999	0.9995	0.9976	0.9903	0.9851	0.9668	0.9038	0.7660	0.6184	0.5289	0.2364	0.0341
22	1.0000	1.0000	1.0000	1.0000	1.0000	1.0000	1.0000	1.0000	1.0000	1.0000	1.0000	1.0000	0.9999	0.9996	0.9979	0.9965	0.9910	0.9679	0.9018	0.8113	0.7463	0.4629	0.1271
23	1.0000	1.0000	1.0000	1.0000	1.0000	1.0000	1.0000	1.0000	1.0000	1.0000	1.0000	1.0000	1.0000	0.9999	0.9997	0.9995	0.9984	0.9930	0.9726	0.9371	0.9069	0.7288	0.3576
24	1.0000	1.0000	1.0000	1.0000	1.0000	1.0000	1.0000	1.0000	1.0000	1.0000	1.0000	1.0000	1.0000	1.0000	1.0000	1.0000	0.9999	0.9992	0.9962	0.9895	0.9828	0.9282	0.7226
25	1.0000	1.0000	1.0000	1.0000	1.0000	1.0000	1.0000	1.0000	1.0000	1.0000	1.0000	1.0000	1.0000	1.0000	1.0000	1.0000	1.0000	1.0000	1.0000	1.0000	1.0000	1.0000	1.0000

$n = 30$

p	0.05	0.10	0.15	1/6	0.20	0.25	0.30	1/3	0.35	0.40	0.45	0.50	0.55	0.60	0.65	2/3	0.70	0.75	0.80	5/6	0.85	0.90	0.95
$x=0$	0.2146	0.0424	0.0076	0.0042	0.0012	0.0002	0.0000	0.0000	0.0000	0.0000	0.0000	0.0000	0.0000	0.0000	0.0000	0.0000	0.0000	0.0000	0.0000	0.0000	0.0000	0.0000	0.0000
1	0.5535	0.1837	0.0480	0.0295	0.0105	0.0020	0.0003	0.0001	0.0000	0.0000	0.0000	0.0000	0.0000	0.0000	0.0000	0.0000	0.0000	0.0000	0.0000	0.0000	0.0000	0.0000	0.0000
2	0.8122	0.4114	0.1514	0.1028	0.0442	0.0106	0.0021	0.0007	0.0003	0.0000	0.0000	0.0000	0.0000	0.0000	0.0000	0.0000	0.0000	0.0000	0.0000	0.0000	0.0000	0.0000	0.0000
3	0.9392	0.6474	0.3217	0.2396	0.1227	0.0374	0.0093	0.0033	0.0019	0.0003	0.0000	0.0000	0.0000	0.0000	0.0000	0.0000	0.0000	0.0000	0.0000	0.0000	0.0000	0.0000	0.0000
4	0.9844	0.8245	0.5245	0.4243	0.2552	0.0979	0.0302	0.0122	0.0075	0.0015	0.0002	0.0000	0.0000	0.0000	0.0000	0.0000	0.0000	0.0000	0.0000	0.0000	0.0000	0.0000	0.0000
5	0.9967	0.9268	0.7106	0.6164	0.4275	0.2026	0.0766	0.0355	0.0233	0.0057	0.0011	0.0002	0.0000	0.0000	0.0000	0.0000	0.0000	0.0000	0.0000	0.0000	0.0000	0.0000	0.0000
6	0.9994	0.9742	0.8474	0.7765	0.6070	0.3481	0.1595	0.0838	0.0586	0.0172	0.0040	0.0007	0.0001	0.0000	0.0000	0.0000	0.0000	0.0000	0.0000	0.0000	0.0000	0.0000	0.0000
7	0.9999	0.9922	0.9302	0.8863	0.7608	0.5143	0.2814	0.1668	0.1238	0.0435	0.0121	0.0026	0.0004	0.0000	0.0000	0.0000	0.0000	0.0000	0.0000	0.0000	0.0000	0.0000	0.0000
8	1.0000	0.9980	0.9722	0.9494	0.8713	0.6736	0.4315	0.2860	0.2247	0.0940	0.0312	0.0081	0.0016	0.0002	0.0000	0.0000	0.0000	0.0000	0.0000	0.0000	0.0000	0.0000	0.0000
9	1.0000	0.9995	0.9903	0.9803	0.9389	0.8034	0.5888	0.4317	0.3575	0.1763	0.0694	0.0214	0.0050	0.0009	0.0001	0.0000	0.0000	0.0000	0.0000	0.0000	0.0000	0.0000	0.0000
10	1.0000	0.9999	0.9971	0.9933	0.9744	0.8943	0.7304	0.5848	0.5078	0.2915	0.1350	0.0494	0.0138	0.0029	0.0004	0.0002	0.0000	0.0000	0.0000	0.0000	0.0000	0.0000	0.0000
11	1.0000	1.0000	0.9992	0.9980	0.9905	0.9493	0.8407	0.7239	0.6548	0.4311	0.2327	0.1002	0.0334	0.0083	0.0014	0.0007	0.0002	0.0000	0.0000	0.0000	0.0000	0.0000	0.0000
12	1.0000	1.0000	0.9998	0.9995	0.9969	0.9784	0.9155	0.8340	0.7802	0.5785	0.3592	0.1808	0.0714	0.0212	0.0045	0.0025	0.0006	0.0001	0.0000	0.0000	0.0000	0.0000	0.0000
13	1.0000	1.0000	1.0000	0.9999	0.9991	0.9918	0.9599	0.9102	0.8737	0.7145	0.5025	0.2923	0.1356	0.0481	0.0124	0.0072	0.0021	0.0002	0.0000	0.0000	0.0000	0.0000	0.0000
14	1.0000	1.0000	1.0000	1.0000	0.9998	0.9973	0.9831	0.9565	0.9348	0.8246	0.6448	0.4278	0.2309	0.0971	0.0301	0.0188	0.0064	0.0008	0.0001	0.0000	0.0000	0.0000	0.0000
15	1.0000	1.0000	1.0000	1.0000	0.9999	0.9992	0.9936	0.9812	0.9699	0.9029	0.7691	0.5722	0.3552	0.1754	0.0652	0.0435	0.0169	0.0027	0.0002	0.0000	0.0000	0.0000	0.0000
16	1.0000	1.0000	1.0000	1.0000	1.0000	0.9998	0.9979	0.9928	0.9876	0.9519	0.8644	0.7077	0.4975	0.2855	0.1263	0.0898	0.0401	0.0082	0.0009	0.0001	0.0000	0.0000	0.0000
17	1.0000	1.0000	1.0000	1.0000	1.0000	0.9999	0.9994	0.9975	0.9955	0.9788	0.9286	0.8192	0.6408	0.4215	0.2198	0.1660	0.0845	0.0216	0.0031	0.0005	0.0002	0.0000	0.0000
18	1.0000	1.0000	1.0000	1.0000	1.0000	1.0000	0.9998	0.9993	0.9986	0.9917	0.9666	0.8998	0.7673	0.5689	0.3452	0.2761	0.1593	0.0507	0.0095	0.0020	0.0008	0.0000	0.0000
19	1.0000	1.0000	1.0000	1.0000	1.0000	1.0000	1.0000	0.9998	0.9996	0.9971	0.9862	0.9506	0.8650	0.7085	0.4922	0.4152	0.2696	0.1057	0.0256	0.0067	0.0029	0.0001	0.0000
20	1.0000	1.0000	1.0000	1.0000	1.0000	1.0000	1.0000	0.9999	0.9999	0.9991	0.9950	0.9786	0.9306	0.8237	0.6425	0.5683	0.4112	0.1966	0.0611	0.0197	0.0097	0.0005	0.0000
21	1.0000	1.0000	1.0000	1.0000	1.0000	1.0000	1.0000	1.0000	1.0000	0.9998	0.9984	0.9919	0.9688	0.9060	0.7753	0.7140	0.5685	0.3264	0.1287	0.0506	0.0278	0.0020	0.0000
22	1.0000	1.0000	1.0000	1.0000	1.0000	1.0000	1.0000	1.0000	1.0000	1.0000	0.9996	0.9974	0.9879	0.9565	0.8762	0.8332	0.7186	0.4857	0.2392	0.1137	0.0698	0.0078	0.0001
23	1.0000	1.0000	1.0000	1.0000	1.0000	1.0000	1.0000	1.0000	1.0000	1.0000	0.9999	0.9993	0.9960	0.9828	0.9414	0.9162	0.8405	0.6519	0.3930	0.2235	0.1526	0.0258	0.0006
24	1.0000	1.0000	1.0000	1.0000	1.0000	1.0000	1.0000	1.0000	1.0000	1.0000	1.0000	0.9998	0.9989	0.9943	0.9767	0.9645	0.9234	0.7974	0.5725	0.3836	0.2894	0.0732	0.0033
25	1.0000	1.0000	1.0000	1.0000	1.0000	1.0000	1.0000	1.0000	1.0000	1.0000	1.0000	1.0000	0.9998	0.9985	0.9925	0.9878	0.9698	0.9021	0.7448	0.5757	0.4755	0.1755	0.0156
26	1.0000	1.0000	1.0000	1.0000	1.0000	1.0000	1.0000	1.0000	1.0000	1.0000	1.0000	1.0000	1.0000	0.9997	0.9981	0.9967	0.9907	0.9626	0.8773	0.7604	0.6783	0.3526	0.0608
27	1.0000	1.0000	1.0000	1.0000	1.0000	1.0000	1.0000	1.0000	1.0000	1.0000	1.0000	1.0000	1.0000	1.0000	0.9997	0.9993	0.9979	0.9894	0.9558	0.8972	0.8486	0.5886	0.1878
28	1.0000	1.0000	1.0000	1.0000	1.0000	1.0000	1.0000	1.0000	1.0000	1.0000	1.0000	1.0000	1.0000	1.0000	1.0000	0.9999	0.9997	0.9980	0.9895	0.9705	0.9520	0.8163	0.4465
29	1.0000	1.0000	1.0000	1.0000	1.0000	1.0000	1.0000	1.0000	1.0000	1.0000	1.0000	1.0000	1.0000	1.0000	1.0000	1.0000	0.9998	0.9997	0.9988	0.9958	0.9924	0.9576	0.7854
30	1.0000	1.0000	1.0000	1.0000	1.0000	1.0000	1.0000	1.0000	1.0000	1.0000	1.0000	1.0000	1.0000	1.0000	1.0000	1.0000	1.0000	1.0000	1.0000	1.0000	1.0000	1.0000	1.0000

Answers

1 Representation of data

Exercise 1A (page 9)

1 (a) 4.3, 5.0, 5.3, 5.4, 5.7, 5.9, 6.1, 6.2, 6.3, 6.4,
   7.1, 7.6, 7.6, 9.2, 9.3.
   (b) (i) Quantitative   (ii) Continuous

2 (a)
```
0 | 4  6                         (2)
1 | 2  5  8                      (3)
2 | 1  5  5  5  7  8  9          (7)
3 | 0  2  4  6  7                (5)
4 | 1  3                         (2)
5 | 2                            (1)
```
   (Key: 2|7 means 27 m.p.h.)

   (b)
```
0 | 3  4  7  8  9  9  9          (7)
1 | 0  1  2  6  8                (5)
2 | 1  1  3  7                   (4)
3 |                             (0)
4 | 2                            (1)
```
   Key: 2|3 means 2.3 hours

3
```
3 | 3  4  0  6                                   (3)
4 | 8  8                                         (2)
5 | 0  0  1  2  3  4  4  6  6  7  8  8  9         (13)
6 | 0  2  3  4  7  7  8  8  9                     (9)
7 | 0  1  4  4  4  5  5  6  7  9                  (10)
8 | 1  6                                         (2)
9 | 1  3  9                                      (3)
```
Key: 7|9 means 79 years

4
```
13 |                               (0)
13 | 7                             (1)
14 | 1  2  3                       (3)
14 | 5                             (1)
15 | 1  1  2  3  4                 (5)
15 | 5  6  6  7  7  9              (6)
16 | 0  0  0  1  1  1  2  3  4     (9)
16 | 5  6  7  7  8  8  9  9        (8)
17 | 0  1  1  1  1  2  3  4        (8)
17 | 5  6  7  7  8  9              (6)
18 | 0  0  1  1  1  2  2  3  4     (9)
18 | 6  6  8  9                    (4)
```
Key: 17|9 means 179

5
```
2996 | 2  5                        (2)
2997 | 2  4  5  6  9               (5)
2998 | 0  1  3  4  5  7  8  8      (8)
2999 | 0  1  3  3  4  6  7  8      (8)
3000 | 0  7                        (2)
```
Key: 2997|4 means 299.74 thousand km s^{-1}

6 (a)
```
132 | 2  9                                           (2)
133 | 2  6  8  9                                     (4)
134 | 1  1  2  2  2  4  5  6  7  7  7  8  9          (13)
135 | 0  1  1  3  3  3  4  4  6                      (9)
136 | 2                                              (1)
137 | 0                                              (1)
```
   Key: 134|7 means 1.347 kg
   (b) There would be only one leaf, or two if the
   stem were split.

7
```
            | 62 | 0  5
            | 63 | 0  0
            | 64 | 5  5  5  5
            | 65 | 0
         3  | 66 | 0  0  3  5  5
         0  | 67 |
   8  8  0  | 68 | 0  0  5
      0  0  | 69 | 0
   5  0  0  | 70 | 5
            | 71 |
      5  0  | 72 |
      5  3  | 73 |
         0  | 74 |
      5  5  | 75 |
         5  | 76 |
         0  | 77 |
```
Key: 68|5 means 68.5 inches

Exercise 1B (page 17)

B means 'class boundaries', H means 'bar
heights', F means 'frequency', FD means
'frequency density'; MP means 'mid-point'.

1 B: 30 40 50 60 70 80 100
   H: 1.2 3.2 5.6 7.2 2.0 0.4

2 B: 4.5 9.5 14.5 19.5 24.5 29.5 34.5 44.5
   H: 0.4 1.0 1.6 2.8 3.4 2.2 0.3

3 MP: 134.5 144.5 154.5 164.5 174.5 184.5
   H: 1 4 11 17 14 13

4 (a) 0, 2.5 and 2.5, 5.5
   (b) B: 0 2.5 5.5 8.5 11.5 15.5
       FD: 6.8 2 1.33 0.67 0.25

5 B: −0.5 9.5 19.5 29.5 34.5 39.5 49.5 59.5
   H: 0.6 2.1 5.1 7.2 9.6 8.2 3.1

6 Assuming data correct to 1 decimal place
   MP: 9.45 10.45 11.45 12.45 13.45
   14.45 15.45 16.45
   H: 1 4 7 6 9 8 7 3

7 (b) 2.875, 3.875

(c) B: 2.875 3.875 4.875 5.875 6.875

7.875 8.875

H: 3 4 6 7 10 4

8 (a), (b) B: 16 20 30 40 50 60 80

FD: 3 4 4.4 4.7 3.2 1.25

9 (a) 4 cm   (b) 7   (c) 3.0

Exercise 1C (page 21)

1 (a) (i) about 150   (ii) about 35

(b) 130 cm

2 Plot at (30,0), (40,12), (50,44), (60,100), (70,172), (80,192), (100,200).

(a) 32%   (b) About 51 m.p.h.

3 Plot at (−0.5,0), (9.5,6), (19.5,27), (29.5,78), (34.5,114), (39.5,162), (49.5,244), (59.5,275).

(a) 28% or 29%   (b) 24

4 (a) Plot at (0,0), (16,14.3), (40,47.4), (65,82.7), (80,94.6)

(b) 10(.4) million

5 (a) About 58 poor days and 14 good days.

(b)

$x < 2$	$2 \le x < 3$	$3 \le x < 4$	$4 \le x < 5$
15	27	64	72

$5 \le x < 6$	$6 \le x < 7$	$7 \le x < 8$	$8 \le x < 9$
86	70	16	10

6 Assuming x is correct to the nearest mile, plot at (0,0), (4.5,12), (9.5,41), (14.5,104), (19.5,117), (24.5,129).

(a) 8 miles   (b) 14 miles

7 Plot at (7,10), (7.05,73), (7.10,150), (7.15,215), (7.20,245).

Between 7.012 cm and 7.175 cm.

8 Plot at (2.95,7), (3.95,62), (4.95,134), (5.95,144), (6.95,148).

9%; about 3.07

Miscellaneous exercise 1 (page 24)

1

0	0 0 6 8	(4)
1	1 1 2 4 6 7 8 9	(8)
2	0 1 5 6 7 8 9	(7)
3	1 3 4 6 7 8	(6)
4	2 2 3 5	(4)
5	5 7	(2)
6	2 3 6	(3)
7	2 5	(2)
8	2 4 5 6	(4)

Key: 4|3 means 43

The diagram indicates how the scores are distributed. But it does not indicate the order in which the scores occurred.

2 B: 0 30 60 120 180 240 300 360 480

FD: 0.07 0.1 0.13 0.27 0.7 0.42 0.3 0.1

About 286 s, obtained from the cumulative frequency diagram or by proportion.

3 Plot at (110,2), (120,12), (130,34), (140,63), (150,85), (160,97), (170,100). 123 cm

4 (a) B: 3.95 5.95 7.95 9.95 11.95

13.95 15.95

F: 3 3 4 11 8 1

(b) Plot at (3.95,0), (5.95,3), (7.95,6) (9.95,10), (11.95,21), (13.95,29), (15.95,30). 11.4; 3.3%

5 Groups: 1.0–2.4, 2.5–3.9, 4.0–5.4, 5.5–6.9, 7.0–8.4, 8.5–9.9, 10.0–11.4, 11.5–12.9

F: 13 16 18 15 6 8 2 2

B: 0.95 2.45 3.95 5.45 6.95 8.45 9.95 11.45 12.95

H: 13 16 18 15 6 8 2 2

For example: most times are between 1 and 7 seconds.

6 (a) Plot at (5,16), (10,47), (15,549), (20,1191), (25,2066), (30,2349), (40,2394), (50,2406).

(b) About 74%

(c) End boundaries unknown. Use (say) 2–5, 50–70.

7 (a) F: 17 11 10 9 3 4 2 4

(b) B: −0.5 9.5 19.5 29.5 39.5 49.5 59.5

69.5 99.5

FD: 1.7 1.1 1.0 0.9 0.3 0.4 0.2 0.13

(c) Plot at (−0.5,0), (9.5,17), (19.5,28), (29.5,38), (39.5,47), (49.5,50), (59.5,54), (69.5,56), (99.5,60). 42

(d) It assumes the data are evenly spread over the class 30–39. There are two each of 31, 33 and 39, and one each of 32, 36, 37, so the assumption is not well founded.

8 (a) Street 1. Plot at (61,0), (65,4), (67,15), (69,33), (71,56), (73,72), (75,81), (77,86), (79,90), (83,92).

Street 2. Plot at (61,0), (65,2), (67,5), (69,12), (71,24), (73,51), (75,67), (77,77), (79,85), (83,92).

(b) 69.8 dB on Street 1, 72.3 dB on Street 2.

(c) Street 1 appears less noisy, in general, than Street 2. For example, there are 56 readings under 71 dB for Street 1, but 24 for Street 2.

```
9   0 | 2  2  3  4  5  5  6  8                    (8)
    1 | 0  1  2  2  2  3  4  6  6  6  9           (11)
    2 | 0  2  3  4  4  4  5  5  9                 (9)
    3 | 4  5  9                                   (3)
    4 | 0  1  4  8                                (4)
    5 | 0  6  8                                   (3)
    6 | 1  6  7  7                                (4)
    7 | 2  6                                      (2)
    8 | 2  5                                      (2)
    9 |                                           (0)
   10 | 4                                         (1)
   11 | 8  8  9                                   (3)
```
Key: 4|8 means 48

Assuming data correct to the nearest second
B: 0 19.5 39.5 59.5 79.5 99.5 119.5
FD: 0.97 0.6 0.35 0.3 0.1 0.2

10 (a) Using 6 equal classes,
       B: 12.75 14.25 15.75 17.25 18.75
       20.25 21.75
       H: 1 2 2 2 7 11
       Although data appear to be correct to
       2 decimal places, having boundaries
       12.745–14.245 would be awkward.
    (b) Plot at (12.75,0), (14.25,1), (15.75,3),
       (17.25,5), (18.75,7), (20.25,14), (21.75,25).

```
(c) 12 | 76                                      (1)
    13 |                                          (0)
    14 | 82                                       (1)
    15 | 61                                       (1)
    16 | 53  97                                   (2)
    17 | 30  71                                   (2)
    18 |                                          (0)
    19 | 12  35  41  61  72                       (5)
    20 | 02  21  27  34  40  52  57  69           (8)
    21 | 04  13  25  38  43                       (5)
```
Key: 16|53 means 16.53

2   Measures of location

Exercise 2A (page 30)

1 5.4 kg; 5.7 kg

2 40

3 (a) 27.5 m.p.h.   (b) 1.1 hours

4 13.5

5 £500 approximately

6 4.7 s; 5.0 s.
   Data not evenly spread over class 4.0–5.4.

7 34

8 116, 110.5.
   On average females score higher than males.

Exercise 2B (page 34)

1 10.5

2 71.43 inches. Students appear taller, on
   average than the population. This can be
   explained by the large values 75.5, 77.5, 76.5
   and 77.0.

3 (a) 11.3   (b) 105.5

4 0.319

5 3.59

6 24.3

7 Assuming the end boundary is 100,
   59.2 m.p.h.

8 (a) 0–2.5, 2.5–5.5, 5.5–8.5, 8.5–11.5,
       11.5–15.5
   (b) 3.56 minutes

9 503.46 ml

10 £12.89; £12.39

11 412

Exercise 2C (page 39)

1 (a) 0   (b) No mode.   (c) 2–3   (d) Brown

2 (a) Mode   (b) Mean   (c) Median

3 It could be true for mean or mode, not the
   median.

4 (a) Roughly symmetrical
   (b) Skewed   (c) Skewed
   (d) Roughly symmetrical

5 (a) Mean 4.875, median 5, mode 6. The data
       set is too small for the mode to give a
       reliable estimate of location. The median
       gives a better idea of a 'typical' mark than
       the mean.
   (b) It has a 'tail' of low values.

Miscellaneous exercise 2 (page 40)

1 (a) 2.56; exact   (b) Both 2

2 (a) There would be no entries for stems 12,
       13, 14 and 15.

(b)
```
 4 | 0 0 0 1 2 2 2 6 6 8 8 9 9 9   (14)
 5 | 0 2 2 4 7 9                   (6)
 6 | 4 5 6                         (3)
 7 | 3 5 6                         (3)
 8 | 5                             (1)
 9 | 2 4                           (2)
10 |                               (0)
11 | 2                             (1)
```
HI 1.66; Key: 5|3 means £0.53

(c) £0.52; £0.617; modes: £0.40, £0.42, £0.49

(d) Median, since it is not affected by extreme values, *or* mean, since it involves all values.

(e) £0.236

3 (a) Both 22.0–23.9

(b) Not supported since modal classes the same. Either $mean_1$ (23.21 °C) is greater than $mean_2$ (22.43 °C) or $median_1$ ($\approx$23 °C) is greater than $median_2$ ($\approx$22 °C).

4 (a) Histogram

(b) Data inaccurate, grouped data, may not be evenly spread over classes.

(c) About 69 s

(d) No change in median, mean increases.

5 (a) B: −0.5 29.5 39.5 49.5 59.5 69.5 79.5 89.5 100.5
FD: 0.4 0.7 1.3 2.5 4.6 7.8 10.5 2.9
Negatively skewed

(b) 72.5   (c) About 77
The marks are higher for Mechanics, indicating better performance.

6 (a) About 20.4 hours

(b) Individual values unknown, data inaccurate, data may not be evenly distributed over the classes.

(c) 21.0 hours

(d) It has a 'tail' of low values.

7 $\bar{x} = 3.6$, me = 4, mo = 3 and mean is between mode and median.

8 (a) $\bar{m} = 453.9$, $\bar{t} = 462.9$, $\bar{d} = 9.0$; yes

(b) me $m = 294.5$, me $t = 266.5$, me $d = 5$; no

9 (a) There should be no spaces between bars; areas are not proportional to frequencies; incorrect scale on vertical axis.

(b) B: 4.5   9.5   12.5   15.5   18.5   28.5
FD: 2.8   6.0   5.0   1.3   0.8

(c) 12.9 m

10 Change by + or −0.06 depending on the order of the frequencies.

3   Measures of spread

Exercise 3A (page 52)

1 (a) 17, 9.5   (b) 9.1, 2.8

2 2.2

3 3

4 £15,420, £23,520

5 Street 1: 70.1 dB, 4.8 dB;
Street 2: 72.6 dB, 4.6 dB
Street 2 is usually noisier, with less variation.

6 Monday: $Q_1 = 105$, $Q_2 = 170$, $Q_3 = 258$
Wednesday: $Q_1 = 240$, $Q_2 = 305$, $Q_3 = 377$
Wednesday has greater audiences in general, with less variation.

7 Fat content 0: $Q_1 = 41$, $Q_2 = 53$, $Q_3 = 61$; interquartile range (IQR) = 20; range = 65.
Fat content 1: $Q_1 = 30$, $Q_2 = 37.5$, $Q_3 = 49$; IQR = 19; range = 46.
Fat content 0 has generally higher rating; has greater spread at extremes.

8 (a) Negative skew   (b) Positive skew
(c) Roughly symmetrical

9 Box plots are preferred since they give visual comparison of the shapes of distributions, the quartiles, IQRs and ranges. Histograms will indicate the general shape of the distributions and will give only a rough idea of quartiles and so on. However, means and standard deviations can be estimated from a histogram but not a box plot.

10 (a) £38.73, £43.23, £49.24, £54.15, £58.42.
(c) Slight negative skew

Exercise 3B (page 57)

1 (a) 4; SD is 2   (b) 5; SD is 4.899

2 (a) 3.489   (b) 4.278

3 50.728 g, 10.076 g^2

4 ±1.2

5 149.15 cm, 5.33 cm

6 (a) Anwar: mean = 51.5,   SD = 34.13
Brian: mean = 47.42   SD = 27.16

(b) Anwar is better; his mean of 51.5 is greater than Brian's 47.42 (Anwar scores more runs than Brian).

(c) Brian is more consistent since his standard deviation of 27.16 is less than Anwar's 34.13.

7 $\overline{f} = 137.2$ lb, SD (female) is 16.52 lb,
$\overline{m} = 166.44$ lb, SD (male) is 19.48 lb
Both distributions have negative skew.
Females are lighter than males by about 30 lb
on average and less variable than males.

Exercise 3C (page 62)

1 0.740, 1.13

3 797.4 min^2

4 250.77(5) g, 3.51 g
Increase the number of classes; weigh more
accurately; use more packets.

5 (a) 71, 12   (b) 34.8, 4.2

6 0.7109

7 −17.2, 247.36

8 135.7 cm, 176.51 cm^2

9 Mid-class values are 18.5, 23.5, 28.5,
33.5, 38.5, 46, 56, 66. Mean 37.49 years,
SD 11.86 years. In the second company
the general age is lower and with smaller
spread.

Miscellaneous exercise 3 (page 63)

1 23.16 cm, 1.32 cm; 22.89 cm, 1.13 cm
House sparrows have smaller variability; little
difference in means.

2 (a) Set B (b) Set B
(c) 39.5 g, 125 g^2
(d) Individual data values not given.

3 (b) 0.060 cm
(c) 1.34 approx.; close to 1.3

4 (a) The standard deviation is zero,
which implies that all data values are
equal.
(b) Ali caught 12.84 kg, Les 12.16 kg and Sam
2 kg so Ali won.
(c) 3.12 kg

5 (a) 1.854 cm; 1.810 cm, 1.886 cm
(b) Negative skew
(c) 1.850 cm, 0.069 cm

6 (a) 18.69 m, 36.20 m^2
(b) 18.92 m, 36.20 m^2

7 (a) 26.9 years, 13.0 years
(b) 22.4 years
Median preferred since distribution
skewed, more information given by median.

8 (a) 8.5 minutes, 9.25 minutes
(c) 10 minutes
(d) (i) and (iii) not true, (ii) and (iv) true

4   Probability

Exercise 4A (page 73)

1 (a) $\frac{1}{2}$ (b) $\frac{2}{3}$ (c) $\frac{1}{2}$ (d) $\frac{1}{2}$
(e) $\frac{1}{6}$ (f) $\frac{5}{6}$ (g) $\frac{2}{3}$

2 (a) $\frac{1}{2}$ (b) $\frac{3}{13}$ (c) $\frac{5}{13}$ (d) $\frac{5}{26}$ (e) $\frac{9}{13}$

3 (a) $\frac{1}{6}$ (b) $\frac{5}{12}$ (c) $\frac{5}{12}$ (d) $\frac{25}{36}$
(e) $\frac{11}{36}$ (f) $\frac{5}{18}$ (g) $\frac{1}{6}$ (h) $\frac{1}{2}$

4 (a) $\frac{1}{5}$ (b) $\frac{2}{5}$ (c) $\frac{1}{3}$ (d) $\frac{1}{2}$

Exercise 4B (page 80)

1 (a) $\frac{3}{51}$ (b) $\frac{4}{51}$

2 (a) $\frac{1}{2}$ (b) $\frac{5}{7}$ (c) $\frac{3}{7}$

3 (a) $\frac{9}{25}$ (b) $\frac{4}{25}$ (c) $\frac{12}{25}$ (d) $\frac{21}{25}$ (e) $\frac{3}{5}$

4 (a) $\frac{1}{3}$ (b) $\frac{2}{15}$ (c) $\frac{8}{15}$ (d) $\frac{13}{15}$ (e) $\frac{3}{5}$
No

5 (a) $\frac{11}{221}$ (b) $\frac{10}{17}$ (c) $\frac{7}{17}$ (d) $\frac{77}{102}$

6 (a) 0.27   (b) 0.35   (c) 0.3375

7 (a) $\frac{8}{15}$ (b) $\frac{7}{15}$ (c) $\frac{3}{5}$ (d) $\frac{2}{5}$
(e) $\frac{9}{16}$ (f) Yes   (g) No

8 (a) 0.24   (b) 0.42   (c) 0.706

9 (a) 0.12   (b) 0.44   (c) 0.048   (d) 0.34
(e) 0.03   (f) 0.07   (g) 0.32

10 (a) $\frac{1}{16}$ (b) $\frac{15}{16}$ (c) $\frac{671}{1296}$

11 0.491

12 0.5073 (note that this is bigger than 50%)

13 0.75

14 0.0317. Very small; the test has to be much
more reliable for it to give any reliable
evidence about a rare disease.

Miscellaneous exercise 4 (page 82)

1 0.110

2 (a) $\frac{1}{15}$ (b) $\frac{2}{9}$ (c) $\frac{14}{45}$ (d) $\frac{31}{45}$; $\frac{1}{120}$

3 (b) $\frac{2}{3}$

4 0.58

5 (a) $\frac{1}{2}$ (b) $\frac{5}{11}$

6 (a) 20%   (b) 10%

7 (b) (i) $\frac{23}{189}$ (ii) $\frac{166}{189}$

8 (a) $\frac{3}{20}$ (b) $\frac{9}{35}$ (c) $\frac{7}{12}$

10 (a) 0.030   (b) 0.146   (c) 0

11 $\frac{1}{2}$

12 $\frac{1}{4}$;   (a) 0.0577   (b) 0.1057   (c) 0.6676

13 (a) $\frac{43}{138}$ (b) $\frac{11}{138}$

14 (a) 0.32 (b) 0.56

15 (a) $\frac{3}{8}$
   (b) (i) $\frac{27}{125}$ (ii) $\frac{8}{125}$ (iii) $\frac{38}{125}$

16 (a) $\frac{1}{8}$ (b) $\frac{3}{8}$ (c) $\frac{8}{9}$

17 0.017

18 (a) (i) $\frac{1}{5}$ (ii) $\frac{5}{13}$ (iii) $\frac{17}{25}$ (iv) $\frac{1}{2}$
   (b) $\frac{21}{25}$

5 Permutations and combinations

Exercise 5A (page 91)

1 (a) 120 (b) 56 (c) 840 (d) 15 (e) 5040

2 5040

3 24; (a) $\frac{1}{4}$ (b) $\frac{1}{2}$

4 120

5 720

7 (a) 24 (b) 6 (c) $\frac{1}{4}$

8 119, $\frac{1}{120}$

9 34 650

10 (a) 720 (b) $\frac{1}{45}$

11 64, $\frac{21}{32}$

12 16

Exercise 5B (page 96)

1 22 100

2 215 760

3 (a) 56 (b) 48

4 70, 63

5 0.25

6 0.0128

7 (a) 0.222 (b) 0.070
   (c) 0.112 (d) 0.180

Exercise 5C (page 100)

1 (a) 3 632 428 800 (b) 259 459 200
   (c) 39 916 800 (d) 457 228 800

2 (a) 1024 (b) 210 (c) 0.205

3 (a) 5.346×10^{13} (b) 3.097×10^{12}
   (c) 0.0579

4 (a) 13! (b) 43 545 600
   (c) 609 638 400

5 (a) 1260 (b) 540 (c) 300 (d) 120

6 (a) 39 916 800 (b) 20 736 (c) 1 814 400

7 (a) 12 (b) 115

Miscellaneous exercise 5 (page 101)

1 3 628 800, 45

2 (a) 40 320 (b) 1152

3 83 160

4 360

5 (a) 1440 (b) 2880

6 (a) 240 (b) 480

7 210

8 210, $\frac{2}{7}$

9 (a) 0.112 (b) 0.368

10 (a) 360 (b) 60

11 432

12 (a) 24 (b) 120

13 (a) 70 (b) $\frac{1}{35}$

14 (a) (1,1,8), (1,2,7), (1,3,6), (1,4,5), (2,2,6),
   (2,3,5) (2,4,4), (3,3,4)
   (b) $\frac{1}{4}$

15 1260

16 0.0109

6 Probability distributions

Exercise 6A (page 107)

1
x	0	1	2	3	4
$P(X=x)$	$\frac{1}{16}$	$\frac{4}{16}$	$\frac{6}{16}$	$\frac{4}{16}$	$\frac{1}{16}$

2
d	0	1	2	3	4	5
$P(D=d)$	$\frac{6}{36}$	$\frac{10}{36}$	$\frac{8}{36}$	$\frac{6}{36}$	$\frac{4}{36}$	$\frac{2}{36}$

3
x	1	2	3	6	10
$P(X=x)$	$\frac{1}{6}$	$\frac{2}{6}$	$\frac{1}{6}$	$\frac{1}{6}$	$\frac{1}{6}$

4
h	1	2	3	4	5	6
$P(H=h)$	$\frac{23}{36}$	$\frac{7}{36}$	$\frac{3}{36}$	$\frac{1}{36}$	$\frac{1}{36}$	$\frac{1}{36}$

5
m	1	2	3	4	6	8	9	12	16
$P(M=m)$	$\frac{1}{16}$	$\frac{2}{16}$	$\frac{2}{16}$	$\frac{3}{16}$	$\frac{2}{16}$	$\frac{2}{16}$	$\frac{1}{16}$	$\frac{2}{16}$	$\frac{1}{16}$

6
Number	0	1	2
Probability	$\frac{5}{12}$	$\frac{1}{2}$	$\frac{1}{12}$

7

c	1	2	3	4
$P(C = c)$	$\frac{1}{13}$	$\frac{16}{221}$	$\frac{376}{5525}$	$\frac{4324}{5525}$

8

Score	3	4	5	6	7	8
Probability	$\frac{1}{216}$	$\frac{3}{216}$	$\frac{6}{216}$	$\frac{10}{216}$	$\frac{15}{216}$	$\frac{21}{216}$

	9	10	11	12	13	14
	$\frac{25}{216}$	$\frac{27}{216}$	$\frac{27}{216}$	$\frac{25}{216}$	$\frac{21}{216}$	$\frac{15}{216}$

	15	16	17	18
	$\frac{10}{216}$	$\frac{6}{216}$	$\frac{3}{216}$	$\frac{1}{216}$

Exercise 6B (page 109)

1 $\frac{1}{20}$

2 0.3

3 0.15

4 $\frac{1}{8}$

5

x	1	2	3	4	5	6
$P(X = x)$	$\frac{1}{4}$	$\frac{1}{12}$	$\frac{1}{4}$	$\frac{1}{12}$	$\frac{1}{4}$	$\frac{1}{12}$

6 $\frac{1}{21}$

7 $\frac{20}{49}$

8 0.2

Exercise 6C (page 110)

1 (a) 130   (b) 40   (c) 120
(d) 160   (e) 360

2 (a) 105   (b) 105   (c) 245

3 12, 31, 34, 18, 5, 0 (0 is better than 1 because it makes the total 100)

4 0.468, 103

Miscellaneous exercise 6 (page 111)

1

Number	0	1	2	3
Probability	$\frac{248}{1105}$	$\frac{496}{1105}$	$\frac{304}{1105}$	$\frac{57}{1105}$

2 (a)

x	0	1	2	3	4	6
$P(X = x)$	$\frac{1}{4}$	$\frac{1}{3}$	$\frac{1}{9}$	$\frac{1}{6}$	$\frac{1}{9}$	$\frac{1}{36}$

(b) 120

3 (a) $\frac{1}{18}$ (b) $\frac{17}{36}$ (c) $\frac{11}{17}$

4 (b) 8.3

5 $\frac{1}{8}$

7 The binomial and geometric distributions

Practical activity (page 121)

Points to consider are: is p constant? For example, is a student likely to improve with practice? Does p vary from one person to another, even if it is constant for a particular person? Do different goalkeepers at football differ in how effective they are at stopping penalties? The binomial distribution will only be a suitable model if p is constant: this condition may not be met in either of the games.

Exercise 7A (page 121)

The answers might change in the fourth figure, depending on whether you use a calculator or tables.

1 (a) 0.0819   (b) 0.0154   (c) 0.0001

2 (a) 0.2561   (b) 0.2048   (c) 0.0005

3 (a) 0.2119   (b) 0.4728   (c) 0.0498

4 (a) 0.0017   (b) 6

5 (a) 0.2461   (b) 0.4102
(c) 0.0196   (d) 0.9102

6 (a) 0.0781   (b) 0.0176

7 (a) 0.6496
(b) The students are not chosen independently.

8 0.0545; no (the outcomes are still green and not-green)

9 0.1143; breakages are not independent of each other (if one egg in a box is broken, it is more likely that others will be).

10 0.0652; for example, P(hurricane) is constant for each month.

11 (a) 0.7648   (b) 0.1811
(c) 0.9947   (d) 0.2352

12 (a) 0.8338   (b) 0.1209
(c) 0.3823   (d) 0.1662

13 (a) 0.1503   (b) 0.9894   (c) 0.6172

14 0.2039. The adults must be independent of each other as to whether they are wearing jeans; the probability that each adult is wearing jeans must be the same. (Do not say there must be only two outcomes; this is automatically implied by the question.)

15 More than one relevant outcome on each trial.

16 (a) The boys are not chosen independently of each other.

(b) The probability that a day is warm is not the same for each month.

17 A, B, C and D are not independent events.

Exercise 7B (page 127)

1 (a) 0.0720   (b) 0.0504   (c) 0.1577

2 (a) 0.1440   (b) 0.0864   (c) 0.4704

3 (a) 0.0320   (b) 0.9920   (c) 0.0003

4 (a) 0.0199   (b) 0.7763   (c) 0.2237

5 (a) 0.3206   (b) 0.1673
  (c) 0.1673   (d) 0.8327

6 (a) 0.0808   (b) 0.1594   (c) 0.8406

7 (a) 0.3056   (b) 0.0711   (c) 0.0541

8 (a) 0.0453   (b) 0.2711   (c) 0.5811

9 (a) 0.0478   (b) 0.3487   (c) 0.3660

10 (a) 0.0988   (b) 0.1317   (c) 0.1646

If the people arrive in groups, their choices of footwear may not be independent of each other.

11 (a) 0.3894   (b) 66

12 (a) 0.2288   (b) 88

13 (a) 0.0558   (b) 0.2791

14 0.34

15 0.25

Miscellaneous exercise 7 (page 129)

1 0.580

2 (a) B(10, 0.4)   (b) 0.820   (c) 4

3 (a) (i) 0.2   (ii) 0.134
  (b) (i) 0.2   (ii) 0.082   (iii) 0.328

4 (a) 0.337   (b) 0.135

5 0.286

6 Geometric; 0.333, 0.222, 0.148, 0.099; 0.983;
  (a) 108   (b) 144

7 (a) 0.0625, 0.25, 0.375, 0.25, 0.0625
  (b) 0.273   (c) 0.313

8 (a) Geometric (b) 0.105   (c) 0.422
  (d) Either the probability of scoring a goal remains constant or whether one kick is successful is independent of the result of any other kicks.

9 Trials in which the only possible outcomes are 'succeed' and 'fail' are repeated, with the probability of a 'succeed' being the same for all trials, and all trials being independent of one another.

   (a) 0.035   (b) 0.138; 83

10 (a) 0.041   (b) 0.185   (c) 0.774   (d) 0.023

11 (a) 0.116   (b) 0.386   (c) 0.068

12 For example: probability that each hen lays an egg is the same each day for each hen; or hens lay eggs independently of each other, or independently of whether they laid an egg the previous day. $\frac{5}{6}$; 1.07, 4.02, 8.04, 6.70

13 (a) 0.9   (b) 0.08
   (c) 0.14   (d) 0.3;   0.747

14 0.088. Complete boxes might be damaged, for instance by dropping, after the eggs have been put in them.

15 (a) 0.002 46   (b) 1.68×10^{-5}
   (c) 0.001 64   (d) 0.001 64
   (e) The number of trials needed before a success is obtained does not depend on the number that have so far taken place.

8 Expectation and variance of a random variable

Exercise 8A (page 138)

1 (a) $1\frac{7}{8}$ (b) 0.05

2 4, 3.6

3 $5\frac{1}{9}$, $1\frac{35}{81}$

4 (a) $\frac{7}{3}$, 0.745
  (b)

y	2	3	4	5	6
$P(Y = y)$	$\frac{1}{36}$	$\frac{1}{9}$	$\frac{5}{18}$	$\frac{1}{3}$	$\frac{1}{4}$

  $\frac{14}{3}$, $\frac{10}{9}$

5 $E(A) = £95,000$, $E(B) = £115,000$; choose B.

6 (a) 0.3, 0.51   (b) 5.7, 0.51
  (c) $E(Y) = 6 - E(X)$, $Var(Y) = Var(X)$. The distribution of Y (the number of unbroken eggs) is the reflection of the distribution of X in the line $x = 3$.

7 $1\frac{25}{36}$, 1.434

8 0.2, 2.8, 1.4

9 $a = b = 0.15$, $\sigma = 1.7$

10 (a)

x	1	2	3	4
$P(X = x)$	$\frac{1}{6}$	$\frac{5}{36}$	$\frac{25}{216}$	$\frac{125}{216}$

   (b) 1.172; 0.5177, −20.56

11

w	0	1	2
$P(W = w)$	$\frac{1}{3}$	$\frac{8}{15}$	$\frac{2}{15}$

0.8

12 (b)

h	0	1	2	3
$P(H = h)$	$\frac{11}{48}$	$\frac{7}{16}$	$\frac{13}{48}$	$\frac{1}{16}$

(c) $E(X) = \frac{7}{3}$; $E(H) = \frac{7}{6}$ (d) $\frac{13}{18}$

Exercise 8B (page 144)

1 (a) 2.8, 2.408   (b) 0.4550

2 0.84, 0.9073

3 10.5, 6.825

4 0.2581

5 1.6

6 0.1407

7 4

8 (a) 2   (b) 1

9 £37.50

10 (a) 4   (b) 4

11 0.196

Miscellaneous exercise 8 (page 146)

1 (a) 2.56, 1.499   (b) 122.9

2 0.5

3 (a) 0.0769   (b) 13.00

4 3, 1.2, 0.3456

5 1.3, 1.01, 3.8, 0.76

(a)

z	3	4	5	6	7	8
$P(Z = z)$	0.15	0.16	0.33	0.19	0.14	0.03

6 (a) 25

(b) For example, it may be near a station where taxis tend to congregate.

7 (a) 0.8901   (b) 280, 18.67

8 (a) 0.1426   (b) 0.6226

(c) 1.712, 1.467; assumes 5% true for each run.

9 (a) 0.8704

(b)

x	1	2	3	4
$P(X = x)$	0.4	0.24	0.144	0.216

) 2.176, 1.377

a) $\frac{1}{8}$ (b) 3

9   Correlation

Exercise 9A (page 150)

1 (a), (c) and (d) are bivariate. (e) could be classed as bivariate, but graphs of time series are generally not referred to as scatter diagrams.

2 Some of these answers may be open to debate, especially in particular circumstances.

(a) Positive

(b) Positive

(c) Little, or slight positive or negative

(d) Positive

(e) Negative

(f) Zero

(g) (Perfect) Positive

3 (a) The best and worst do well or badly in both subjects; little relationship between the others.

(b) Strong negative correlation; it's cold in London and Vancouver at the same time.

(c) Linear relationship up to $v = 50$, thereafter quadratic.

(d) No particular pattern except on a very cold day (ice) and a very hot day (lots of holiday traffic)

4 (a) Positive correlation; taller students will tend to weigh more.

(b) No obvious relationship.

Exercise 9B (page 155)

1 (a) 1; the points lie exactly on a straight line with positive slope.

(b) −1; the points lie exactly on a straight line with negative slope.

(c) 0; the points do not show any particular pattern.

(d) 0.851; the points lie close to, but not exactly on, a straight line with positive slope.

Exercise 9C (page 160)

1 (a) 0.95 (b) −0.943 (c) −0.150 (d) 0.978

(e) −0.964   (f) −0.904   (g) 0.992

(h) −0.904; $p = 4x+1$, a linear relationship

(i) 1; $x = w^2$, a non-linear relationship. The data points in 1(g) are related by $t = 3w^2+0.56$.

(j) 0.820

(k) 1; all the points except (7,16) are in a perfect straight line.

2 (a) Other shapes might be better still – for example a curve, or separate straight line segments.
  (b) There could be a strong non-linear relationship between the data.
  (c) The line might not pass through the origin.
  (d) Causality can not be established; both x and y might depend on some other, unchanged, factor.

3 −0.746; general downward trend.

4 0.818; points lie fairly close to a straight line; unchanged

5 −0.535. Any relationship between f and A is likely to be non-linear. The scatter diagram shows a strong non-linear relationship. (The situation is a classical problem in operational research, and a typical model for the relationship is $A = pf + \dfrac{q}{f}$. In this notional problem, $p = 80$ and $q = 2000$.)

6 −0.727. Suggests fairly strong linear correlation; but the scatter diagram shows that, although the proportion of defectives decreases quite rapidly at first, at higher levels the expenditure has to increase much more in order to make much reduction in the number of defectives.

7 (a) 0.985   (b) 1.00 (0.99998)   (c) 0.990.
  Therefore $y = ax^2 + b$ is best.

8 $r = -0.440$. Some suggestion that the smaller the sodium content the higher the rating, but the correlation is quite low so the result must be considered inconclusive.

Exercise 9D (page 168)

1 0.536, or $\frac{15}{28}$

2 −0.536, or $-\frac{15}{28}$

3 The ranks are opposite. r_s is multiplied by −1.

4 $r = -0.886$ or $-\frac{31}{35}$. Strong negative rank correlation.

5 0.143 or $\frac{1}{7}$. Little correlation/relationship.

6 0.548 or $\frac{23}{42}$. There is some agreement between the judges.

7 (a) 1
  (b) The student is good at judging the age of one person relative to another but is not very good at estimating their actual ages.

8 0.486 or $\frac{17}{35}$. Suggests that there is agreement, but it is not strong. In fact the actual scores, as opposed to the rankings, of Universities B, C, D and E are very similar, and the close agreement between the tables is displayed by the value of r, which is 0.914.

9 (a) −0.107 or $-\frac{3}{28}$
  (b) −0.929 or $-\frac{13}{14}$.

There is little relationship between the views of Ashish and Bella, whereas Ashish and Clive have opposing views: they tend to rank films in opposite orders. To distinguish between these two situations it is better to avoid the use of the word 'disagree', which can be ambiguous.

10 No difference; the rankings would stay the same. The answers would change; the transformation is non-linear.

11 (a) See for example Fig. 9.15 (a).
  (b) See, for example, Fig. 9.7, the diagram labelled 'strong'.

Miscellaneous exercise 9 (page 170)

1 (a) 0   (b) Fair to strong positive

2 (a) 1   (b) −1.

3 (a) (i) −1   (ii) 1
  (b) P and Q

4 −0.657

5 −0.385; disagree, no evidence that one causes the other.

6 (a) 0.429
  (b) Q, because the rank correlation coefficient between P and Q is positive whereas that between P and R is negative.
  (c) positively correlated, 6 8 1 5 7 2 4 3.

7 0.393; eliminate Z, result B, A, C.

8 (a) −0.865   (b) −0.905
  (c) Arif different, relation between h and d is non-linear.
  (d) Beth same, ranks are unchanged.

9 (a) −0.975, strong (but not perfect) linear correlation.
  (b) −1, rankings in perfect agreement.
  (c) Scatter diagram: it shows a clear non-linear relationship.

10　Regression

Exercise 10A (page 181)

1　(a) $y = -13 + 1.9x$　　(b) $y = 28.1 - 1.63x$
　 (c) $y = 8.06 - 0.106x$　(d) $y = 0.143 + 2.57x$
　 (e) $t = 27.45 - 1.52w$　(f) $y = 11.05 - 1.206x$
　 (g) $t = -33.2 + 21w$

2　7.0

3　Out of range. No information as to the range.

4　8.04. Some, but not all, calculators will give this answer directly.

5　(a) $t = -0.614 + 0.0747d$　　(b) 1.6 s

6　$y = 84.2 + 1.16x$. a is the percentage of trains which would run on time with zero investment; b is the expected increase in percentage for every increase of £1000 in investment.

7　$x = 43.4 - 0.41v$; 29; expected decrease (increase) in x for every litre of weedkiller; out of range (there may be a sudden decrease in the number of weeds if any weedkiller is present); x would become negative.

Exercise 10B (page 185)

1　(a) $y = 66.5 + 0.278x$;
　　　$x = -4.375 + 0.625y$
　 (b) $y = 1 + 0.8x$;
　　　$x = 0.172 + 1.104y$
　 (c) $y = 2.51 + 2.69x$;
　　　$x = 0.756 + 0.353y$
　 (d) $y = 31.37 - 3.87x$;
　　　$x = 7.94 - 0.248y$

2　(a) $y = -13.57 + 1.148x$; 36
　 (b) $x = 15 + 0.810y$; 72

3　(a) $y = 25.8 + 0.645x$; $x = -0.123 + 0.988y$
　 (b) 70 inches
　 (c) (i) 73.4 inches　　(ii) 68.4 inches
　 (d) 0.798, reliable
　 (e) 64.1 inches
　 (f) Fathers taller than average generally have sons who are taller than average but not so much as their fathers; fathers shorter than average generally have sons who are shorter than average but not so much as their fathers. Hence there is a 'regression towards the mean'.

4　−0.965.　　(a) 5 °C　　(b) 41 °C
　 ndon tends to be an exception to climatic neralisations because of the Gulf Stream.)

5　$r = 1$. $y = -4 + 5x$. Because $r = 1$, the two lines coincide, so $x = 0.8 + 0.2y$

6　(a) False, unless $r = \pm 1$.
　 (b) True
　 (c) True, unless r is too close to 0.
　 (d) False; there is no guaranteed relationship between r and b apart from their having the same sign.

Exercise 10C (page 190)

1　$y = -9.8 + 1.3x$;　(a) 39.6　(b) 30.6

2　$x = 129.24 - 11.124y$;　(a) 89.2　(b) 3.53

3　(a) 4.22　　(b) 6.355 (use t on m)

4　26.9 °C (use R on t)

5　It is difficult to be dogmatic without knowing exact details of the experiments being carried out, but it is likely that (a), (e), (f) and (g) would involve controlled variables, and that (b), (c) and (d) would not.

Miscellaneous exercise 10 (page 191)

1　(a) $y = 3.07 + 1.17x$　　(b) y is controlled

2　(a) $s = 1.05$; $0.55t$; 2.9
　 (b) close to straight line, positive gradient

3　(a) $g = 12.8 + 0.869h$
　 (b) h is controlled; 25.6

4　(a) $x = 0.0840y + 31.2$; 45
　 (b) 103; impossibly high, unreliable because of extrapolation

5　(a) 0.786
　 (b) Crop yield with no fertiliser; rate of change of crop yield with fertiliser.
　 (c) 1.6; x is independent, so use y on x.

6　(b) F　　　　　(c) 0.979
　 (d) Yes, strong correlation
　 (e) $a = 39.6$, $b = 11.4$　　(f) 79.5
　 (g) Unreliable because of extrapolation.

7　(b) 0.98; strong linear correlation
　 (c) $y = -39.8 + 1.92x$
　 (d) Lines similar as r close to 1; 7.47 a.m.
　 (e) Outside data range, unreliable

8　(b) $v = 1.54 + 2.68t$　　(c) 0.988
　 (d) The product moment correlation coefficient suggests that a single line gives a good fit, whereas the scatter diagram suggests two straight lines.
　 (e) For example: $v = 3.3t - 0.05$　　(f) 5%

9　(b) 19　　(c) 5

(d) Negative gradients so negative correlation

(e) r close to 0 so unreliable

10 (b) −0.848; not a good model.

(c) Little relationship for $70 \le t \le 75$; drops steadily for $t \ge 75$.

(d) Probably sensible but causality cannot be proved.

(e) t is controlled; therefore l on t; $l = 510 - 5t$, 77

(f) Estimate is reliable, $r = -0.995$; less reliable, extrapolation is dangerous.

(g) Transformation from F to C is linear, so r doesn't change; for example: temperatures are likely to be rounded to nearest integer.

Revision exercise (page 197)

1 (a) Frequency densities: 1.6, 1.2, 0.833, 0.6

(c) 39.88 mm, 28.2 mm

2 (a) 1800, 2987.5, 1168

(b) 0.964; the data indicate that there is a strong positive correlation between the variables height and mass.

(c) $w = 0.603h - 39.1$, 57.3 kg

3 (a) Two mutually exclusive, exhaustive outcomes; repeated, independent trials; constant probability of success; variable is the number of goes until success occurs.

(b) 0.191, 0.514   (c) 170   (d) 57

4 (a) $\frac{16}{52} = \frac{4}{13}$

(b) $P(S = 0) = \frac{4}{13}$, $P(S = 2) = \frac{5}{13}$, $(S = 5) = \frac{4}{13}$ $2\frac{4}{13}$, $3\frac{153}{169}$

(c) Geo $\left(\frac{4}{13}\right)$, 3.25   (d) 0.332

5 (a) Dice is fair, all six faces are equally likely to turn up.

(b) $2\frac{11}{12}$

6 (a) $\frac{3}{4}$

(b) Assume constant probability of success, independence of outcomes. (i) $\frac{3}{16}$ (ii) $\frac{37}{64}$

(c) The probability of success may vary.

7 (b) 16, 7.2   (c) 26 or 27

8 0.75

9 (a) 0.0148   (c) 10

(d) Slightly surprising; it would happen less than 1 in 20 times.

10 (b) 3.8, 2.6

11 (a) −0.915

(b) The value in (a) suggests that as the car gets older its price decreases.

12 (a) 50 400   (b) $\frac{1}{15}$ (c) $\frac{3}{10}$ (d) $\frac{1}{3}$

Practice examinations

Practice examination 1 (page 201)

1 0.881; the magazines are in good agreement

2 (i) (a) 29   (b) 42   (c) 21

(ii) Medians are quite similar; men's scores are more spread out.

(iii) For example: Cumulative frequency graphs include more information, and can be used to find other percentiles, but box-and-whisker plots are easier to use for comparison of key features.

3 (i) 720   (ii) 48   (iii) 144

4 (i) The variable measures the number of trials until a 'success' is obtained; the trials are independent with constant probability of success. For example, the number of throws of a die until a 6 turns up.

(ii) (a) $\frac{16}{243}$ (b) $\frac{32}{243}$

(iii) 0.002 28

5 (i) 0.258   (ii) 0.649   (iii) 3.6   (iv) 0.503

6 (i)

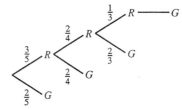

(ii) Missing probabilities are $\frac{2}{5}$, $\frac{1}{5}$, $\frac{1}{10}$

(iii) 1

7 (i) (Frequency densities are 29, 23, 7.5, 4.2, 1.2)

(ii) $4.985 billion; use of class centres is an approximation

(iii) The distribution is positively skewed.

(iv) Approximately two-thirds of the companies are worth less than the mean.

8 (i) 0.855

   (ii) The points lie fairly close to a line of positive gradient.

   (iii) $y = 14.3 + 0.802x$ (iv) A, $y \approx 82$

   (v) Although the pmcc is quite high, the diagram indicates considerable uncertainty in using a straight line for prediction.

Practice examination 2 (page 205)

1 (ii) 0.45, 0.3

   (iii) No; for example, $n = 3$ and $np = 1$ give $p = \frac{1}{3}$, but $P(X = 3) \neq \frac{1}{27}$

2 (i) −0.685

   (ii) The two passengers tend to have opposing priorities.

3 (i) 6006   (ii) 0.793

4 (i)

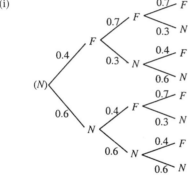

   (ii) (a) 0.196   (b) 0.288

5 (i) $\frac{1}{8}$

   (ii) (a) Constant probability of success in independent trials, and number of trials to first success required.

   (b) 8

   (iii) (a) 0.109   (b) 0.979

6 (i)

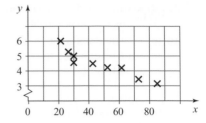

   (ii) −0.983; the points lie close to a straight line of negative gradient.

   (iii) $y = 6.15 - 0.0358x$ (iv) 4.36

7 (i) 0.203   (ii) (b) 0.136   (iii) 0.316

   (iv) For example: P(shell is good) must be constant, but there may be variations in manufacture.

8 (i) For example, assume no car is older than 25 years.

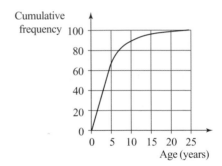

   (ii) (a) 32%   (b) $8\frac{1}{2}$ years

   (iii) 4.8 years

   (iv) The position of the final point plotted does not affect the values read off, but the mid-point of the last class interval is affected and this is used in the calculation of the mean.

Index

The page numbers given refer to the first mention of each term, or the blue box if there is one.

addition law
  of mutually exclusive events, 72
arrangement, *see* permutation
average, 27

b, *see* regression coefficient of y on x
b', *see* regression coefficient of x on y
binomial distribution, 120
  expectation, 141
  parameters, 116
  variance, 141
bivariate data, 148
box plot, 50
box-and-whisker diagram, 50

class, 10
  boundaries, 11
  width, 13
coded values, 34, 157
combination, 92, 93
  solving problems, 96
comparing correlation coefficients, 168
complement, 71
conditional probability, 74
continuous variable, 4
controlled variable, 188
correlation
  negative, 149
  positive, 149
correlation coefficient
  comparing, 168
  interpretation, 160
  product moment, 154
  Spearman's rank, 164, 165
covariance, 153
cumulative frequency graph, 19

data, 1
  raw, 5
datafile, 1
dependent variable, 180, 188

discrete variable, 4
dispersion, measures of, 44

event, 68
expectation, 134
  of a binomial distribution, 141
  of a geometric distribution, 143
expected value of a random variable, 134
extrapolation
  of regression line, 181

factorial n, 87
failure, 113
five-number summary, 50
frequency density, 13
frequency distribution, grouped, 10

geometric distribution, 126
  expectation of, 143
geometric progression, 124
geometric sequence, 124
grouped frequency distribution, 10

histogram, 12

independent events, 77
independent variable, 180
interquartile range, 45

least squares, 176
  regression line, x on y, 184
  regression line, y on x, 177
lower quartile, 45

mean, 30–1, 134
mean, assumed, 34
mean, calculating, 32
mean, mean absolute deviation from, 54
measure of central tendency, 27
measure of location, 27
median, 27

mid-class value, 33
middle quartile, 45
modal class, 36
modal value, 36
mode, 36
multiplication law
   for independent events, 78
   of probability, 74
mutually exclusive events, 72

negative correlation, 149
negative skew, 51

ordered stem-and-leaf diagram, 5
outlier, 37, 52

parameter
   of binomial distribution, 116
   of geometric distribution, 124
permutation, 87–8, 90
   solving problems, 96
positive correlation, 149
positive skew, 51
probability, 67
probability distribution, 103
product moment correlation coefficient,
      153
   calculating, 156

qualitative variable, 4
quantitative variable, 4
quartile, 45
   lower, 45
   middle, 45
   upper, 45

r, see product moment correlation coefficient
r_s, see Spearman's rank correlation coefficient
random variable, 103
   expectation, 134
   standard deviation, 135
   variance, 135
range, 44
   interquartile, 45
rank, 163
   correlation, 163
   data, 5

regression line
   coefficient of x on y, 184
   coefficient of y on x, 177
   method of least squares,
      x on y, 184
      y on x, 177
relative frequency, 67

sample space, 66
sampling
   with replacement, 77
   without replacement, 74
scatter diagram, 148
selection, see combination
sigma notation, 31
skew, 37, 50
   negative, 51
   positive, 51
Spearman's rank correlation coefficient,
      164–5
standard deviation, 55
   of a random variable, 135
statistics, 1
stem-and-leaf diagram, 5
   back-to-back, 8
   key, 5
   ordered, 5
success, 113
summation notation, 31
S_{xx}, S_{xy}, S_{yy}, 154, 156

tree diagram, 75
trial, 113

upper quartile, 45

variable, 1
   continuous, 4
   controlled, 188
   dependent, 180, 188
   discrete, 4
   independent, 180
   qualitative, 4
   quantitative, 4
variance, 54–5
   of a random variable, 135
   of a binomial distribution, 141